THE PAGES IN BETWEEN

*A Holocaust Legacy of
Two Families, One Home*

ERIN EINHORN

A TOUCHSTONE BOOK
Published by Simon & Schuster
New York   London   Toronto   Sydney

TOUCHSTONE
A Division of Simon & Schuster, Inc.
1230 Avenue of the Americas
New York, NY 10020

First Touchstone hardcover edition September 2008

TOUCHSTONE and colophon are registered trademarks of Simon & Schuster, Inc.

For information about special discounts for bulk purchases,
please contact Simon & Schuster Special Sales at
1-800-456-6798 or business@simonandschuster.com.

Designed by Laura McBride

Manufactured in the United States of America

1   3   5   7   9   10   8   6   4   2

Library of Congress Cataloging-in-Publication Data

Einhorn, Erin.
The pages In between : a Holocaust legacy of two families,
one home /Erin Einhorn.—1st ed.
p.   cm.
"A Touchstone Book."
1. Frederick, Irene, 1942– 2. Jews—Poland—Bedzin—Biography. 3. Hidden children
(Holocaust)—Poland—Bedzin—Biography. 4. Holocaust survivors—United States—
Biography. 5. Einhorn, Erin—Travel—Poland. 6. Children of Holocaust survivors—
Biography. 7. Holocaust, Jewish (1939–1945)—Poland—Bedzin—Personal narratives.
8. Holocaust, Jewish (1939–1945)—Influence. 9. Karwowski, Honorata, d. 1995.
10. Righteous Gentiles in the Holocaust—Poland—Biography. I. Title.
DS134.72.F73E35 2008
940.53'18092—dc22
[B]   2008015629
ISBN-13: 978- 1-4165-5830-9
ISBN-10:   1-4165-5830-6

For Irena
for trusting me with your story, and for knowing why
I thought it was interesting

THE PAGES
IN BETWEEN

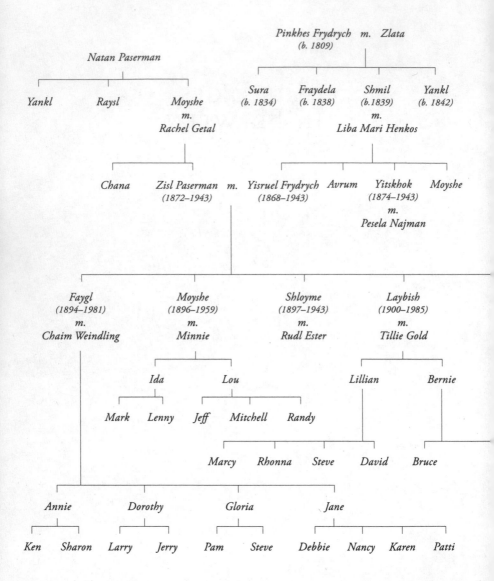

GENEALOGY

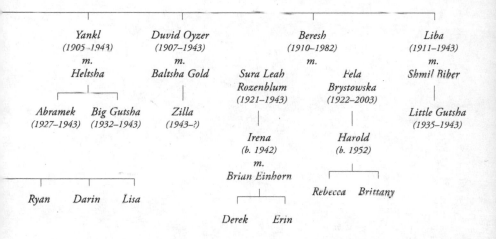

Yankl	Duvid Oyzer		Beresh		Liba
(1905–1943)	(1907–1943)		(1910–1982)		(1911–1943)
m.	m.		m.		m.
Heltsha	Baltsha Gold	Sura Leah Rozenblum (1921–1943)	Fela Brystowska (1922–2003)		Shmil Riber

Abramek	Big Gutsha	Zilla			Little Gutsha
(1927–1943)	(1932–1943)	(1943–?)			(1935–1943)

Irena
(b. 1942)
m.
Brian Einhorn

Harold
(b. 1952)

Ryan	Darin	Lisa

Derek	Erin

Rebecca	Brittany

CHAPTER ONE

M ONTHS LATER, WRESTLING THE PERSONAL AND HISTORICAL
demons my search had set free, I would look back on the first
six weeks I lived in Krakow—lovely weeks spent strolling the square—
and wonder if I had known something then, if a part of me had seen the
future and divined the grief about to visit my family. I would look back
on entire days devoted to "cultural reconnaissance" and wonder if I wasn't
just savoring a last dance before an end to the party. It seemed easier at
the time to attribute the delay in my search to something cosmic, to believe it served some purpose beyond the drag of my own fear. But if I had
been honest with myself, if I had allowed even a hint of self-awareness,
I would have had to acknowledge that those cheerful spring days were
little more than creative diversions. Because as bold as I pretended to be,
and as brave as I was to have made it that far, I recognize now that I was
just afraid to continue. It was one thing to concoct an adventure, to boast
to friends that I would locate the family who saved my mother from the
Nazis. It was entirely another to begin that adventure—born, as it was, of
a lifelong dream—and expose it to the looming possibility of failure.

It's not that I didn't know where to begin. I knew that if I boarded a train in Krakow and rode it two hours to the west, I could arrive in a city where I could switch to a bus that would take me to a town where I could wander around in search of the house that my family used to own. I knew that if I found the house, I could approach the people who lived in it and ask them, after all these years, if they could direct me to the people who had made my life possible. It was in that house, in the small city of Będzin, Poland, where, in 1945, after his liberation from Auschwitz but before his departure from the country, my grandfather last saw the family who had saved his daughter. And so it would be to that house that I would return to find them again. But half a century had passed with our families on opposite sides of an ocean, and if these people were alive at all, I feared they had moved, disappeared without a forwarding address. And then what would I do? I worried that I'd never find them, that I'd be forced to go home with nothing.

But even more daunting than the prospect of never finding the family was the thought that its members were not only alive but living in what had been my family home. Of this I had been warned: "Be careful," hissed the man beside me one night in a Krakow bar when I told him why I had come to Poland. "You're wading into dangerous waters." He spoke of other foreigners he'd known, other Jews who'd returned, who'd tried to claim land seized first by the Nazis, then by the Soviets. They'd been spit on, accused of trying to steal a home from a family who had committed no crime. I assured this man that I had no interest in restitution, no desire to claim family property, but he told me it might not matter, that my motives might be questioned. His warnings were echoed by others, in other conversations, in other Polish bars. I heard of blistering debates over Jewish property in the Polish parliament. I heard that in towns where jobs were becoming increasingly scarce, Jews were once again becoming the scapegoats of choice. I feared my search would be viewed in this context and so I invented excuses. With a little more time, I reasoned, I could be more careful. I could form the right words.

But the first cold buds that had appeared on the trees soon after I arrived had already unfolded into blooms and were starting to curl into leaves. In the six weeks that I had been living in Krakow, March had become April, April had become May. And even my mother, who always insisted she had no interest in the family who had saved her life, had started to wonder, in her weekly calls from Detroit, when I would make my move. I told her, as I had told myself, that I was waiting for the right moment, but it sounded more like a lie when I said it out loud, and I knew I'd exhausted my excuses. And so, on a sunny morning in early May—the year was 2001—I reluctantly took my first few diffident steps toward whatever would happen next.

"We have to be cautious," I told my flatmates, Krys and Magda, who agreed to come with me as interpreters. This was a delicate matter. We would take good notes, then retreat to plan an artful approach. "We have to stay under radar," I insisted. Krys and Magda looked at each other, smiled at me, and both burst out laughing. "Sure thing," Magda chortled. "Whatever you say." They giggled down the stairs from our apartment and all the way to the train station, but I could barely swallow. My hands wobbled as I bought three tickets and handed them, crumpled and clammy, to the conductor on the train. I tried to watch out the window, to focus on the blur of muddy fields and abandoned factories in the passing scene. I tried to hear above the grinding gears of the belching train a piece of Krys and Magda's Polish banter, but there was no room in my head for anything beyond the nervous pounding of my own quickened heart. It was a sound track I knew, the drum in my head from days spent clinging to a notch of stone or a hairline crack on a granite cliff. I'd taken up rock climbing to confront my fear of heights and had willed myself to the tops of soaring cliffs. I had scrambled to the infinite tips of desert spires but had never learned to suppress those moments of panic when my hands would become so sweaty I could barely hold on, when I would become intensely aware of the empty space below me, and when all I could do was close my eyes and regret my decision to relinquish the solid comfort of earth. I would stand there, my toe jammed into a thimble-like pocket, two fingers pinching the tiniest crimp of rock, and listen to the pulsing beat of terror in my head. Then I would focus on the small task—the next move, the next handhold. And this was the lesson I applied now, sitting on the train beside Krys and Magda. I tried to relax, to calm my breath, to steady my hands.

As my flatmates laughed and chatted in Polish, I tried to divine at least the subject of their conversation, but after weeks of struggling to memorize strange-sounding verbs, I was still learning basic phrases. Discouraged, I dug through my bag for the photograph my mother had given me a few weeks before I left for Poland—an ordinary studio portrait, yellowed with age and printed on a scalloped-edged postcard from the 1940s. There was nothing outwardly remarkable about the three people in the picture, posing stiffly in front of a blank screen, but there was something so arresting about them that I'd taken to examining the photo as though it were a clue to a mystery, an insight, perhaps, into the child at the center of the frame. It was my mom at age three, her round little head tucked into a white knit cap, sitting between a man I recognized as her father and a pretty woman I had never seen before. "Is this your mother?" I asked when Mom first handed me the picture. I thought I could see a vague reflection of my own features in the woman's oval face and high cheekbones. But no, Mom said. Her mother would have been dead by the time the picture was taken. I remember standing silently in my mother's study that day, stunned that something as precious as this had appeared, as if out of the air, out of time. I thought I'd seen everything my mom had kept from her childhood and couldn't quite figure how she'd never shown this to me before. Did she not know she had it? Had she forgotten? Had she been wanting to keep it to herself?

"I used to think maybe she was my mother," Mom said, sounding distant even as she stood beside me. "But it couldn't have been her." We stood for another few minutes looking down at the photo, its unanswered questions. "I've wondered if maybe she's the woman who saved me." She turned the card to show me the back, where, in a handwriting that was like my mother's but had less confidence, a younger version of her had written her best guess about the picture: *Daddy, me and Polish lady caregiver,* it said. Now, on the train, I turned the card over to admire my mother's lovely script, the loopy lines of her pen along the top edge of the card.

The picture caught Krys and Magda's attention, and they leaned in. Magda reached over to tilt the picture toward the window's light. I watched as she considered the image, squinted slightly, and pulled the picture closer to her face before pronouncing her verdict: "Your mom looks sad," she said, handing the photo back to me. I hadn't noticed this before, but sure enough, when I looked down at the picture again, I could see that my mother's eyes looked puffy, as though she'd been crying. "Look how she's holding on to her coat," Magda said, pointing. It was another detail I'd somehow failed to notice despite hours of staring at the picture. I blushed with the shame of my inattention, but Magda was right. With her small right hand, Mom was gently fingering the white fur trim on her coat, holding on to its softness for comfort. My grandfather, on his daughter's left in the photo, looked dashingly handsome in a dark suit and dark tie. His face, unsmiling, was smooth and proud. The woman in the picture was the only one who seemed happy to be there. She wasn't smiling exactly, but the quiet edges of her painted lips were slightly upturned. "You're sure this isn't your grandmother?" Krys asked. "They look so much like a family, a mother, a father, a child." But no, I said. The woman in the photo was unknown.

Będzin was much bigger than I'd thought it would be, and much more urban. I'd pictured chickens and goats in the streets, but the bus from the train station dropped us on the side of a smog-choked highway beside a city center where three- and four-story buildings made of concrete and brick jostled for space along the crowded sidewalk. A young town his-

torian named Jarek Krajniewski was overjoyed by our interest in his city
and led an enthusiastic tour of its medieval castle and decaying neighborhoods. I'd made contact with Jarek a week earlier to arrange for this
tour, and thrilled in walking the streets where my family story began.
People seemed friendly. They waved to Jarek. They greeted us warmly.
But I still couldn't shake the warnings in my head. I worried that people
were watching us, that they could tell I was a Jew. I avoided eye contact. I took photos only covertly. I spent so much time glancing over
my shoulder that I nearly knocked into Jarek when he suddenly stopped
walking and grinned. "What's wrong?" I asked, glancing around. "That's
it," he said, gesturing with his chin. "That's the house you asked about."
I studied his face for a minute, not sure what he was saying or when I
had asked about a house. Then I remembered that I told Jarek my family's old address when we met through a mutual friend in Krakow. That's
when I realized where I was: the house I came to Poland to find.

I followed Jarek's gaze to a wide three-story town house of pinkish
brick, covered with a layer of grime. It was the only building on the block
that wasn't flush with the sidewalk. It sat, strangely, twenty feet back
from the street beyond a square of grassless lawn, a large, thick tree, and
a jarringly ugly aluminum shack. The house seemed almost to be hiding.
Like the city itself, the house was much bigger than I'd thought it would
be, and much more modern, but it was also dingier than I'd expected.
Its bricks seemed coarsely placed, its rows of windows—seven across the
top, seven through the middle—seemed to droop, to gape vacantly back
at me. Upstairs, a sweatshirt hung drying from a balcony rail.

I felt suddenly winded. I realized I had been holding my breath and
sharply released a lungful of air. We stood planted on the sidewalk,
watching the house, waiting. I think it was Magda who broke the silence: "Do you think they're still here?" she asked.

"I doubt it," I said, my eyes still fixed on the house. "It's been a long
time."

It had been a long time. It had been fifty-five years, five months, two weeks, and three days since my grandfather invited the family to live in his house, then left Poland forever. And yet there was a chance that behind one of these windows, I could still find the people who had saved my mother's life. After all these years, they could still be here, drying their laundry on the balcony rail. I could hear the heartbeat pulsing in my head again. I was back on the cliff, praying for an easy way down, an easy way out.

"Doesn't look like anyone's home," I said, as though saying it could make it true.

"What do you mean?" Krys asked. "Let's see if they're here."

"Oh, no," I said. "Not today. I just wanted to see the house and to—"

My friends were already bounding down the brick path toward the building's central archway. I tried to stop them, tried to yell for them to return, but they continued into the staircase on the left side of the archway and intrepidly knocked on the first door they saw. I hung back, afraid of what would happen, hoping no one would answer. I cringed when the door edged open and a woman's face appeared. I nearly ducked behind the stairs so I wouldn't be seen.

Jarek introduced himself, asking the woman if she knew a family named Skowroński who used to live here. The woman hesitated, skeptically eyeing the strangers in front of her, then slowly nodded. She said something in Polish, pointed toward the sky, then disappeared back into her apartment. It was the news I had both feared and secretly hoped for.

"They're dead?" I asked.

"No," Krys said, laughing, patting me playfully on the shoulder. "They live upstairs." I was dumbfounded. Upstairs? They were still here? But how? And what if we went upstairs and they slammed the door? My friends had already started up to the second floor as I hurried to catch them. "Listen," I said. "Maybe we should send a letter first. It'd be less confrontational." The first approach was crucial. It needed to be handled with care, not rushed like this, but my friends were almost giddy as they rang the bell beside a door on the second landing. That was when I noticed that the small tag beside the doorbell said: SKOWROŃSKA, HONORATA. That was the name of the woman who had saved my mom. She couldn't still be alive, could she? If she'd been an adult during the war, she'd be . . .

I should have brought water with me. I was starting to feel light-headed. The stairwell had a faint stench of urine and rot. The iron railings were twisted as though beaten and bruised. On the turquoise walls, ribbons of graffiti swirled around the badly chipped paint. I just wasn't ready for this, not yet. I wanted to leave the house and put an end to this stressful day—to go back to Krakow and write a carefully worded letter to introduce myself to the family to assure them that my intentions were innocuous. When no one answered the door, I felt enormous relief and pleaded with my friends to leave with me. I argued that we would miss our train back to Krakow, but they wanted to talk to the neighbors. They wanted to ring another bell, then another, until we were joined in the narrow stairwell by an old man and his wife who lived across the hall and an even older lady who came out to investigate the commotion. Jarek addressed them in what seemed like a formal tone, asking if they knew that their neighbor Mrs. Skowrońska had sheltered a Jewish baby during the occupation. The neighbors seemed surprised, but yes, they seemed to be saying, "She did shelter a Jewish child." Then they all started talking at once, smiling and nodding and interrupting one another to tell the story they'd heard from their neighbor. I picked out a few words. I heard *Baby. Jewish. War.*

"Mrs. Skowrońska told them about your mother," Magda whispered to me. "She talked about her all the time. She's dead now, but her son still lives here." My friends started pointing at me and saying *córka,* which means *daughter.* "She's the daughter of the baby who lived with Mrs. Skowrońska." The neighbors started gesturing with their hands, telling more of the story. The old man pointed to the Skowrońska door, but we told him that no one was home. "Oh, they're home, they're home," the old man seemed to be saying as he stepped around us to the door and knocked. No one answered, so the old man knocked again, this time harder. *"SKUV-ROYN-SKI!"* he yelled, pounding like a cop without a warrant. *"MASZ GOSCI!"* *You have guests.*

The man continued to pound on the door, and the muted sound of his fist against the wood echoed up and down the stairs. That was when I really started to fluster. I needed subtlety, not seven people in a stairwell and one of them pounding on the door. What if someone actually opened the door to this? *"SKUV-ROYN-SKIII!!!"* The man raised his voice to a shout. "Really," I said. "If they're not—" Then the door opened and a confused older face emerged. I saw blue eyes, startled and wide, tucked into a blanket of soft creases. The owner of the eyes blinked as though he'd been sleeping. Then everyone started talking at once, pointing and nodding—Krys, Magda, Jarek, the old man with the pounding fist, his wife, the lady across the hall—they were a buzzing cacophony of Slavic confusion interrupted for me only by the same few words: *Mother. Baby. War.* And now they were pointing at me. They were pointing at me and saying *córka,* daughter. I blushed. Everyone was talking except me and the man with the startled blue eyes. While they talked, we kept looking at each other. Finally, I put out my hand and said in broken Polish something I hoped was: "Hello, sir, nice to meet you." He took my hand and told me the meeting was his pleasure.

"My name is Erin," I told him. His name was Wiesław (VYE-swahf). He invited us into his living room, a small rectangular space with two windows facing the street; a beat-up sofa; a square table with a collec tion of mismatched chairs; and a large ceramic heater in the corner. Krys, Magda, Jarek, and I stood awkwardly in the middle of the room, not sure if we should stand or sit, if we should say something or wait for him to speak. Wiesław stood wordlessly, as though trying to decide if we were real or if he was dreaming in his sleep. He kept blinking. Not sure what else to do, I reached into my bag for the photo of my mother at three, with her father and a dark-haired woman. I handed the picture to Wiesław, who started.

"My God," he said, closing his eyes and opening them again. *"To moja matka."* That's my mother. I smiled, touched his arm, and pointed to the girl in the picture.

"And that's *my* mother," I told him. *Moja matka.*

Wiesław looked from the picture to me and then back to the picture. This was my proof. He took me in his arms and started to cry. "She was my sister," he told me. Tears welled in his eyes. "I was her big brother. Is she still alive? Is she okay?"

I turned to Magda for translation, then answered, "Yes, of course." I could feel tears forming in my eyes, too. "She's doing well."

I had been worried he would hate me. Instead, I'd just brought his long-lost sister back to life. "How old is she?" he asked as my friends translated. "She's fifty-nine," I said. He shook his head and marveled. Did she marry young? How many children did she have? When was she coming to Poland to see him? He asked if I had a picture of her today, and I pulled from my bag a snapshot I had taken in February of Mom in her kitchen, smiling and cute. "She looks so young! She's so pretty!" he said. "You're really going to bring her to see me?"

My face was starting to hurt from grinning. I couldn't wait to bring her here, couldn't believe this was happening. I thought of Mom at home, how she hadn't exactly agreed to come to Poland. I thought of something else I knew about her that I couldn't tell him yet. "It's expensive to come over," I said. "It's very far. But she'll come. She told me she wants to come." Wiesław put his hands on my shoulders and told me that his mother had waited her life for this moment. She'd prayed that someday the girl she loved as a daughter would return. And that was when I did something I would later live to regret. I smiled up at Wiesław's soft blue eyes and, searching for the words to address him in Polish, promised that no matter what happened, no matter what it cost me, I would bring him his sister. I would bring my mother to Będzin and the two would meet again.

CHAPTER TWO

I RENA FRYDRYCH WAS EIGHT YEARS OLD, ALMOST NINE, THE FIRST time she heard the story of her life. She was sailing with her father and stepmother aboard a transatlantic ocean liner bound for New York harbor. She was thin on the details, or maybe she didn't remember them, but I pictured a sun-drenched deck, the taste of salt in the air, and a little girl with flaming red hair, maybe a blue dress— it was her favorite color—trembling and suspiciously looking up at a man she barely knew. As she would later recall, the man—her father, Beresh Frydrych—having lost his wife, his parents, three brothers, a sister, their children, their spouses, and nearly every friend he'd ever had, turned to his only child, his only living tie to home, and began a tale with a sentence that is almost as famous in my family as the events it describes: "You were born in Poland in 1942," he told her. "And things did not look good for the Jewish people."

He must have gone on to describe how he and his family were moved from the apartment building they owned in the small Polish city of Będzin (pronounced BENjin in Polish, benDEEN in Yiddish) to a nearby ghetto and how he and his wife were rounded up one morning on their way to work. Or maybe those details came later, as Mom grew older and could understand more. But she never wanted to hear any of it, and now, as I retell it, I stand by none of it. I can't even say what language my grandfather was speaking that day. Probably Swedish, Mom said. They had been living in Sweden, and she figured she must have forgotten Polish by then. She couldn't remember when she learned to speak Yiddish. But like most of the details in this story, even that can be seen only through the rheumy eyes of distant memory.

> Irena Frydrych's parents met in the Bedzin, Poland ghetto and fell in love in 1940. It was not a time for romantic illusion. The Jews of Bedzin were crowded into the ghetto. They lived among rats, vermin, constant fear—certainly not the candies and flowers of young love. But it was here, a year after Germany invaded Poland, that Beresh Frydrych and Sura Leah Rosenblum found one another. "They decided to get married because it was war time," Irena recalled from stories she'd heard. "In war time, you don't know what is going to happen. My parents wanted to be together."

I wrote this story for my high school newspaper, the West Bloomfield High School *Spectrum,* in January 1991. At seventeen, I interviewed my mother at the kitchen table, using an old black tape recorder with buttons like toes, and crafted her memory into a narrative. Research that I did in college and after turned up factual errors. The Jews of Będzin, for example, weren't forced into the ghetto until 1943, so my grandparents weren't necessarily in the ghetto when they decided to get married. But the story, as I wrote it then, was the product of perfect folklore. It was the sum of what my mother had told me, based on what her father had told her. Like most family stories, it was more memory than truth. It was colored by half a century's agenda and spin, and written, because I was young and dramatic, with excessive sentimentality. But this was the story I knew, or thought I knew. And ten years later, when I attempted to find out what actually happened, it was all I had to go on.

> Dirty grey snow covered the ghetto when baby Irena was born, Feb. 20, 1942. She was born in a cellar, in silence. If anyone knew of her existence, she would be killed. While her parents worked, they left Irena in the care of an elderly aunt, sharing a crib with a baby cousin named Gitte who was born a few months earlier. When the Germans patrolled the streets, pillows shoved in the babies' faces muffled their cries. The babies remained hidden. They rarely saw sunlight. They learned, instinctively, to be silent. But their lives, from the moment of their births, were doomed.
>
> Irena's parents stayed alive for three years in the ghetto by virtue of their work papers. As long as they had papers, they had hope of survival and of keeping their daughter alive. But eventually, even papers couldn't save them. Beresh and Sura Leah were on their way to work one morning when they were rounded up and herded at gunpoint with hundreds of others onto a slow-moving train bound for somewhere. Their own fate was bleak. But what about Irena's? There'd been no time to arrange for her care.
>
> Beresh spotted a window on the train and pleaded with his wife to escape with him, to go to their daughter. It was a desperate effort. There were guards on both ends of the car—guards with orders to shoot—

but Beresh urged his wife to join him. "My father was a pessimist," Irena would recall decades later. "He always thought the worst was going to happen. He knew when he went on that train that he was going to end up dead."

Sura Leah was terrified. She didn't know where the train would take her but she knew the chances of surviving a jump were slim. Her husband begged, but she refused. Eventually, he went without her, slipping through the thin window of the cattle car under a shower of Nazi guns. He landed hard on the grass and escaped to the woods. Blood poured from his leg where a bullet pierced his flesh but there was neither time for nor access to treatment. He bandaged his leg with the armband—JUDE—that labeled him a Jew, then swiftly made his way back to Bedzin, to his only child.

He made contact with a gentile woman with whom he'd traded goods for bread. He knew this woman was reliable—or hoped she was—and lavished on her his every possession. He gave her his money, his jewelry, the deed to his factory and apartment. He gave her the address of his relatives in the United States and made her promise to contact them if he failed to return after the war. Then he handed her his daughter and pleaded with her to keep the baby safe. A few days later, he was captured again, and again forced onto a train. This time, though, he didn't jump. He rode the train to its final destination.

The woman who'd agreed to look after Irena asked her sister to look after Gitte and both girls became daughters to strangers. But Irena had something that

Gitte did not: she had blue eyes, red hair, Aryan features. Gitte had dark eyes and dark hair that betrayed her Semitic blood. Soon there were whispers. Gitte's caretaker became scared. Terror-stricken, she carried her dark-haired charge onto a streetcar, set the baby on a seat and left the train without her, never asking after her again. Whether Gitte survived is impossible to know. A kindly woman may have scooped her up from the seat and saved her, maybe left her on the steps of an orphanage. She could still be alive today. Or that day could have been her last.

For Irena, red hair served as a handy disguise. The woman who agreed to look after her dropped Irena off in the country at the home of her own mother. This old woman introduced the baby as her daughter's girl, telling her friends that her daughter had to work in the city and could not care for the child herself. And there, in the countryside, Irena was loved.

Beresh, meanwhile, was taken to Auschwitz, where he reunited with his brother, Gitte's father. The two vowed to stay together, to support one another. When they heard that the German manufacturing company Siemens was looking for workers trained in the tool trade, they both volunteered. Both brothers had run the family brass factory at home in Bedzin and both brothers were confident that they would be selected for this lifesaving assignment. But though Beresh's brother was the brain of the family and though Beresh boasted how much better his brother knew the trade than he, when Siemens questioned the brothers about the tool trade, Beresh passed the test and his brother did not.

The elder brother went instead to the gas chamber, leaving Beresh to survive the camp on his own. Of everything Beresh would lose, of all the agonies he would suffer, this would be the moment that would trouble him most through the rest of his life—that he had passed the test and his brother had not.

Beresh worked for Siemens until the end of the war, making munitions that would continue his own enslavement and enrich the German corporation that was at once saving his life and destroying it. He was liberated in 1945 and returned home to Bedzin, where he hoped somehow to find Sura Leah, waiting for him with a survival story as dramatic as his own. But she was not there and neither was the city of his birth. Bedzin had become a city of people who despised him. He hadn't realized the hate that would have grown for a once-wealthy Jew. He wanted to leave. But first he had to find his daughter.

Irena walked and ran. She spoke and sang and could recite the Polish alphabet. Her fair white skin was splashed with thousands of freckles from summer days in the country. She loved the woman who took care of her and knew nothing of the man who arrived one day, claiming to be her father. She was three years old and frightened of this stranger.

Beresh took Irena, kicking and screaming, to an orphanage for surviving children, then traveled to Germany, where he could earn money for passage to the United States. His relatives in the States were relieved to learn that he and Irena had survived and urged them to move to Sweden, where the wait for visas would be shorter. Then, when Beresh had money enough to make it as far as Sweden, he returned again to Poland to collect Irena from the orphanage.

"I remember when he came for me again," Irena recalled. "This was the second time I had seen this man. Each time I see him, he takes me away from where I'm comfortable. I screamed." She remembers the incident vividly and can still picture the hurt expression on her father's face. But she feared him. "I screamed the whole time he was there. The minute I saw him, I started to scream and I didn't stop screaming until he left. When he left, I stopped screaming."

She was screaming when she met her foster family in Sweden. Her father made arrangements with the cantor at the Jewish synagogue in Stockholm who knew of a warm Jewish family that could care for a young Polish girl. Their name was Keijler. While Beresh worked to earn money for the boat, he lived in a boarding house with other holocaust survivors. Irena stayed with the Keijlers. "He had nothing," Irena said of her father. "He went to work to try and rebuild his life but he had to start from scratch. He had nothing, like a newborn baby."

Irena remembers the Keijlers as warm people whose home smelled of baking sweets. She'd survived terrible trauma but emerged unscathed. "I was always loved. I was lucky that way," she said. "Whoever took care of me, loved me . . . I think that's what saved me." It was love that made her father risk his life repeatedly to save his daughter. The chocolates he brought every Saturday of the four years they spent in Sweden were filled with love. Irena ate the candy quickly and, although she was shy, would smile often.

"It wasn't until we were on the boat, crossing to America, that he told me about my life," Irena said. Father and daughter traveled the Atlantic together in December 1950. "He told me I was born during the war time and that things did not look good for the Jewish people . . ."

In Sweden, Beresh met Fela Brystowska through his cousin and married her after two months. She was a beautiful young woman who'd been captured by the Nazis at 17 but survived the horrors. She would be a new mother to Irena. The three would settle in Detroit, Michigan, near Beresh's family. Irena Frydrych became Irene Frederick. Beresh became Bernard and Fela became Faye. They adjusted to society and all became American citizens.

The family had seen more and endured more than most read about in a lifetime, but they had survived. Irene went to school and learned English. She grew up and went to college and met her husband, Brian. They would have two children: the first, a boy named Derek. The second, a girl to whom they would give the Hebrew name Sura Leah, they would name Erin. She would one day write down the whole story. Bernard Frederick died of a stroke in 1982. He was 74. Faye Frederick lives happily in Atlanta, Georgia. My mom, Irene, who never met her mother or even saw a picture of her, has always been there for me.

The story was the pride of my senior year. It won national high school journalism awards. I lavished attention on its every detail, then basked in the way my friends and teachers responded. The day that article ran in my four-hundred-circulation high school monthly was the day I decided to go into journalism. I wanted to discover fascinating narratives and tell them. And in the years to come, I would do just that, reporting for much larger publications. But this story, my mother's story, lived inside me like an organ. I relished its dramatic arc, its tale of love in a time of desperation, of lives begun with no hope of survival, of a father's daring leap from a moving train, and of a Polish mother's courageous sacrifice. But the prize for me had always been the happy ending: the family's triumphant reunion, stepping out of the ruins of war to set sail for new lives in a new country, a child learning the story of her worst years, just as her best years were about to begin. That parts of this story may have been wrong never occurred to me. That my mother may have deliberately misled me, cleaned up the story's messier aspects, was not a concept I paused to consider. But what if the ending wasn't exactly happy? What if I had swept the story too forcefully into my own fantasy of how it must have been? What if my mother had told me a version she preferred to believe instead of one that was actually true?

It all started to unravel for me in the thick of a summer heat wave in 1999. My mom and I were driving from her house in Detroit to mine in Philadelphia. I was twenty-six. She was fifty-seven. And we were, after years at emotional war with each other, finally, if tentatively, friends. This meant we were willing to sidestep most of the mother-daughter land mines most of the time. We were transporting an antique cabinet that Mom had bought for me in Michigan without considering how she'd get it to my door. I was grateful for the gift, but it had languished in her garage for a year until I could find time to fly out for a weekend and drive it back with her. We fired up my brother's discarded Ford Explorer and prayed the air-conditioning would last. Temperatures were in the hundreds. The air was sticky and wet. When the AC quit outside of Toledo, Mom and I were left to maintain our tenuous peace through nine hours of sweat and irritation.

"Do you have to drive so fast?" she shouted over the noise of the wind through the windows.

"I am not driving fast!"

"Well, slow down!"

"I'm going seventy. How slow do you want me to go?"

The conversation went something like that through most of Ohio. We snapped, then we sulked, then we fished around for something to talk about. I tried movies, but she'd seen only chick flicks. She probed my love life, but there was nothing I wanted to tell. Eventually, I tried an open-ended question: "Have you ever driven across the country?" I asked, hopeful.

"Yes," she said, still eyeing the speedometer. "When we first got here. We went to California. My father thought there were jobs there."

I gave my mother a puzzled look. This was a detail of her life I'd never heard before. "You didn't go straight to Detroit? Wouldn't the jobs have been there in 1950?"

"I don't know," she said. "He wanted to go to California, so we went to California."

Mom and her family spent a few weeks in Detroit when they first arrived in the United States, she told me. They attended a family wedding there. But my grandfather had a sister in California whom he wanted to visit, so a relative—an uncle Abe—volunteered to make the drive with them across the Rockies. I'd never heard of Uncle Abe, but he was reportedly the father-in-law of my cousin Jane, whom I had heard of. I wasn't entirely sure why he drove or why Jane's sister Dorothy came, or why Dorothy brought her son Jerry, or how they managed to cram my mother, her father, his wife, Dorothy Jerry, and Abe into a single car that must also have been carrying luggage and food. I asked these questions, but Mom didn't know. "I didn't even speak English," she protested. "I was just there." She had a fair point, I agreed.

"So how was it?" I asked.

"What? The drive? I only remember fighting with Jerry," Mom said. She smirked when I asked what the fights were about. "Kid stuff, whatever kids fight about," she said. Her patience with my questions was faltering, but she had to give me something. We had six hours left to drive. I kept at it. I asked if they stopped anywhere, if they saw the Grand Canyon, but Mom protested again. "I was young!" she said. "I don't remember."

This was how it always happened. I would ask for details, something to color the sketch I had of her childhood, and she would tell me that she had been young, that she didn't remember. I had never understood this. From what I could tell, her long-term memory was extraordinary. She could rattle off trivia about movies and songs from the 1950s. She knew the names of my kindergarten play pals, the names of their mothers, cute things they said. But she didn't know if she'd seen the Grand Canyon?

Then Mom surprised me.

"Oh, I do remember something!" she said. "I remember my uncle made me cry."

I turned to look at her. "This Abe guy made you cry?"

"He didn't mean to," Mom said. "He was just teasing, but I had a photo of my foster mom from Sweden, and he kept pointing and laughing that she had a pimple."

Only it wasn't a pimple, Mom said. It was a smudge on the picture, on the nose. Mom must have held it too long and damaged the print. She tried to explain this, to correct her uncle, to insist that her foster mom was really very pretty, but she didn't speak English, and she wasn't understood.

"They were all laughing," she said. "That's when I cried."

I pictured my mom at eight: the little girl in the backseat, struggling to be understood, being laughed at instead. I pictured her clutching her photograph, sleeping with it beside her pillow, rubbing away at the smudge on its beloved subject's face only to find that her sticky fingers deepened the damage. I could feel the pierce of her grief. "What a terrible story!" I said. But Mom waved me off. "It was a long time ago," she said. I took my eyes off the road for a second and settled them on her, hoping to see beyond her nonchalance to the place in her head where she stored the memory, that ache of being eight, confused and completely unable to defend a woman she loved as her own mother. Something in her eyes, maybe? But no. I wasn't psychic, and Mom wasn't playing. I looked again. Still no. Not that I knew what the imprint of childhood pain might look like, but there was nothing unusual on my mother's round face, just the same faded freckles on the soft folds of pale skin, the same light blue eyes behind trendy wire frames, the same crown of red-brown hair—darker than when she was a child—pulled back from her face with a pair of drugstore barrettes. Having told her story, Mom had moved on. Not me. The power of her story lodged in my throat. "You must have been frustrated," I said. She gave me a questioning look, as if she'd already forgotten what we were discussing. Then she answered distractedly: "I guess so. That's why I was crying, but you know." She shrugged. "Kids cry."

I spent the rest of the drive trying to join my mother in light conversation. She recycled her favorite topics of home decorating, family, and Hollywood gossip and what so-and-so at work—*can you believe it?*—had said to her. She nagged me about my driving speed and cross-examined me on my lack of a boyfriend. Was it because I didn't wear lipstick or because I talked too much? But as much as I tried to participate in her cheerful chatter, I couldn't shake her story. That little girl, just weeks after arriving in a new country, crammed in the back of a nasty road-trip car packed with people and luggage and stink, her sweaty hands destroying the only picture she had of a woman who had cared for her as long as she could remember. There was this cousin—a little brat, no doubt—who was picking on her, and an uncle—a man she'd only just met—making fun of her. And she didn't even know the language to defend herself!

Her anecdote was simple, a single moment in what must have been a five-day ride. It was a moment so insignificant to her that she'd never mentioned it before. But hearing it that day for me was like picking up a book I'd read a hundred times and realizing there were pages stuck together, pages that, when pried apart, revealed an entirely new drama. The pages in between changed everything. Through all the dramatic tellings I'd heard of my mother's story—the unspeakable setting into which she was born and the fantastic odds she'd beaten to get out of Europe at all—I'd never given much thought to what happened later, once she reached the United States. The war story's final scene had always featured Mom, her hair in pigtails, her Swedish flag in one hand and little suitcase in the other, jumping up and down as she spotted the Statue of Liberty. She'd only ever told me how lucky she was, how she was always loved. She'd told me this repeatedly, like a politician getting a sound bite on the news. He won't answer questions, only repeat his quote. "I was always loved." Her mantra. And I believed her. Why wouldn't I? But now the story had a new dimension. She must have entered the American public school system as a big-nosed, red-haired, motherless Jewish girl whose only language was Swedish and only dress a hand-me-down.

There was no question she was lucky. She'd escaped a genocidal scourge that had killed one and a half million children. Only about a dozen kids from her city in Poland were known to have survived. But to say she'd escaped unscathed? She'd been "saved" and united with her family in the United States, but she must have pined for the world she'd left behind in Sweden, maybe even for the one before that in Poland. Her hair was cut into bangs so she would look more American. Someone scrubbed her face to help rid her of freckles. Her name was changed from a lovely, roll-off-the-tongue name, Irena (airENnaah), to the harsh, blunt I-rene. The woman who had just married her father would be the fifth mother she would have. And here was this uncle, a member of the "real family" everyone had been so intent on connecting her with, and he was making fun of her. The more I thought about it, the more it upset me. "Did you stay in touch with her?" I asked a few miles outside of Philadelphia. My voice was cracking from the heat, from yelling over the hot wind, and from a large scoop of emphatic grief.

"With whom?" she asked.

"The lady in Sweden, Mom. The one you were crying over."

"Oh, no. Not really."

"But she was your mother!"

"Eh," Mom said. "I was young."

It wasn't that I thought my mother had lied about her happy ending, at least not deliberately. The more I considered it, the more certain I was that the version she'd told was the one she believed, the one that came filtered through decades of convincing herself that if no one saw her scars, she must not have had any. She had masterfully enlisted me into her concept of herself as a woman without a painful past, a woman who had always been loved. And I was invested in the story. But if the ending was wrong, I wondered, what else was? My mind raced over the details. Had my grandparents really fallen in love amid the ruins of war? Or were they among the couples who believed—falsely, as it turned out—that married women would fare better in the ghetto? And how was it that my grandfather was able to jump from a train, like he said? If you could jump, wouldn't everyone have jumped? He bandaged his leg with his Jude armband? Really?

The story's characters seemed suddenly flat; its narrative seemed pocked with holes. The tale I had seen forever as family history transformed that day into a mystery, into a series of clues I needed to decipher. And as I considered them, I felt the same anticipation that rushes over me whenever I stumble into a big-headline news story. When the phone rings with an unbelievable tip or when a possible scandal emerges from behind a passing remark, an urgent sort of mania sets in, a frantic thirst for the rest of the details, for the other glimmers of facts that can be pried from cryptic documents or begged from unwilling sources. The story almost torments me until I know enough and can prove enough to put it into the paper and out of my head. And that, I knew, was what I needed to do with my mother's story, with my family's story. I needed to pursue it. For me, if not for my mom.

By the time we began setting the table at my house that night for a late dinner of Chinese takeout, I announced that I had made a decision: "I'm going to find your foster family in Sweden."

Mom looked at me incredulously. "They're dead!" she protested.

"Maybe so," I said. "But they had a daughter. She'd be alive. I'll find her."

Mom adjusted her glasses and peered at me across the table, as though by seeing me better, she could understand my thinking. "The daughter didn't even like me."

"That was fifty years ago. She'd be thrilled to see you now. And I'll go to Poland, too. I'll find the family who hid you there."

Mom cocked her head to the side, clearly trying to decide if this was a real plan or another in a series of proposals that I would discuss for months, then abandon. For years I had talked of a great adventure, of a yearlong journey that would take me to Peru, perhaps, or to China. I could see Mom trying to decide how to respond to this latest idea, weighing whether objecting would discourage or only embolden me, but on my side of the table, in my head, I was already searching the Internet for grants. I was already asking my editor for time off. I was already packing my bags. Mom may have seen this, may have realized that this scheme was different from my others. Or she may have been too drained from the long drive to argue. She exhaled audibly and settled her eyes on mine. "You want to find them, Erin?" she said, a resignation in her voice. "Then go find them. But the family in Poland only did it for the money. They asked my father to send them a Chevrolet. And the family in Sweden . . ." She stopped for a second to think about them. "Well, anyway, they're gone now. If they were alive . . ." She picked up a plastic container of egg drop soup, poured the contents into a bowl, and lifted her spoon to start eating.

"If I find them, will you come over and meet them?" I asked.

"I don't know, Erin." She sounded tired now. "I'm hungry, and I'd like to eat."

I could tell she wasn't thrilled about the idea. I knew she'd prefer to have me home, where I would be safe. She wanted me married. She wanted grandchildren. But if the other options were China or Peru, she'd rather have me in Poland. Despite this, I decided to take her ambiguity as a full-fledged go-ahead. As we tackled our greasy Chinese dinner with splintered wooden chopsticks, I even decided that a part of her was proud that I'd taken an interest in her life. Then again, I may have invented that. Either way, I had been wanting to live abroad since the year I graduated from college and watched my friends go off to join the Peace Corps or teach English in Japan. I had made what I'd thought at the time were wise choices, applying for reporting jobs, taking positions that offered the best career prospects. I worked for a newspaper in Detroit, covering murders in my hometown until my union there went on strike. I moved to Philadelphia to cover the suburbs, zoning meetings, and school boards for *The Philadelphia Inquirer*. Two years later, I took a job with another Philadelphia paper, the *Daily News,* taking on big-city pols with a notebook and pen. It had been interesting and challenging—even fun—but I still craved a youthful adventure, and this was my chance. As I reached for a second helping of moo shu vegetables, I made another announcement. "I'll go at the end of the year," I said, never more certain of anything.

CHAPTER THREE

ANYONE PASSING THE SMALL WHITE HOUSE WITH BLUE SHUTTERS on Genesee Avenue in Los Angeles would have seen the little red-haired girl at the door that day, her freckled nose against the screen. They'd have seen the shine of her new dress, the pretty gleam of her newly cut hair, maybe even the sadness of her light blue eyes. It was her birthday. She was nine. And the last thing she wanted was a party. She'd told her family that she didn't want anything. No presents. No cake. She wanted to go back to Sweden, to Shprinsa Keijler and her sweet-smelling cinnamon rolls, to the apartment next to the park where Shprinsa used to push her on the swing. She didn't want to be in America, didn't want to be in Los Angeles, thought the bright sun here made everything look fake. She hated the kids at school, how they teased her, made fun of her clothes. She suffered when they called her stupid. More than anything, she wanted to be left alone.

When her cousin Sharon, a sixth-grader, appeared in her class one day to invite the younger kids to a birthday party, she wanted to shrink under her desk, to hide until everyone stopped staring. She avoided the eyes of her classmates for the rest of the week, hoping they'd forget about the party. But then her stepmother went out and bought her a new party dress, a fancy one with blue and white stripes on the skirt and delicate yellow flowers woven into the fabric. Her cousin Annie, Sharon's mom, baked her a cake with nine candles. And that morning, when she came into the kitchen for breakfast, there was a box for her with a doll in it. She'd already started knitting the doll a new dress, like she used to do with Shprinsa in Sweden whenever a new doll arrived. Shprinsa would sit beside her and praise her perfect stitches, her careful rows of knits and purls. And as she knitted that tiny dress, she started thinking that maybe the party wouldn't be so bad, that maybe if her classmates saw her in her party clothes, they would know she was normal, like them. They might even want to be her friend. By the time she was dressed for the party, she was even looking forward to it: her first celebration in America.

Her parents and cousins had been fussing for weeks over her cheerless, quiet ways. But this morning, getting ready for the party, she seemed a different child entirely. She even joined her stepmother in singing a song in Yiddish about a bird on a tree branch that her stepmother had taught her on the ship to America. It was the first time, her cousins noted, that they'd seen her smile. She had a lovely smile with a darling dimple that puckered like a kiss on her right cheek. The adults remarked on how nice it was to see her starting to warm. But then the hour of the party arrived before any of the guests, and the dimple began to go flat. It was still visible after ten minutes. A stubborn hint of it remained after twenty. But when an hour passed and still no child had arrived, the dimple vanished like grass beneath a cold sheet of snow. She stood by herself at the screen door, her stony face against the mesh, her eyes on the sidewalk, where she hoped still to see one of her classmates arriving with a ribbon-wrapped gift. Still more time passed, and she looked down at her toes, at the red leather shoes she'd adored when she'd chosen them in Sweden. Now they looked ugly, old-fashioned, nothing like the white and black saddle shoes her classmates wore. She could feel tears creeping onto her lashes, but she blinked them away. The kids could still come, and she didn't want them to think she was a baby. She wouldn't cry, she refused to cry, even after her stepmother and aunt suggested she cut the cake so that she could have a piece, even after Sharon and her brother, Kenny, started saying how much fun it would be to have a party "with just us family." She stood wordlessly, tearlessly, a sentry at the screen door, until there was no denying the only conclusion: No one was going to come.

Stinging with shame, she took hold of the heavy front door with her small hands and heaved it closed with an angry slam. Eyes she'd struggled to keep dry now flooded with salty tears as she ran to the bathroom. She flipped the lock and sat down on the toilet to sob. If they were knocking on the door, calling her name, she was unaware. If there was a fuss in the hallway over whether she should be punished for slamming the door, she couldn't have known. All she heard was the choking of her own despair. She sobbed for everything she'd lost and for everything she wanted. She sobbed for how much she hated her father, who was icy and harsh and had never asked if she wanted to come to America; for her stepmother, who talked to her like a baby, who tried to teach her those babyish songs. She was not a baby. And she wasn't stupid. She could knit and sew and ski and do a somersault on a balance beam, and none of those stupid kids in her class could do that. She sobbed for Shprinsa, who was missing her birthday. And she sobbed because it just wasn't fair, because nothing would ever be fair again.

It was, my mother would tell me decades later, one of the most difficult moments of her life. She was unimpressed, even bored, by the indescribable events that surrounded her birth. Years later, with Shprinsa and Sweden a distant memory, she claimed no particular recollection of being moved from place to place. She didn't remember being stashed in an orphanage, uprooted to a foster home. She would tell me—whether or not she was speaking the truth—that she was not affected at all by refugee life in Europe. But this party, its uneaten cake, she remembered as clearly as any event that happened before or was yet to transpire. The war crimes of my mother's life were not, in her mind, committed by fascists. They came at the hands of cruel American children.

This could be why she tended to gloss over the war years, why everything that had happened to her in Europe was overshadowed by her later zeal to fit in, her need to spend hours in front of a mirror practicing precise American diction, like a TV newscaster. She had to have the right clothes, to wear her hair the right way. After college, she became a teacher because that was the right kind of job for a woman who wanted children (she had secretly wanted to be a doctor). And she wanted to have the right kind of past, one that had been easy. By the time I was born, twenty-two years after the fateful birthday party, there was almost no way to detect that my mother was anything other than what she seemed: a goofy wife, an overprotective mother, a self-taught craftswoman with a knack for refinishing furniture who lived in the suburbs of an American city. She had impeccable English grammar and no perceivable accent. Even the Jewish nose wasn't there anymore. She did away with it in college, dropping years of babysitting cash on an adorable replacement nose, a tiny button of a thing that held her small, round glasses and made her face look open, happy, symmetrical. She developed a wry sense of humor and laughed at other people's jokes. Only a few people knew where she came from. Even some of her closest friends had no idea.

It was no surprise, then, that in years of trying to assemble the story of my mother's life, I managed to misread even the details she provided. She'd told me about the birthday party, about bursting into tears when she realized that no one was coming, but I considered that an everyday tale of childhood rejection, the kind known to misfit children the world over. In the same way I'd tidied the ending of my mother's war story, I'd also failed to connect her war years to the taunted-child stories they preceded. I failed to consider how the events of her early years would have compounded and intensified the thorny transition she would have to make later when she arrived in yet another new country and had to make yet another new set of friends. But now the whole of her life was coming together for me like the careful stitches on the dresses that, decades after she knitted them for her dolls, would be worn by mine. I could see more clearly how each stitch of her life affected the next, how everything—from the choices she'd made to the rancorous fights she would later have with me—was woven from the same ball of yarn.

I used to wonder, back when I was in high school and she and I were entangled in a malicious multiyear hostility, how it was that we became such adversaries, why we were both so ready to scream at each other with the slightest provocation. But now, looking back, I could see that the bulk of our legendary clashes began with her wanting me to fit in as badly as she had wanted to fit in herself. I was too loud as a kid, too rude, always talking back to my teachers and shouting at her in the grocery store. She would be furious with me and would smack me when we got home. She was horrified when, at sixteen, embracing feminism, I stopped shaving my legs and gleefully grew a forest of thick black hair in my armpits. She wouldn't go out with me in public, afraid her friends would see us. She begged me to dress like everyone else, to stop parading around in garishly colored clothes. I had a generous appetite, and though I was a competitive tennis player, she worried that I would become fat. She bribed me to go on diets. The more she tried to fit me into her picture of the pleasant, well liked child, the more loudly and creatively I rebelled against her. And the more I rebelled, the more she expanded her methods of control. It was no longer enough to scrutinize my calories. Now she had to openly call me fat, to shame me into dieting. Instead of mocking my clothes, she would stand in front of the door and forbid me from leaving until I had changed into something less galling. I started lying to her, not because I was doing anything I needed to hide, but to retain some power for myself. And then we started fighting over everything; over tennis, where she viewed every lackluster match I played as an insult to her; over school, where I thought straight A's earned me the right to cut classes; and over basic issues of respect. She grounded me. She issued orders. She took away the keys to the car. And so it went: a multifront conflagration that raged for most of a decade. After I left for college, after I graduated and moved to another state, and after peace reigned again in her home, it would all seem very petty, but at the time, even minor disagreements called for rampant crusades whose soldiers insisted on warring until blood soaked the very personal battlefield.

This was part of why our drive through the heat wave had such an effect on me. She'd only ever tried to give me the luxuries she hadn't had—a stable household, the right clothes, a mother who stayed at home to read to her children. And I, at thirteen, had called her a disgrace to the women's liberation movement. I'd told her she should go out and get a job, like any other master's-degree-holding woman with any self-respect. I remember the hurt on her face that day. We were sitting in her SUV, parked in the lot of a local mall, bickering about something. I was going through an angry phase. The week before, I'd discovered that the girls at school whom I considered my friends were planning a surprise party for a girl named Christine who was moving to Chicago. When I asked why I wasn't invited, I was told: "Because Christine doesn't like you, and none of the rest of us do, either." I'd come home crying and told Mom the whole story. I'd said I was going to ruin the surprise by telling Christine about the party, but Mom talked me out of it. "You can be bigger than that," she said. But now, in this parking lot of the local mall, with her daughter accusing her of wasting her life, passing judgment on a mother's every sacrifice, the hurt on her face shifted to disgust, and she shot back the meanest of retorts: "You're a nasty little girl," she told me. "No wonder your friends don't like you." It was an episode that would define our relationship for years to come. It was the reason I refused, well into my twenties, to disclose to her the details of my life. I never wanted to give her anything that could be used against me in anger.

It was shameful, the things we did and said to each other, the way we used our intimate knowledge of each other to launch precision strikes at wounds left raw. But it all had a different context now, at least for me. Mom seemed more real, more interesting, more whole. I didn't know how she really felt about my traveling to the lands of her early life. I wasn't sure what she would have done if I'd told her I wouldn't go without her expressed support. But this was something I thought I could do for us these years later, a bold gesture to seal the quiet truce we'd reached after years of distance and perspective. I thought we could take a trip together, something we would always remember, and while I learned about her life, she could learn about mine. My plan was to go to Poland first, to settle in, find an apartment, then try to reconstruct her life from the beginning, from Będzin, where she was born, to the ghetto, to the place where she went into hiding, to the orphanage, to Sweden, to California, and, eventually, to Detroit. I would find people who knew her at every stage and locate whatever documents remained. After mapping the course, I would call for her. She still hadn't agreed to join me, but I knew I could coax her onto a plane and convince her to meet me in Europe. Together, we would retrace her life.

That was my goal, anyway—one I planned to set in motion within months of its genesis—but there were delays. I was offered a new beat, covering Philadelphia's City Council. I worked long hours in City Hall, trying to bring to life for readers of a big-city tabloid the art of politics in a ward-controlled town. I spent my weekends on rock-climbing trips to the mountains. The trail of my mother's childhood was over fifty years cold, but after so much time, I reasoned, what difference would a year make? Even two? Then, in the summer of 2000, a year after our drive through the heat wave, Mom left me a message saying she had news. I meant to call her back. I even dialed her number once and heard a busy signal, but it took me two days to connect with her, and when I did, she sounded annoyed. And so it was in this tone, this mad-at-me voice, that she delivered the news without any sugarcoating or any kind of hope: "I have cancer," she told me almost accusingly. "I'm dying."

I was sitting at my desk—an old gray iron thing coated with decades of nicotine, in a ratty corner of the City Hall press room. Everyone else had gone home for the night. I had just filed my story and found a minute to call her back but was supposed to meet someone for dinner. I looked at my watch. I was about to be late. An ambulance screeched past the window and raced around City Hall, its lights flashing into and out of the room. I still hadn't said anything, was still searching for something to say. "I wasn't going to tell you," she said. "You're obviously very busy, but you need to tell this to your doctor. It could affect you medically."

I pulled the receiver away from my head and looked down at it as though I were looking at her. "That's why you're telling me?" I didn't know if I should be angry, if I should cry, if I should ask questions or wait until later. I told her she had my support, whatever she needed, but she didn't seem to care. I could hear her voice quiver, like she was starting to cry. "Do you want me to come visit?" I offered.

"That would be nice," she said. A few minutes later, before I could complete any of the thoughts I was trying to compose, she told me she had to go, that she was hanging up. I sank deep into my chair, looking at the phone, listening to cars honking outside and the sound of water rushing through a pipe on one side of the room: Someone in another part of the building was flushing a toilet. I kept thinking that the phone would ring again, that it would be her telling me she was kidding, that she was trying to punish me for not calling sooner. But I knew she wouldn't do that. I'd heard the unmistakable note of panic in her voice.

Mom had a slow-growing kind of lymphoma. Her doctors said she could die in as few as ten years. She felt fine physically but had just been told at fifty-eight that she wouldn't see her seventies. Worse, there was nothing anyone could do. Chemo wouldn't make a difference. Radiation was for other kinds of cancer. Mom was despondent. When I arrived in Detroit a few days later, she started listing all the better ways to die, sudden ways, appliances in bathtubs, heights that could be jumped from. I didn't think she was serious, but my father and brother and I begged her to get therapy, to talk to someone. She wasn't interested. She had no respect for "closure" or "feeling the pain" or anything that smacked of psychobabble. "People are just so whiny these days," she'd say. "They all had terrible mothers. It's always the mothers. They do drugs. They drink. It's not their fault. It's their mothers' fault." She'd wave her hand as if swatting a fly. "People should get over themselves," she'd say. It was how she'd handled the events of her youth and how she planned to handle this.

I remembered her reaction to the Baby Jessica adoption case in the 1990s, when an Iowa father who hadn't consented to the adoption of his daughter sued to get the girl back from the Michigan couple who had welcomed the infant into their home. The case dragged on for two years, until the Michigan Supreme Court ordered the adoptive parents to return Jessica to the couple who had conceived her. But by then the girl was a toddler and profoundly attached to the only parents she'd known. Child advocates fretted over how this turbulence would affect her, invoking the crucial early years of child development and warning that an upheaval like this would haunt Jessica later. But the court had spoken. With TV cameras rolling, a police officer pulled Baby Jessica from the arms of her adoptive mother. "Mommmmy!" she cried in an unforgettable wail, her little arms outstretched. Katie Couric was near tears after watching the wrenching clip during a broadcast. Nearly thirty states changed their adoption laws to redefine the rules of consent. The climate for adoption in America would never be the same. Everyone following the case was affected by it—everyone, that is, except my mother. "The kid'll be fine," Mom said after watching the agonizing scene. "I don't know why everyone's making such a big deal about it. The same thing happened to me. I was fine. She'll get over it." Mom turned off the

TV in disgust and waved a finger at me. "Like I've always told you," she said, "if you don't make a big deal out of it, it won't be a big deal."

Now, however, she was sick and suffering. She had no symptoms of her illness, but she was living under the cloud of doom cast by its diagnosis. Eventually, we convinced her to see a therapist, but she went in, answered the woman's questions, and, inevitably, was asked about her childhood. Then came the story: Poland, ghetto, hiding, orphanage, foster home, survivor parents who woke up screaming. Now she could add terminal diagnosis to the batter and come home smug. "The shrink's surprised I'm as normal as I am," she chirped. After one session, she was cleared of the "crazy" charges pinned on her by her family, and forever excused herself from therapeutic obligations. She went back to feeling sorry for herself, to sitting on the sofa in the dark and crying. Meanwhile, she warned us, we were to tell no one she was sick. She didn't want anyone's pity. Just as she never let on about the ordeals of her childhood, she refused to even hint to her friends that she was anything other than perfectly healthy.

From Philadelphia, I started calling my mother every night, trying to cheer her up, to remind her that the doctors had said she would live ten years, that a decade was a long time. But was it? I'd been so involved in my own life, in writing stories, in scaling cliffs, that everything else seemed like it could wait, like there would be time. But now? Ten years. My mother's life could be measured in raw mathematical terms. One year equaled 10 percent, two years equaled 20. I called her in September 2000 and proposed again that we plan a trip to Poland and Sweden, certain she'd refuse. "Next summer, maybe?" I suggested, bracing for her answer.

Mom's response was bleak. "I might be dead by then," she said.

"Okay, Mom." I sighed. "If you're not dead by then, will you come?" She gave me a weak response like "we'll see," but it was enough. I requested a leave of absence from my job, bought myself a plane ticket, and immediately threw myself into making sure that nothing else could delay the project I wanted to do for us both. I signed up for a Polish language class, found someone to rent my house, and excitedly started making contacts in Poland, calling friends of friends.

By December 2000 I was deep in the throes of packing and good-byes, anticipating my approaching adventure with a mix of delight and apprehension, when my mom again called with news. This time a lump removed from her leg had revealed the cancer was growing faster than predicted. This time, she said, she'd be starting chemotherapy. Everything in my life went from moving too quickly, from speeding dizzily toward a euphoric future, to smacking hard against a callous now. I wanted to go to Poland; I desperately wanted to go and, after a year of delays, was ready to do so. My plane was scheduled to leave in three weeks. But my mother's news changed everything. I felt a sinking drain of disappointment, then a punch of guilt. It was wrong to think of me at a time that was just about her. I wondered if I should move to Detroit instead of Poland. And then I felt a flash of panic. This could be my last chance to research my mother's roots in her lifetime. When I asked my mother what she thought I should do, she insisted that I proceed with my plans. But I worried that this was less advice for me and more a reflection on her concern that my moving home would raise suspicions among her friends. She was still determined to conceal her illness. "You should go," my father said. "If you need to come home, you can come home." But what did he mean by that?

The questions streaked around me like the view of the world from the end of a twirling rope swing, everything in a dizzying blur. And soon there was another problem. Or not exactly a problem, but definitely an added complication. I didn't mean for it to happen. In fact, I'd done just about everything I could to prevent it from happening, but somehow, at the worst of all possible moments, I had met a man, the first in years whom I thought I could actually fall for. I'd gone to the corner bar near my house one night in the middle of this spinning whirlwind because I needed to sit and relax for an hour with a glass of wine and a plate of food. My house was too quiet, too small. The walls felt like coffin walls. In the bar, the music and shouting canceled each other into a quiet hum of white noise. When the man beside me struck up a conversation, I tried to ignore him, but he persisted. I tried to give him a section of the newspaper I was reading in hopes that he would leave me alone, but then for reasons I couldn't entirely explain, I felt compelled to confide in him. I told him of my possibly doomed adventure, of my mother's disease, of the packing and shopping and research I needed to get done in the few short weeks before I was scheduled to leave. He listened and didn't try to offer advice, didn't try to solve anything. He just let me talk.

A computer programmer who played bass in an indie rock band, David had a captivating smile that featured a single, adorable baby tooth where an adult incisor should have been. He had an infectious laugh, soft red hair, and big broad shoulders on his tall, bulky frame. He met me again the following night and let me vent some more. We talked about work and politics and, well, I didn't mean for it to happen, but I couldn't help but wonder if this relationship could have meant something if only I weren't leaving, bound for either Poland or Detroit. I cursed our bad luck, our terrible timing. Almost as soon as I met this man, I began trying to separate myself from him, to convince us both that our new flame was destined for extinction. I wasn't exactly succeeding, however, and on top of everything else, I found myself looking for ways to spend a portion of my last days in Philadelphia with him, enjoying our fated affair while I could.

Leaving in January no longer seemed like a viable option, so I called the airline, postponed my flight until March, and when my leave from work began, moved in with my parents in Detroit. I would have about eight weeks to hang out with my mom and decide what to do. When I arrived, I found her in the kitchen, mashing a pot of potatoes for lunch. I bounded up the three steps to the kitchen and greeted her excessively, as usual. "MOMMY!" I grabbed her and flung my arms around her the way I did when I was small and clung to her the way other kids clung to blankies and dolls. I would throw my arms open all the way behind my back: "I love you THIS much!" I'd returned lately to this greeting from our happiest years together, when I was four and it was just the two of us, after my brother, Derek, started school but before I did, before I got older and meaner and things became ugly. When we put it to rest after the four-year breathing period of college and the five years since, when I actually started wishing I lived closer to home, I exuberantly, though with a decided air of irony, returned to loud, excessive expressions of love.

I asked how she was feeling. "Not great," she said. "But Dad's being nicer since I started the chemo. He doesn't think I'm faking anymore."

"No one thinks you're faking, Mom."

"He thinks he can cure me with a pep talk."

Mom could use a pep talk, I thought, but I declined to make this point. My mother's illness was no longer diagnosis without symptom. Now there were fevers and side effects from the chemo and frustration over all the things she didn't have energy to do. The house she'd bought with my father's sister to renovate and lease had a light fixture that needed to be rewired. She'd promised my brother she would help him build a bathroom in his basement. But she was tired. And she looked thin, like never before. It had been only two months since I'd seen her at Thanksgiving, but the difference was dramatic. For years I'd teased her about the subtle curve at the top of her back, the round curl marking the first stage of osteoporosis. I called it "the Mom shelf" and rested my arm on it when we were standing together. "What am I? A public leaning post?" she'd ask me. "It's just the right height, Mom, thanks," I'd say with a peck on her cheek. Now, though, when I rested my arm on her shoulder, the proportions were off; my arm went too far. She played tennis almost every day until just before the chemo started, her Ping-Pong, slap-at-the-ball strokes somehow managing to befuddle the best players on the ladies' club circuit. When I worked at her club in high school, her friends would come off the court, dripping from an hour of chasing Mom's drop-shot-lob combinations, and hiss at me: "I am never playing with your mother again!" But skin that had stretched to accommodate the muscular skill of a perfectly executed forehand now flabbed around bone and little else.

What was happening to my mother's body was distressingly clear, and I was grateful that I was with her and not in Poland. We had not had a chance to spend this much time together in years, and we soon settled into a routine. We watched daytime TV. We drank tea. We cleaned out the half-empty food boxes in the pantry. She wasn't sick all the time. She had bad days when she felt nauseated and sick. But there were plenty of good days, even great days, when I would take her to the mall for exercise and watch her delight at a good sale. There were days when she felt so strong and refreshed that she would take on projects she had set aside, and I would help her grout the new tile in my brother's basement or entertain her while she refinished his cabinets.

It was on one of the good days that I sat my mother down and asked if she'd consent to an interview. She said no at first but eventually relented. "I'll give you an hour, but you better make it quick," she said as I hurried to set up a microphone at the kitchen table. Mom was not cooperative. She snarked at me when I asked questions that she considered stupid. She insisted she didn't remember Poland beyond shadowy images that could have been dreams. She claimed to have no memory of an orphanage. She was a little more helpful on the subject of Sweden and offered a few details about her years there, but when I tried to ask about her father, she rebuffed my efforts and largely shut down. "He was taciturn," she said, refusing to elaborate. It was only when I asked about her mother, who was killed when she was a baby, that she had anything thoughtful to say. "I never met my mother," Mom said in a tone that could reasonably be described as wistful. "I've never seen her name written, never seen a picture. It's as if she never existed."

After about twenty minutes, I could tell that her patience was waning. I knew she wouldn't put up with many more questions, but there was something I had been needing to ask her for months. Though I had tried to broach the subject during casual moments, while driving in the car or half listening to daytime TV, I had been afraid of her answer and left the question unasked. But now I scrounged up the courage. I inquired about the trip I'd been planning, the research I hoped to conduct. "Is it something you want me to do?" I asked. I shifted in my chair, anxious to hear what she would say, unsure what I would do if her answer suggested she didn't approve.

Mom considered the question as though she had never considered it before. She looked out the big kitchen window at her snow-covered backyard. She glanced down at her cooling cup of tea. Then she looked back at me and pursed her lips. "Well," she said, bobbing her head. "You're a writer. I can see why you think it's interesting."

"And you? Do you think it's interesting?" I asked.

"No," Mom said, shaking her head. "I don't think it's particularly interesting."

By the end of February, Mom looked much stronger than she had a month earlier. Color returned to her freckled cheeks, and she began knitting an ambitious green afghan to match the new sofas we bought on one of our exercise trips to the mall. Her new vigor inspired me to start making plans again, and I told her I was thinking of driving to Atlanta to visit her stepmother. My grandma Fela had a trove of family records and the best knowledge of family history, but Mom was concerned that I would say something about the cancer—her most adamant secret. If Fela knew about the cancer, she would call every day, Mom said, maybe twice or three times a day. Mom wanted her secret kept from her stepmother more than from anyone else. I promised that I would guard my every utterance during my stay in Atlanta, then I set off on a twelve-hour drive to the South.

There are legions of holocaust survivors who never speak of scars cut too deeply. But there are others, like Fela Brystowska Frydrych, who married my widowed grandfather in Sweden after the war, who tend to speak of them constantly. In contrast to my mom, from whom every scrap of detail had to be extracted like a splinter lodged deep beneath layers of skin, my grandmother told me her story in vivid and horrifying color: how she hid in a basement with her brothers and sisters; how they left their sick mother behind when the gestapo arrived; how she lay on the floor of the transport train as her father told her he didn't think he would survive; how he was counting on her to honor his family name.

In an interview that stretched across two days, for an hour on Saturday night, after *Shabbos*, and then another two hours on Sunday, Grandma Fela told me her story in a clear and mostly calm voice, set to the music of her thick Yiddish accent and her immigrant's grammatical quirks. She spoke faster when recalling happy memories, the songs her family sang on *Shabbos* nights, and she slowed to the measured pace of a funeral procession when describing the moments that were the most bleak: how she stood in the gas chamber at Auschwitz until a last-minute change of plans, when a phone rang and the women in the chamber, shivering and naked, were suddenly, instead of being gassed, ushered out to sit on the frozen ground. She told me how she and her sister walked barefoot through the snow for more than five hundred miles from Auschwitz to Bergen-Belsen, how she wanted to stop, to rest, whatever the consequences, but how her sister pleaded with her to keep walking, to keep living, to keep staying together so that neither sister would have to live through this savagery alone. Then she told me how her sister died in her arms of typhus a day before liberation, how she wished that she could die, too, how she still sometimes wished she had.

When we were done, I asked my grandmother if I could look through the documents she had saved over the years, and she opened a door in the maple cabinet that held her good china and produced a tattered red folder stuffed with paper. Some of the pages were in English, but the ones that looked the most interesting—yellowed letters penned on tracing paper; typed documents with dates and notarized signatures; long handwritten missives addressed to my grandfather—were in a mix of Polish, Yiddish, German, Swedish. I asked if I could make copies, but Grandma Fela didn't want anything leaving her house. "I've looked after these papers for twenty years, since your grandfather died," she said. "I don't want anything to happen to them." I assured her that I would be careful, that I would keep everything in order and return it all to her within the hour. Still, she refused. I remembered Mom telling me, years earlier, that I was lucky to have her for a mother. She told me that her stepmother had been wholly unreasonable and would never budge from a position once she'd taken one. Mom's arguments with Grandma Fela were so contentious that they rivaled the ones she would later have with me. Mom told me that I was the manifestation of her stepmother's curse. Grandma Fela had wished for Mom to one day have a daughter who'd be as rude to her mother as Mom had been to Fela. Mom upped the curse for me, hexing me with the prospect of three such daughters. I argued with Grandma Fela for an hour before brokering a compromise in which she let me take the papers to copy, but only if she came along to supervise.

I very nearly didn't tell my grandmother about my possible trip. I had visited Poland once before when I was in high school, on an organized tour of graveyards and concentration camps. Fela had been terrified that something would happen to me, that the Poles would find out I was a Jew and try to hurt me. She called my mother every day of that week in 1990 to make sure I was unharmed. This time I knew Mom would rather I spare Fela my potential plans. But I wanted to know what Fela would say, so I told her that I was thinking of moving to Poland for a year and that, if she wanted, I would go to her neighborhood in Łódź and take pictures of the street where she grew up. To my surprise, she not only didn't object, she seemed to light up at the prospect. "That would be nice," she said with a nod and the slightest hint of a smile. She seemed so positive about it, I thought perhaps she hadn't understood. "Grandma, did you hear me say I might go to Poland for a *year*?" I said.

My grandmother calmly shook her head. "You won't go for a year," she said.

"I won't?"

"No," she said. "You'll get there. You won't like it, and you'll come home."

I stayed with my grandmother for several days, stopping to visit and interview some of my cousins and other relatives in Atlanta, then drove north to Washington to view the archives at the United States Holocaust Memorial Museum. In the reading room there, I flipped through old photographs of Będzin from before the war that an archivist had suggested might be helpful, but without knowing the names of the people in the pictures, they were too abstract for my purposes. I returned them to the research desk. "Do you have anything else on Będzin?" I asked. The archivist looked annoyed. I'd heard him complain earlier to a colleague that everyone was "going surfing" and they were "having a wave." The archives were flooded with researchers anxious for details about their families before the last of the survivors passed on. This man had been inundated with requests from amateurs like me. "You must have something," I pleaded. "Well, we have this," he said, dropping two bound volumes onto the counter. "Look through them and bring them back." I carried the two books to a table and examined their titles. They were a collection of identification photos from the Będzin ghetto— photocopies of the original pictures. According to a note in one of the books, the originals could be found in the archives at the Yad Vashem museum in Jerusalem. The copies were fuzzy and small, crammed in twelve to a page, but they were a good start. I opened the first volume, an index, and flipped to F for Frydrych.

Frydrych, Abraham, I read. *Frydrych, Blima Jente, Frydrych, Mojzesz.* No one I'd heard of. Cousins at best. My grandmother's maiden name was Rosenblum, so I plowed ahead to the R's, where I found the name spelled with a Z: *Rozenblum, Majer Szulim, Rozenblum, Wigdor,*

Rozenblum, Srul. Then there it was, spelled differently from how I'd imagined, but decidedly her: *Rozenblum, Sura Leja, born Feb. 2, 1921, photo number 190.* That was her birthday, and this was unmistakably her: my grandmother, the one my mother had spent a lifetime imagining. There was a picture of her in here? I picked up the other book, the one with the photos, and flipped to the page where photo 190 should be. Only it wasn't there. I flipped to the front of the book. *Photo 1, photo 2.* I flipped each page, scanned each picture. *Photo 80, 81, 82 . . .* Then, about seven pages back from where it should have been, I found it: *Photo 190, Sura Leja Rozenblum, Feb. 2, 1921, Bedzin, Poland.* The photo was small and dark, a two-inch photocopy of a photograph. Her features were hard to decipher, but there she was: the woman for whom I'd been given my Hebrew name, the one whose picture my mother had always wanted to see. She was gazing pleasantly out from the page, looking out at me, her granddaughter. A shiver shot down my spine as my mother's words scrambled in my head: *I've never seen her name written, never seen a picture . . .* I reached for my cell phone. *"Mom,"* I whispered, struggling to keep my voice down in the library. "You're *never* going to guess what I'm looking at!" She gasped when I told her, and asked what she looked like. "I'll be home in a couple of days," I told her. "You can see for yourself."

I stopped for only a day in Philadelphia, saying a final good-bye to David, kissing him through the car window as I prepared to pull away. In the hurried weeks before I'd gone home to Detroit, David and I had spent parts of sixteen intense and wonderful days together in Philadelphia. We'd had a frenzied fling ahead of a fast-approaching deadline, but now that deadline had arrived. It was sad to wonder if David and I could have worked out, if he and I could have meant something to each other. But for now, at least, we would have to wait. "Maybe next year," I told him before starting the engine. "Yeah," he said. "Maybe next year." Then I set out for Detroit, bringing my mother the photo she had waited a lifetime to see.

Mom was in high spirits and apparently good health—she told me she'd gained five pounds—when I walked exhaustedly through the door. "Let me see it!" she said, surprising me with an actual display of enthusiasm. She was anxious, though probably not as anxious as I was. I set down my bag on the dining room table and made a small drama of unzipping my filing case to unfurl the awaited document. This was an important moment: a daughter bringing her mother a longed-for prize. I cursed myself for not having a tape recorder ready. Dad looked over Mom's shoulder as she studied the tiny, dark picture near the bottom of the page. They both squinted and leaned in closer. I watched Mom intently, curious whether she would catch a glimmer of recognition or see something of her mother in herself. Mom studied the picture and then: "Brian!" she said, addressing my father as her face took on a copious smile, the dimple on her right cheek puckering tightly. "Do you see who she looks like?"

My father gave the page another look, moving his eyes from the photo to Mom and then from the photo to me. "No," he said, after ruling us out. "Who does she look like?"

Mom was laughing and putting her hand on my father's shoulder. "Brian," she said, "she looks like your mother!"

Dad laughed and looked again. "You're right. She does!" he said.

This was not the reaction I'd hoped for. It wasn't just that I wanted Mom to embrace me and thank me, but they were also wrong. Sura Leah Rozenblum looked nothing like Sally Einhorn, my father's mother. "It's just the hairdo," I argued. We had many pictures of my grandma Sally from the 1930s, her dark hair piled high on her head, her eyebrows tweezed to eternal surprise. "That was the fashion of the time," I said. But my parents had made up their minds and were giggling over this happy coincidence as my father went off to find an old picture of his mother.

I couldn't help but feel disappointed, like they'd ruined my moment. Ultimately, I think Mom was grateful for the picture, pleased she'd seen it at last, even if her reaction wasn't quite what I'd imagined. But there was no question: This was the first success of my adventure. I wondered how many other treasures were out there waiting to be found. I looked at Mom, huddled with my father as they compared her mother's picture with his. She was getting better, looking stronger. There'd be two more treatments and then recovery. The doctors said she'd be cancer-free by July. We talked of her coming to Poland in September. She was worried that her immune system would be weak and she wouldn't want to fly, so I looked up transatlantic cruises for her on the Internet and told her she could travel in luxury on the *QEII*.

"That's the boat I came over on!" Mom said, showing, for the first time, a real interest in the trip. Mom had come over on the *Queen Elizabeth*, not the *Queen Elizabeth 2*, but it was then I knew that I had no more reasons to delay my adventure. Mom was in good hands. She had my dad. She had my brother, Derek, and she had my aunt Fran, my father's sister who lived nearby. They'd pitch in. If something happened, I could be home in a day. I'd be only a plane ride away.

And so it was that on a chilly day in the middle of March, my parents took me to the airport and hugged me at the gate. "If you need anything, Mom, just call. I'll be home," I told her. "Even if you just miss me, I'll come back." When we pulled apart, our faces were streaming with tears, which made us laugh. We were both criers. We had sat beside each other in movies and blubbered in concert through the sad parts. There was one movie in particular when we turned to look at each other in the midst of a particularly heart-wrenching scene and saw that we both were soaked with tears. We burst out laughing at the sight of it and now did the same thing in the airport, laughing as the tears on her face mixed with the tears on mine. "You two are something else," my father said through an eye-rolling smile.

Mom wrinkled her nose at him. "We're allowed to cry," she said.

"Yeah," I said. "Leave us alone." Then I gave my mother a long, extended hug and turned reluctantly to board the plane.

CHAPTER FOUR

A T FIRST THE OLD FEARS CLAIMED TOP BILLING: APPREHENSIONS about leaving home, leaving my mom, my family, the boyfriend who could have been. Then, halfway across the Atlantic, they began to have company. There were new fears sidling up to mingle with the old ones. Now it wasn't just what I'd left behind. It was also what stood before me: the new country, the new language, the new rules, and—looming largest of all—the fear that I'd ignored for months. Now, headed for Poland, I could no longer escape the fact that I was moving to a country I had been taught to hate. I'd been trying to get over it, to get out from under the massive chip hefted heartily onto my shoulder by my grandparents, my parents, and every Jew I'd ever met who had ever told me a story about Poland. I'd been looking for a way to approach the country with an open mind, a giving heart, a scale set to zero that could fall where it would, but I'd only ever heard one thing about Poles: that they hated me, that they hated all Jews, that they always had, that they'd collaborated with the Nazis, aided in our demise, and that by 1945 they'd rejoiced in having what they had always wanted: a country free of Jews.

This had always sounded strange to friends of mine at home. We were taught in school that Germany had invaded Poland, triggering the war, then killed and destroyed and burned viciously through Europe with an evil unknown to preceding generations. What wasn't taught in school, what really couldn't be taught, were the millions of much smaller and more personal cruelties that had happened in the streets, in the neighborhoods, in the villages of countries that were occupied during the war. These were the places where people fearing for their lives had made choices that ultimately betrayed their neighbors, where pointing fingers exposed the hiding places and where petty neighborhood rivalries from before the war morphed into wartime murder and spiteful slaughter. And so people like my grandparents, the survivor generation, emerged from the war with a blazing hatred for the Poles who they once had befriended, for their former neighbors who they felt had double-crossed them. And they passed that hatred on to their children. It was why, I suspected, Art Spiegelman, the son of a survivor from Sosnowiec, the town next to the one where my mother was born, drew the Poles as pigs in his holocaust comic book, *Maus,* and the Germans as comparatively pleasant cats. The implication from our parents and grandparents was that the Germans, while evil and calculating in the war, were basically intelligent people who were swept catastrophically into nationalistic frenzy, while the Poles were anti-Semitic pigs. There was a reason—I had been told many times with a wink—that the Germans located the death camps in Poland, that the German people never would have stood for such horror on their own land. Poles, I was told, had welcomed these camps. They'd embraced the chance to see Jews die around them. Even my mother, who was saved by a Polish family, told me the family only did it for the money.

The reasonable part of me didn't believe this. People don't risk their lives for money alone, and such horrible, sweeping statements couldn't possibly apply to an entire population without benefit of nuance or exception. But these perceptions were there, coloring my expectations.

I delighted in the prospect of unearthing my family roots, but the thought of living in Poland had me trapped in my seat on the plane, cranking my jaw into a sour clench and searching in vain for an exit. I tried to read, but the words jumbled on the page. I attempted to sleep, but my eyes stayed open, refusing to rest. My only choice was to agonize through eight hours of transatlantic worry. When the plane finally arrived at the Amsterdam airport, I was so exhausted from the ordeal and so emotionally sapped that I couldn't bring myself to continue the journey—at least not on that day—and without really thinking much about it or making any specific plans, I decided to skip my connecting flight to Warsaw. Like a red-eyed drone, I dragged my bags through customs, and rather than checking them in again for my connecting flight, I wearily hoisted them onto a train to the center of town. I found a small hotel with a small room and a welcome respite of peace. Then I collapsed, fully clothed and completely drained, into a deep, enervated sleep, visited by dreams:

It was 1990. I was seventeen, in Poland on a tour of concentration camps with a busload of Jewish-American high school kids. I wasn't shocked by the ovens or piles of hair, which I'd expected. It was the houses. Out there in the field. Houses that looked as though they'd seen what there was to see. Damn Poles! I cursed them. They'd rather stew in the stench of death than do something to stop it.

It was 2000. I was twenty-seven, in a class at the Polish American Cultural Center in Philadelphia. I came to learn the language, but it was the last day of class in December, the teacher was dressed as Santa Claus, and we were all singing Christmas carols in Polish. The director of the center stood to make a speech. "Who has a last name that ends in *ski?*" he asked as some hands waved. "See," he said when most hands stayed down. "People think Polish names end in *ski,* but here, we're all Polish, and some of us have other names." People—he meant the rest of America—don't understand Poles. But we—all of us here—are all Polish and united by this: our culture. He meant the carols and the

twelve-course *Wigilia* feast we were enjoying, a Christmas Eve tradition. I looked around the room, mostly third- and fourth-generation
Polish Americans. I was one of a few—maybe the only—student with
a parent actually born in Poland. I had more of a claim to that country
than they, but this pan-Polonia, one-people, one-nation speech didn't
include me. These carols, this feast, were never part of my family tradition. I never would have been welcome in this man's unified Christmas
culture. I wondered about the people around me. Who among them
had aunts or uncles in the houses near Auschwitz? Who had a cousin
in Będzin after the war who may have confronted my grandfather: *You,
Jew? What are you doing here? How come they didn't kill you?* Who had
relatives in the mob in Jedwabne, locking their neighbors in a barn
before torching it?

Jedwabne. It was the place on the lips of everyone I called for advice
that year about Poland. As I reached out to people who knew the country, nearly all of them mentioned the book *Neighbors* by Polish-born
historian Jan Tomasz Gross, which proved, when it came out in 2000,
that the murders of sixteen hundred Jedwabne Jews—nearly every Jew
in that small town—on a night in 1941 were not the work of Nazis,
as previously believed. Despite the plaque in the town that, for years,
mourned the mass murder at the hands of German aggressors, *Neighbors* showed that the slaughter came at the hands of local men who'd
lived their lives beside their eventual victims. The book had triggered
a humbling wave of soul-searching in Poland that was followed—as
these things often are—by a backlash from those who questioned the
book's claims. They called Gross a liar and steamed with fury when the
Polish president issued an apology. I couldn't figure the fuss. Didn't
everyone know that Poles killed Jews? Didn't everyone know about the
Kielce pogrom? About the forty-two Jews killed by a Polish mob in
1946, a year after the war? Didn't everyone know what had happened
over twenty years later, when twenty thousand Jews had to flee persecu-
tion in Communist Poland? I couldn't understand why the book was so

controversial. And now, as I contemplated a long stay in that country, I couldn't remember why I'd been so excited about it.

I was thankful for my Amsterdam reprieve. There, no one I knew was sick. There were no awkward good-byes to say, no questions of staying or leaving. For that moment there were no historical bogeymen with whom to contend. Amsterdam was just me and my thoughts. I wandered along the canals, stopping in cafés to write and read and imagine myself in dreamy, romantic terms. I fancied myself the solitary writer, floating around the great cities of Europe. I bought a beat-up copy of *A Moveable Feast* to read in dark corners of smoky coffeehouses, indulging Hemingway's take on the intellectual coffeehouse existence of the Paris of his youth. I coveted his life—a poor, young writer in love with his wife, trying to do good work and write, in his words, "one true sentence." I wondered if I should spend my year in Paris instead of Poland, if maybe I should hang around Amsterdam instead. I was enjoying myself so much that the last thing I wanted to do was visit the Anne Frank Museum. There'd be time enough for the holocaust later, and I doubted that seeing Anne Frank's magazine clippings would do much to enhance my understanding of the period. It had always bothered me that the deaths of eleven million never seemed to affect people the way the death of this girl had, but the other travelers in my hotel encouraged me to go, and what else was I doing? So I got in line outside the quirky building where the world's most famous holocaust victim had spent much of the war.

The hiding place surprised me. I had pictured it tighter, more cramped, not an apartment of interlocking rooms on two floors. But more interesting than the space were the photos in the interpretive exhibit. There were poster-sized pictures of Nazis marching into Amsterdam, sepia-toned snapshots of Jewish businesses with their windows smashed, and one picture in particular that stopped me. It featured a group of people with Jewish stars on their coats, being herded along the street. Epiphanies don't usually arrive in a single moment. They're

never precisely a sudden light that appears upstairs in a window. Later, you see that the light was always there, burning dimly by itself. But this moment in the Anne Frank Museum—as I examined a photo of sad-looking Jews—truly appeared to me in the form of a blinding light, a quick second when something missing was suddenly, stunningly there. And it threw me. My shock came not from the picture's foreground—the march of the doomed captured in many such photos. What was new for me was the background, which was not the ugly scene of rubble and smoke typical of war photography. Instead, this march took place on a sweet scene of Amsterdam quaint, on a little street like the ones I'd been walking and admiring. Delete the foreground, and this photo could have been a postcard: an Amsterdam canal, a canal boat tied nearby, a small arching bridge, a stretch of narrow homes, all frozen in delicate gray. But insert the people in the foreground, and everything changed. I looked from the photo to the window beside it and saw the same scenery outside in vivid color—the same quaint street, the same little bridge.

I felt like a fool. Here, I'd been so blissful, so much more comfortable than I'd expected to be in Poland. And now I saw myself for what I was: a sucker for marketing. It wasn't that I didn't know bad things had happened in Holland. I did know. I think I even knew that 75 percent of Dutch Jews had been murdered. But when I'd thought about the Netherlands, I'd thought about other, more pleasant things—windmills, tulips, open fields. I'd never thought to hate the Dutch for what they did to Anne Frank. And yet I'd always blamed the Poles for Auschwitz. Poland was the scene of the worst of the slaughter. It was home to the death camps and to the postwar pogroms. But Poland was not the only graveyard in Europe. It was not the only country with Nazi collaborators. And it was not the only country still home to anti-Semites. But unlike Holland, on the sunny side of the Iron Curtain, Poland hadn't made it to the Travel Channel. It never had a chance to recast its brand.

This wasn't enough to void my fears about Poland. I was a long way from pardoning Poles for sins I knew they'd committed, but when I boarded an eastbound train the next day, I did so with a little perspective. If I wasn't prepared to paint all of Europe with the same brush I'd put to the canvas of Poland, I was compelled to at least give Poland the same chance I'd give to Norway or France. At that moment I made a vow: I would not go to Poland to dwell on death. I was not a holocaust survivor and had no claim to my grandparents' anger. I would focus on the present, on seeing now instead of then. I might as well be going to Paris, I thought as I dug the Hemingway out of my bag to read on the train. Like it or not, this play had opened on many a stage.

I arrived in Krakow on a bitter and windy evening in late March, a night more winter than spring. A chill blew across the tracks, and I pulled my coat tightly around me as I scanned the platform for someone who looked like she was looking for me. In her last e-mail, Magda had written that she would find me, but she hadn't said how. A friend of a friend had given me Magda's name, and we had been corresponding for weeks. I'd asked her in an early e-mail if she knew of an open apartment in Krakow, and she'd mentioned an available room in the three-bedroom flat she shared with Krys. It would not be up to American standards, she warned, but the rent would be cheap, everyone would speak English, and they would show me around. "I'll take it!" I replied without hesitation. "It sounds perfect!" And it did. But now, as I eyed the faces of travelers rushing around me, finding their parties, hugging hello, collecting their luggage, and disappearing down the stairs in the middle of the platform, I wondered. I knew nothing of these people and they nothing of me. The train moved on, pulling loudly out of the station. More people called to one another, hugged, and vanished down the stairs until I was the only one standing, alone and shivering, on a platform that was suddenly, eerily still. I wondered if I'd told Magda the wrong time, if maybe she hadn't read my last e-mail. I wondered

if it was too late to find a hotel. Then a petite woman appeared at the top of the stairs in a black beret, a bomber jacket with a fake fur collar, clunky black boots, and red lipstick. She had the look of a French resistance fighter, indignant but chic. She scanned the platform, settled her eyes on me, and lifted her eyebrows as if to say *You her?* I paused, then waved. She strolled confidently my way, hand extended.

As Magda led me and my suitcase from the train station, she delivered a play-by-play of the hazards on our way: the train station cabbies who overcharged, the "hooker district" that I should avoid at night, the ubiquitous dog doo on the sidewalk. She had an easy laugh and a cutting, sharp sensibility that I welcomed. We crossed a commercial boulevard, lit by the lamps of a few open stores, and turned down a smaller lane to emerge on a dark and quiet street—Ulica Staszica—that ran for only one block. Ours was the corner building: a heavy gray structure, slightly wider than its four stories. The building looked as though it had been elegant once, with curled ornaments around the windows and small decorative columns above the door, but it was showing its age. The next day I could see that the soaring skylight in the lobby was clouded with dirt and guano. The curving staircase, hugged by a hand-carved banister, was naked where small brass hooks once held a rug in place. Each smooth marble stair sagged in its center.

Magda and I heaved my suitcase to our third-floor flat, where she showed me my room, which was spacious and airy and had walls the color of bright spring green. We cooked dinner together in the high-ceilinged kitchen with a floor painted red and an old ceramic wood-burning stove in the corner. I showed Magda pictures of my friends and family, and she ran to grab the framed photo of her boyfriend in London that she kept by her bed. I told her about David, about our daily e-mails, but confessed that I wasn't very sure of our prospects. I liked him, I told her, but I didn't think we knew each other well enough to sustain a long separation. I could tell that Magda and I would be friends and that despite our different backgrounds, we had a great deal in common. But in the swirl of my fears about Poland and Poles, I had no frame of reference for Magda.

It was my first night in Krakow when I noticed the silver charm on the chain around her neck. "Is that a *chai*?" I asked. The charm looked like the Hebrew symbol for life.

"Oh, this?" Magda rubbed the charm between her fingers. "I've worn this for years," she said. "I have one here, too." She stood, untangled her arm from the sleeve of the hooded sweatshirt, and pushed aside the strap of her tank top to reveal a tattoo of the same Jewish symbol, inked on her shoulder, entwined in a tattooed vine. I sat stunned, looking at her shoulder, not sure how to react. If Magda were Jewish, wouldn't she have mentioned that in her e-mails? We'd been chatting by e-mail for weeks. Wouldn't that have come up? And if she weren't Jewish, then what was she trying to say? And why was she trying to say it with a tattoo?

Magda's eyes twinkled a laugh as she saw me processing these questions. "No, I'm not Jewish," she said. "And yes, I know that tattoos are forbidden in Jewish law." She shook her head at my dumbfounded expression. "You're all so surprised," she said, picking up the wine to refill her glass. "It's not so strange." Magda's father was the director of a museum in a city that had been heavily Jewish before the war, she told me. In researching the history of his town, her father became something of an expert on the Jews of Poland and, in the process, made Jewish friends through whom he visited Israel in the 1980s. He brought back books on biblical archaeology that Magda remembered devouring. "At some point," she said, "I realized that Israel and all this ancient history has a connection with Poland because these people lived here for many centuries and established this great culture." In high school, she went to Israel herself, spending six months learning Hebrew—and serving as an informal interpreter between the Russian and American teens in her program, since she was the only student who had studied both English and Russian in school, Russian before 1989 and English after. She came back to Poland inspired to immerse herself in as much Jewish culture as she could find in her home country.

There was a hint of boredom in Magda's voice as she told her story. She had been a tour guide in the Krakow Jewish quarter. She had worked in a Jewish bookshop and now, at twenty-five, while finishing her master's in ethnology, she was working in a Jewish cultural center. Over the years, she had met a great many people like me—Jews with chips on our shoulders—while none of us had met anyone like her. Magda was not the first person I'd known to become engrossed in a culture not her own. She was hardly different from the legions of suburban American white boys who dressed and talked like gangsta rappers. Magda's tattoo of a *chai* was not unlike the Japanese and Chinese symbols for peace or love or fortune that have long graced the ankles and shoulders of my white friends at home. But a Pole drawn to Jewish culture went against everything I thought I knew about the country that my family had fled—and Magda was just a small piece of it.

As I would soon learn, my flatmate was just one character in the complex drama playing out in Krakow at the time. As I set out over the next few days to explore the city, I did what most Jews do when they visit Krakow and went looking for Kazimierz, the old Jewish quarter. I had read about the Jewish quarter's infamous spectrum of kosher-style restaurants that serve matzo ball soup and potato kugel to the high-pitched strains of Jewish klezmer tunes. But actually seeing these places had an effect on me that I hadn't anticipated. I stood in the center of Kazimierz, on a plaza that was once the beating heart of a sixty thousand-strong Krakow Jewish community, and gawked at storefronts—once home to Jewish tailors and butcher shops—that now boasted an odd assemblage of gentile-owned Jewish-themed cafés. At home, I'd been to Mexican restaurants adorned with plastic cactuses and pink sombreros. I'd seen Chinese restaurants painted with cartoonish murals of people in triangular hats. I'd seen many cultures adopted and appropriated, but I had never seen my own culture used that way. And here, in a city of fewer than two hundred Jews, half a mile from what had been the Jewish ghetto during World War II and roughly an hour's drive from Auschwitz, was an entire plaza full of these restaurants: Noah's Ark, Klezmer Hois, the Alef, the Ariel, the Esther.

Some had facades adorned with iron menorahs. Others had paintings of men in black hats on their interior walls. Signs on their doors were printed in either Hebrew letters or a Hebrew-like script. Most offered klezmer concerts. Several had souvenir shops selling crude paintings of Jewish minstrels and foot-high wooden carvings of pious Jews. The guidebooks characterized Kazimierz as a Jewish Disney World, as if Epcot had a "Jewland," but I was actually reminded of Santa Fe—not so much a theme park cast randomly into a Florida swamp, but more like a blooming commercial flower of ethnic kitsch that had pushed through the soil of what really belonged there. The old city and its vanished inhabitants were now little more than nutrients for an opportunistic organism that found a way to repackage the past, to resell it, to thrive off it, regardless of why the old city had died. It was unsettling, but it was also harmless. I wouldn't have chosen to purchase one of the painted canvases of pious Jews playing the fiddle, but it is worth noting that none of the men in the paintings were rendered with horns on their heads or cash in their hands. Kazimierz was no more Jewish, in my mind, than Taco Bell was Mexican, but I didn't see any swastikas, either. I had, after all, promised myself an open mind.

A few days later, I was in a coffee shop in a different, non-Jewish-themed neighborhood when a young woman sitting near me struck up a conversation. She had seen me reading in English and told me she was leaving for London soon to find work as a barmaid. She wondered if she might practice her English with me. "Certainly," I said, and invited her to join me. But when she asked what I was doing in Poland, I hesitated. I tried to be vague, saying research, then historical research, but she still seemed confused, so I ventured family research.

"Oh, you're Polish, then?" she squealed.

ERIN EINHORN   59

"Mmm, not exactly," I said.

It wasn't that I worried she'd respond violently. I didn't think she'd jump up, yell *Żyd!*, and throw coins at my feet, but while Magda had been wonderful and while I enjoyed meeting her friends, this woman was a stranger. I wasn't sure how she'd react. Eventually, tentatively, I confessed, feeling like a first-timer in a twelve-step program: *My name is Erin, and I am a Jew.* I braced myself for her reaction, but it was not what I'd expected. "You're Jewish?" she gushed. "That's so great!" I looked at her quizzically. "I mean, Jews are so . . . beautiful!" she said. The thrill on her face told me she'd never met an actual Jew before.

I wasn't sure how to respond to her or to the other young Krakovians I would meet in cafés or at parties in my first weeks in Poland. Krakow is a college town. It's home to the second oldest university in Central Europe. The Jagiellonian University, founded in 1364, is the most prestigious school in Poland, and so it attracts the country's top students. If they were talking to me, it meant they also spoke English, so I was meeting a particularly well-educated and youthful segment of Polish life. I couldn't say what the rest of Poland was like, but here, among this demographic, the reaction to things Jewish seemed effusive. "It's a wonderful tradition!" they told me. "Extraordinary how your people have maintained your tradition for so long, through so much!" Few of these people approached Magda's level of interest in things Jewish. Most knew very little about Jewish culture, but they were intensely curious. They asked about customs and rituals and listened to my answers as though I were describing a recent trip to the moon. Many tried to connect. "I'm from Częstochowa," they'd tell me. Or Kielce. Or Rzeszów. "It was a very Jewish city." Often they'd add something like: "My grandmother's best friend was a Jew. Her name was Luba. She died at Belzec." I cynically picked up on the *best friend* line. *Some of my grandparents' best friends . . .* But these young Poles were very possibly speaking the truth. Jews were nearly a third of the population in many major Polish cities in the 1930s. They were roughly a tenth of the population of the country. There were undoubtedly thousands of Polish children who watched in horror as their best friends were taken away. And those kids were the grandparents of the people I was meeting. But were those same kids' parents raising their glasses to toast the deportations? Would those kids have remained friends later, when they had to compete with Jews for jobs or admission to the university?

I remembered my vow to focus on the present, but these were my thoughts—instinctively negative. I knew I wasn't being fair. These young Poles were obviously sincere and seemed determined that I should feel comfortable in their country. "Is it true," they'd ask with concern in their voices, "that Jews think Poles are anti-Semitic?" I'd look down at my shoes, not sure how to answer. "Actually, yes," I'd acknowledge. "That is true." They would shake their heads and cluck. "You'll have to tell them it isn't so." I would nod in polite agreement. Some would tell me with shame in their eyes that they had an uncle or a grandparent who was anti-Semitic. "It's such a pity," they'd say. "We have terrible fights." To these comments, I would agree that it was a pity. Then I'd think of certain relatives who used to make racist remarks at holiday dinners, how I used to shout at them and how I'd be banished from the table for insolence. "But *they're* the bigots. Banish *them*!" I'd whine. "You're right," my mother would whisper as she'd escort me from the room. "They're wrong, but you have to learn to make your point more peacefully." Now I imagined the same scene at Polish dinner tables, self-righteous kids taught tolerance in school, going to battle with older relatives who'd been around, who *remembered* the Jews and what this country was like when the Jews were running everything. As with my smug, racist relatives, the Polish elders are probably relieved when the kids are removed so the grown-ups can go on telling it like it is.

I met my second flatmate, Krzysiek, a week after I arrived. He had been visiting his parents in their village in Silesia and came noisily into the apartment one night while I was sitting in the kitchen with a

stack of Polish vocabulary cards. He was hauling a bag of clothes that
I suspected he'd taken home to wash. Our apartment was terrific. It
had high ceilings and big windows that opened inward like sweeping
French doors. We had a giant iron bathtub with feet like lions' paws.
But among the flat's deficiencies—a bathroom that had only hot water
and a kitchen that had only cold—was a washing machine that took up
half the bathroom but never worked. Krzysiek dropped his things in
his room, which was decorated with a mix of Beatles album covers and
tie-dyed tapestries, then came into the kitchen to introduce himself.
"Krzysiek," he said, extending his hand. His name sounded to me like
Shh-shhhk. He pronounced his name again, then told me to call him
Krys.

Krys sat down in the broken red easy chair that sunk low beside
the kitchen's small table. He had scraggly sand-colored hair, a hint of
a scruffy goatee, oval specs, and a lanky frame that made me think of
Shaggy from *Scooby-Doo*. He opened his mouth as if to say something,
then started to fidget. "Are you okay?" I asked, eyeing him across the
table.

"Yeah. It's just . . ." He stopped speaking and winced. "Would you
mind if . . . Can I smoke here?"

I wasn't sure why he felt he needed to ask me. I shrugged. "It's your
place," I said.

Krys's face lit with joy. "Oh, thank God!" he said, producing a cigarette from a pack in his pocket. Later, he told me that he and Magda
had been apprehensive about living with an American. They'd heard
that Americans never smoked, not even in bars or their own homes,
and that Americans liked to tell other people what to do. These facts
dawned on them a day after Magda invited me to live with them and
triggered a crisis: "We're going to have to smoke in the hallway like
Americans!" We all had our stereotypes, it seemed, and their perception
of my country was not that far from reality. I didn't tell him that we
usually don't let people smoke in the hallway, either.

Like Magda, Krys was a tour guide in the Jewish quarter, but his main job was tending bar in a Jewish hotel, mixing drinks for a clientele of mostly Jewish tourists. The Eden Hotel was the only hotel in Krakow with a known Jewish owner, an American. It had a *mikveh*, a Jewish ritual bath, and a kosher kitchen as well as other services for religious guests. I was anxious to hear Krys's perspective on Kazimierz, so, a few weeks into my stay, I asked him about the comments he'd heard across the bar, how Jewish tourists tended to respond to the theme cafés. "I guess some of them think these cafés are really Jewish. I mean, owned by Jews and run by Jews, and the food you can get is kosher, which is not true," he said. "And when they learn the truth, sometimes they are shocked." In Krys's accent, *shocked* sounded like *chucked*.

"Do they ever get angry?" I asked.

"More like confused," he said. I asked Krys if Jews ever said anything to him about Poles being anti-Semites. He bobbed his head softly. "Sometimes," he said. "But you get used to that. I remember talking to one of my friends, and he said, 'Whatever happens, we are the anti-Semites for the foreigners,' so it's kind of like no use. Whatever we do, people will still regard us as an anti-Semitic nation." It was during this conversation that I began to feel a new sensation washing up against my suspicion. I thought of Krys behind the bar at this Jewish hotel, meeting people like me who immediately assumed that he was a bigot. I asked Krys how he responded to such people. "I don't respond," he said. "What could I say?"

I told my mom on the phone that my preconceptions about Poland may have been too harsh. "Maybe," Mom said. "But my parents had their reasons for hating Poles. They may like us now, but that's easy when there aren't any Jews. We're not a threat anymore." She was right. It was one thing to admire a culture from a distance and another to live in harmony with people who were different, but the crack that started forming with a dose of context back in Amsterdam had started to widen. Krys told me a story about his grandmother, who, when the winds blew a certain way during the war, could smell bodies burning at Auschwitz, a few dozen miles away. Repulsed, she yelled for her children to come inside. I considered the houses around Auschwitz that had so enraged me when I saw them in high school. But what could Krys's grandmother have done? Could she have stopped the killing? Then, on a day trip to Auschwitz for the opening of a new exhibit, I learned from a guide that the homes around the camp had been evacuated during the war. The Poles I'd despised for gazing uncaringly at the camp had actually never existed.

Slowly, as I came to know and befriend my Polish peers, I was starting to feel shame for the biases I'd brought with me. Now, when I saw Jewish tourists in Kazimierz frowning at the theme cafés, I approached them and rebuked them for judging so harshly. I would tell them, as many young Poles had told me, that Poland was the only country in Europe where the penalty for helping Jews was immediate death. I'd tell them that more Poles had been recognized for saving Jews in the war than the citizens of any other country. I wasn't even sure if these claims were true, but seeing the tourists was like looking into a mirror of the not too distant past, and I wanted to do penance for my earlier lack of charity. But another day, I'd go for a walk in the market square and see a vendor selling carved wooden "Jew dolls," foot-high men in black hats and coats, bent over their prayer books or playing violins with sad and wistful eyes. Months later, I would learn that these dolls had a long history in Poland dating back before the war, but when I saw them on sale in the market, they looked to me like Jewish lawn jockeys, mocking and racist. I'd see the banner hanging above the national tourist agency that touted: TOURS OF OLD TOWN CRACOW! WIELICZKA SALT MINES! AUSCHWITZ! And I'd berate myself for giving anyone the benefit of the doubt.

I was riding a confusing roller coaster of contradictions, but it made for interesting hours. I had Polish-language classes in the morning and spent my afternoons exploring this funky medieval city that had been home to Polish kings. Krakow had survived the two world wars that destroyed much of the country, and seemed to glow with whatever magic had protected it until now. I would walk through an open food market, among tin stalls and tables made from wooden crates, to buy bread that all but melted in my mouth; beets that dripped like syrup on the plate; and radishes—the first small ones of spring—that were the sweetest I'd known. Our apartment on Ulica Staszica was just six blocks from the pleasant green park, the Planty, that encircled the old city in the loop once carved by the castle's moat. I would move through the perimeter to enter the old city through a turreted gate and wind my way through narrow cobbled streets to the square in the center. There, four-story buildings of curled gables and soaring pediments stepped back in perfect formation to give the street a rectangular garden in which to bloom. The edges of the market square were striped palates of color—creamy greens, subtle reds, smooth caramels of paint that coated four walls around the chaos of the center, which was alive with the collision of feet and bodies, music and motion.

Walking around, I'd play games with history. Sitting in the upstairs window of a sunlit coffeehouse on Bracka Street, or on the balcony of the little café designed to look like an old tailor shop, I'd wonder if it all could have turned out differently, if there hadn't been a war or a holocaust, if my family had stayed in Poland, if I had grown up here and come to Krakow for school, befriended Krys and Magda on terms less complicated by history, I, too, might have a degree from the same university as Copernicus and Pope John Paul II. I might be able to understand this lisping language of K's and Z's whose grammar demanded a different set of rules for every part of speech. But these were foolish games. There were no what-ifs in history. There was only what was, and as much as I was enjoying the city, and as determined as I was to ignore the specter of death here, I still sometimes caught a phantom image of troops marching through the square or of a heavy corpse hanging from a tree in the Planty. It was a shame. There were thirteen hundred years of history here: Jewish history, Polish history, Austro-Hungarian history. But try as I did, I needed an enormous amount of focus to see anything here beyond the six years that had brought me back. It was hard to walk down the street in 2001 and not see 1941. It was hard to look in the eyes of an old man on the streetcar, holding the handrail, and not wonder what he'd seen, what choices he'd made. It was all a long time ago—a lifetime—but I knew, somehow, it might never be quite long enough.

CHAPTER FIVE

M OM SOUNDED FINE ON THE PHONE—HAPPY, EVEN. HER HEALTH
had improved. She'd had her last chemo treatment and was
beginning to express an interest in my life in Poland. It was early May,
and Mom wondered why, after six weeks, I hadn't yet made my way
to Będzin. I started to give her the answer I had given to others about
wanting to learn the language better and gain a deeper understanding of the culture, but she cut me off. "Aren't you curious?" she asked.
"Don't you want to have a look?" I started to object, to tell her I was
waiting for the right moment, but then I thought I detected a subtle
note in her voice that betrayed an interest in something more than
how I was spending my time. "Are *you* curious, Mom?" I asked. "Do
you want me to have a look?" Oh no, she answered too quickly. "I just
thought you'd have gone by now. That's all."

She didn't want to admit that she cared about my search, but when
I spotted that breach in her painstaking armor of disinterest, I knew
I could no longer justify my constant delays. I quickly got in touch
with Jarek Krajniewski, the historian at the regional museum in the city

where my mother was born, and that was how we all ended up five days later—Krys, Magda, Jarek, and me—standing in Wiesław Skowroński's living room, watching an old man with tired blue eyes staring at a photo of his mother and my mother, frozen in time. "*Siostra,*" he kept saying in a soft, almost agonized voice. "*Siostra.*" Sister. "She used to follow him around," Magda said, translating. Wiesław muttered quietly as he looked at the picture. Magda stepped closer to hear him, then conveyed his words. "She was like his pet," she said. I could hear the pulsing in the veins behind my ears again, only now I wasn't clinging desperately to a rock. Now I was approaching the summit, about to pull myself to safety and turn around to see the sweeping vista of the valley. I could feel a glow in my belly, as though I'd consumed a steaming bowl of soup on a blustery, dark night. I couldn't believe this was happening, couldn't believe how quickly I'd been pulled up the stairs and into this room, face-to-face with a man who had known my mother as a child. I pictured Mom here with me, meeting this man, getting a hug from him even tighter than the one he'd given me. There was no way she could stand here like this and not feel something. Even if she didn't remember him, there was no way she could be immune to the power of a moment like this.

Everyone again started talking at once, drawing me into yet another cloud of Polish commotion. They asked questions of Wiesław and more questions of his answers. Krys and Magda passed on as many snippets as they could, but I shuddered to think how much I was missing. They translated moments from the old man's memory, how he would wake up early to milk the goat so Mom would have fresh milk; how he made her pancakes, her favorite food; how it was his job, when troops marched in the streets, to hide the baby in a dresser drawer so no one could hear her cries. He taught my mother to cross herself so she could play the Catholic child and helped her form her first words, he said. Then, as abruptly as she appeared in his life, she was erased from it. She never wrote or called. Wiesław's family wondered if she was even alive.

"She's alive," I told him, "alive and well." I was smiling and grateful as I told him this in my tentative Polish. I knew I wasn't speaking the whole truth, that Mom wasn't entirely well, but I knew that she would be soon, and then it wouldn't matter.

Wiesław wiped more tears from his face and gazed again at the scalloped postcard in his hand—his mother and my mother, framed in black and white, fifty-five years earlier. When I gave him another picture of Mom today, beaming in full color, he marveled at how young she looked. "She looks younger than fifty-nine," he said. I didn't tell him that she was wearing a flattering wig in the picture, one with more red in it, less gray, than her real pre-chemo hair. Wiesław's mother, Honorata Skowrońska, had died in 1995, he told us, years after suffering paralysis from a stroke. On her deathbed, she regretted that her "daughter" had never returned to see her. "That's so tragic," I said with a sigh when Magda translated this bit for me. "It is," she said, nodding. "You only missed her by six years." I pictured Honorata at the end of her life, feeling angry and forgotten. I'd only recently begun to understand the trauma of my mother's early life, and this was the first time I'd considered the people she left behind, people who, years later, might still have been wondering what came of her.

When it was time to leave, we wrote down Wiesław's phone number and promised to call soon. He shook each of our hands with a formal flourish, then Krys, Magda, Jarek, and I filed back down the stairs and into the sunny cool of a May afternoon. It was a beautiful day, one of the first when we hadn't needed heavy coats. Jarek offered to finish the tour he'd started. He said he would take us to the top of the castle, where we'd have a view of the entire city. But I glanced at my watch. It was just after two P.M., and Mom would be waking up soon in Detroit; I was anxious to get back to Krakow to call her. "Next time," I told Jarek in my best broken Polish. I thanked him for showing us around the city and skipped off with Krys and Magda toward the bus stop.

As we took the bus to the regional train station to catch the express train to Krakow, we were giddy from the rush of the morning. Krys and Magda teased me for having been scared. "What were you so afraid of?" Magda asked as I grinned through my blush. "You know," I said, "that he would come after us with a shotgun." Krys and Magda hooted and laughed. "This isn't America," Krys said. "People don't have guns here."

We'd bought a handful of beers before boarding the train, and I handed one to each of my friends. "Thanks for coming today," I told them. "I can only imagine what would have happened if I had tried to do this without you."

"Yeah," Magda said. "You'd still be standing outside, taking pictures with your spy camera."

"Like a little KGB agent," Krys said.

We cracked open the pop tops on our beers and bumped the cans together in a toast. "To you two," I said. "No!" Krys said. "To you." "No, no, no," Magda said. "To your mother. When is she coming? I feel like I know her already." Through the rest of the ride, we talked gleefully of my mother's expected trip to Poland in September, how Wiesław would react, how Mom would. I was almost running up the stairs when we got back to the apartment. I found him! I actually found him! I couldn't believe how easy it had been. I planned my words, what I would tell her first, how afraid I'd been—how needlessly—how he'd cried and called her his sister. I went straight for the phone when I came in the door and fumbled with the hard plastic slots of the rotary dial. Zero first. All the way around. Then again: 0-0-1 to get an international number. Then the area code. I made thirteen turns around the dial and waited to connect. I let the phone ring twice, then hung up. This was our signal, her cue to call me back, since it was cheaper for her to call me. Krys and Magda settled in around the table, another beer each as I paced the kitchen waiting for the phone to ring. When, after a couple of minutes, the phone remained silent, I tried again before deciding that Mom wasn't home. This was good news—it meant she was feeling strong enough to go grocery shopping—so I gave up and went off to the bar with my friends. We made fantastic plans about how we would call the local TV stations to cover Mom's reunion with Wiesław, then I left Krys and Magda with their drinks to run home and try the phone again.

This time I stayed on long enough to leave a message: "Mom! Call me! I have news!" It wasn't until a few hours later, after I had fallen asleep and was awakened by the ringing phone, that I learned why no one had answered. "Your mother's gone into the hospital," I heard my father saying. His words sounded empty, stripped of meaning. "It's nothing serious," he said. "I don't want you to worry. She probably just needs a transfusion. But I saw that you called and wanted you to know why she didn't call back." I was groggy from sleep and from drinking at the bar and for a minute couldn't place where I was, how far I was from home. I managed to sputter out some questions, but my father didn't know much. Mom had fevers that wouldn't go down. He hadn't wanted to take her to the hospital, and when he did, he regretted it. She seemed to get sicker. "I thought you said it wasn't serious," I said. "It's not," he assured me. But by the time Krys and Magda returned from the bar, tipsy and tittering, I was getting off the phone with the airline. I was leaving in five hours, I told them, watching as their buzz from a night of vodka and beer began to wilt. They both froze where they were standing and stumbled for something to say.

"Just like that? You're going home?" Magda squeaked.

"I'm coming back next week. Don't worry," I said. But they were visibly upset. Magda looked like she might cry. "Really, she'll be fine," I said. "It's no big deal. My dad didn't even want me to come home. But I told her I'd be there if she needed me, and she needs me, so I'm going."

Krys exhaled deeply and went to the cupboard for a bottle of vodka and a single glass. He poured a shot and handed it to me. "Drink this," he said. It was a Polish act of love.

"Thanks," I said, raising my glass to him and saying, "*Na zdrowie*," as he'd taught me. I tossed the cheap booze down the back of my throat. Magda sat down at the table, rubbing her eyes. "It's not serious, really," I told her. "She was fine the last time she went to the hospital. It was routine, a transfusion. I just want to be there for her." I refilled the glass and guided it across the table to Magda.

"But your mother—"

"Look," I cut her off. "Our parents will get sick. They're supposed to die before we will, and it'll hurt when it happens, now or twenty years off. There's no point in stressing before then." I had repeated these words to myself over the past year. They were words I spoke to ward off the wasted energy of worry. But my self-reminder had a morbid screech when spoken out loud. I could tell from the look on Magda's face that it had come off wrong. I stammered around to temper the damage. "Really," I said, "my mother's fine. She just needs a transfusion."

Magda picked up the glass unsteadily. She was already quite drunk. "To your mother," she said, slurring her speech. "To her health." She swallowed and refilled the glass for Krys. Magda looked too sullen to be upset about a woman she'd never met. I wondered if the booze was stoking her pathos or if she was still hearing my words: *Our parents will get sick. They're supposed to die before we will.* She must have been thinking of her own parents: *now or twenty years off.* They were thoughts no one wanted to think. I was glad, actually, that I had a little perspective. There was a lingering nag at the back of my head, a hint of doom, but I pushed it farther back. This was a bad time for me to be going home, just as my real adventure was about to begin. But I would be back soon. I would call Wiesław. I would go see him. I wouldn't tell him Mom was sick. There'd be no reason to distress him. And then who knew what would happen? Mom would visit. She and I would travel the country. I'd take her to the top of the Będzin castle to show her the view of the place she was born. And it would be just as I had dreamed.

CHAPTER SIX

I TRIED TO SLEEP ON THE PLANE BUT NEVER MANAGED TO DO SO and was dragging, nauseated and spent, when Derek picked me up from the airport after ten hours of travel. I wasn't sure how much longer I'd be able to stay awake, but I was eager to see my mother, to run to the side of her bed, to throw my arms around her, and to break the extraordinary news that I had met her long-lost brother. "Mom doesn't know I'm coming, does she?" I asked as Derek and I stepped into the hospital elevator. "She knows," he said dryly. I scowled at my brother. He should have consulted with me before blowing my surprise. Still, it wouldn't matter. I'd kiss her hello and pull up a chair and tell her about our crazy day in Będzin. "He's your brother, Mom! You were his sister! He can't wait to see you!"

"We're on the fifth floor," Derek said, pressing the button in the elevator. "The ICU."

I turned to look at him. No one had said anything about an ICU. "When did she—"

"This morning. She was having trouble breathing."

My father's words on the phone took on a new depth: *Your mother's gone into the hospital.* I swallowed a sour gulp of mucus and followed my brother to the ICU.

Mom had a slab of Plexiglas covering her face, squashing her nose flat and wide against the plastic. Derek told me it was an oxygen mask. It helped her breathe. But she didn't seem to be breathing. She was curled up, gasping for breath. She was panicking, upset. There were two doctors and a nurse in her room, watching, frowning. My father was standing in the hallway, staring through the thick window into Mom's room, cringing at the sight of her rocking back and forth on the bed, twisting herself into different positions in search of a full breath.

"Hey, you made it," he said as he gave me a distracted hug, his eyes still trained on Mom. Her head looked shrunken. Her ears poked out from the sides of the mask, weird and alien. She'd lost a lot of hair. It was spiky and thin.

"Dad, what's going on? Why is Mom wearing a hockey mask?" He looked tired and distressed. An obese doctor with a white Santa beard poked his head out the door. "Mr. Einhorn, I really do think we need to intubate," he said. My father winced. "She doesn't want to be intubated," he said. But the doctor said it couldn't wait. "My daughter just got here," he pleaded. "Can't she go and say hello?" But the doctor shook his head. "We have to do it now. I'm sorry, miss. You'll have to wait." The door slammed shut, and someone pulled a cord to close the beige venetian blinds between us and Mom. Dad sighed and, with a hand on my neck, guided me out toward the hallway. "Let's go sit down," he said.

It was a frightening night, unbearably so, but it was only a momentary scare. By the next day, when I came to see her, Mom was already on the mend. She was hooked up to a ventilator but awake and engaged. A day later, she was sitting up in bed, entertaining us. She soon returned to her throne as queen bee of the family, barking out orders by way of memos on a clipboard. The ventilator tube in her mouth rendered her mute, but she gave commands with exclamation points. *Brian,* she scribbled to my father, *don't forget to change the water softener! Derek: the tile in the basement needs another layer of sealant!* The first time she had me alone, she motioned me over and hurriedly scrawled on her clipboard a request for information about my brother's recent breakup with his girlfriend: *What you'd get on Derek and Corrie?* I hadn't heard much, I said, beyond what Mom had told me the week before when she called me in Poland, devastated. She'd gone to Derek's house, letting herself in with her key, and found the pictures of Corrie missing from the walls. Mom had run to the bathroom and found an empty drawer where Corrie's things had been. "She's gone!" Mom had wailed to me on the phone.

"Oh, Mom, I'm sorry," I said. "What are the chances that Derek will find someone else that you like as well?"

"Zero chance!" Mom steamed. And now she wanted answers. *You're the reporter,* she wrote on the clipboard. *Go report!*

"Yes, ma'am!" I agreed.

When I finally told her about my meeting with Wiesław, she seemed moderately interested, listening as I described the way he'd thrown his arms around me, but the ventilator obscured her usually expressive face, and I couldn't tell what she thought of the news. I tried to show her pictures of Poland, including some of Wiesław and his house—our house—that I'd developed in the hospital gift shop, but when Mom lifted a picture from the pile on her lap, and brought it close enough to her face to see without glasses, she started coughing. The tube irritated her throat. I set the pictures aside and decided they could wait until she emerged from the hospital and put her glasses back on.

When they finally took Mom off the ventilator, five days after she entered the ICU, it was a joyful day. She was smiling and talking. She had her health again. She had her future. She could speak with her voice. The chemo was officially behind her, and the infection or whatever it was that had landed her in the hospital was gone. I was enormously glad I'd come home, glad I'd been able to see her through this, to see the relief on her face as she realized she would pull through. My father and brother went back to work, and now it was just the two of us during the day, hanging out, talking about nothing. I decided against discussing Poland again unless she asked about it. I wanted her to enjoy herself, to get better so we could go home and properly talk about what had happened in Będzin. I would set up the microphone again and try for a second formal interview on the subject. When the hospital priest stopped by, Mom poked me and whispered that she thought the priest was Polish. "Talk to him," she said, then beamed when I wished him good morning in his native language. "I see your lovely visitor is here again," he chirped in his visit-the-sick voice. Now that Mom was feeling better, she played along. "Pray for me, Father!" she said, trying, I think, to sound like a hospital patient on a soap opera. The priest's face lit up. "Why don't we pray together?" he suggested. I watched in amusement as Mom tried to decline without being rude. "Oh, no. You just pray for me," she said. The poor priest backed clumsily out of the room, looking confused. "Oops." Mom giggled when he was gone. "I don't think he'll be coming back."

She was feeling so much better that, after a few days, I called David and invited him to visit. I'd sent him an e-mail from Krakow the night I decided to fly home, and he'd called immediately, full of concern. We'd been talking on the phone every night since then, me in Detroit, he in Philadelphia, slightly lifting a window that I'd assumed had more or less closed when I left. I wouldn't have opened the window again, either, wouldn't have allowed us both to get our hopes up, except that he had sounded so sweet on the phone when he'd called me that night in Krakow. I could hear true worry, as though the ache in my heart were sticking pins into his. I'd never had anyone channel my hurt like that and found it incredibly touching. I called him my first night back at my parents' house and told him about my mother's desperate effort to breathe in a hockey mask, how devastating it was to feel like I was watching her die. These were things I couldn't tell my father because they would only upset him. My brother and I were close, but he's a doctor and he seemed so focused on the science of Mom's disease that I didn't want to distract him with fear. So I told these things to David. And each night, as my mother's health improved, I gave him a daily report and could hear the tension softening on his side of the line as the dissipating worry in my chest lifted the weight from his. I had told David at first that I didn't want him to visit, didn't want Mom to think that while she was sick in the hospital, I was out with some guy she'd never met. But everyone else in my family had a life outside of the hospital. They had jobs and friends. They had lives in Detroit. The whole of my existence in that city were official hospital visiting hours and a late-night call to a man in Philadelphia. So after a week of telling David not to come, I called and announced a change of heart. "Check and see if you can find a cheap fare for next weekend," I told him. "I'll pick you up at the airport." Then, for the next few days, as I cheered on Mom's recovery, I had something to look forward to as well.

It wasn't me who stirred the bad karma, or so I kept telling myself. The distressing turn of events had nothing, I hoped, to do with the way I'd taken things for granted and tempted evil spirits. But still, I felt at least partly responsible when Mom had a sudden setback and found herself, for a second time, with a tube down her throat, hooked up to machines that helped her breathe. I had wanted so badly to spend the weekend with David, to be a little bit selfish. But now it seemed foolish to invite him here, to bring him to Detroit, to my family, to a city where my mother lay sick in the hospital. I tried to reach him the morning of my mother's setback to tell him not to come, that the timing wasn't right, but he had left for the airport before I could catch him and already was flying toward me, anticipating a fun weekend and a chance to rekindle what we'd briefly had. As I drove to the airport and waited for him at the gate, I wasn't sure what to expect. I wasn't even sure what he looked like anymore, this man I'd known for a handful of weeks in the cold of winter. He had been warm and thoughtful, I remembered that. But it was a vague memory, more emotional than cognitive. Then there he was, walking toward me, smiling tentatively beneath his brown leather cowboy hat. I saw the single crooked baby tooth at the front of his grin and a look of quiet hesitation in his eyes. I gave him a hug, too scared to look up and kiss him, not sure if kissing was the right sort of gesture.

Dave was a good sport about the change of plans and agreed to spend the day entertaining himself. I gave him my car and directions to a local museum, then I sat down in a chair at the foot of my mother's bed and glumly listened to the rhythmic waves of her sleeping. This was the day the doctors had planned to move her from the ICU to a regular room, but now she had fluid in her lungs. Her blood pressure had dropped. She was depressed by the setback, and so was I. So were we all. The hospital had started to wear on us. It had been nearly two weeks of sitting here, of waiting. It wasn't just that it was boring or that the room smelled like piss. It wasn't just the constant beeping of the machines or the perky nurses or the boiled food. It was the interminability of it all. For a while, I could get used to it—the relaxed exhale of the ventilator, hypnotic and regular. It was demoralizing to see her gagged by the tube again, but there was a certain comfort in knowing she didn't have to worry about breathing. If nothing else, she looked serene. I would watch her belly rise and then, a second later, would hear the machine gasp and sigh. I would watch the red sensor on her finger go up and down atop her rising and falling gut as she slept. I could handle this for a time. What I couldn't handle was not knowing how long it would last, how long we'd have to wait before she would be better, before we could all go home and return to our lives. I was anxious to get back to Poland, to whatever it was I was supposed to be doing there. I didn't want to lose the momentum with Wiesław Skowroński. Having finally trounced my hesitations and jumped into the river, I was itching to see where the current would take me and was becoming increasingly exasperated with the wait. I just wanted Mom to get better, for this all to be over.

May 31, 2001. I scrawled the date across the top of a blank page in my journal. I'd returned to the roof of my parents' house, my back against the chimney, my bare feet turning black on the shingles like they used to back when the roof was where I retreated to vent my hate for her. I had so much rage and resented her terribly, she who . . . *FUCK!* It was the only word I could think of to write, so I wrote it in big block letters across the top of the page. *FUCK FUCK FUCK FUCK FUCK!!!* It just didn't seem fair. I stabbed my pen at the page, gouging an inky blue divot in the paper. Why couldn't I write now? There was so much I wanted to say, so much to record. Every detail: the bizarre sensation—comical, even—of her icky painted face in the casket. The orangish lipstick not quite staying between the lines. I actually laughed. It made it easier. Like it wasn't really her, it was some other weird-looking lady with bad makeup. The sensation of dirt in my hand, cold between my fingers, curled into my palm. Her face in the newspaper. So cute. Big smile. *The Detroit News: W. Bloomfield resident, teacher, counselor, 59. The Detroit Free Press: Irene Einhorn: Escaped Holocaust.* I told her story again and again that first day. She would not have liked my emphasis on the parts of her life over which she'd had no control, those first nine years. I'm not sure why I did that. I guess I knew her war story would sell better, and I wanted Mom to have display obits. The *Detroit Jewish News* guy asked if he should use their HOLOCAUST SURVIVOR logo. Mom would have hated that. She always insisted that she was not a survivor because she hadn't been in the camps. "I was just a kid. My father was a survivor," she'd told me. "Yes, please use the logo," I said. "That sounds nice." Telling her story was my job now.

Death itself is not that bad. I kept thinking that at the funeral—that death was just a moment in time defined by all these scripted events and uncomfortable conversations. The sting, I knew, would be the happy days later—days that forever would be less happy. My wedding. Why was everybody talking about my wedding? Friends of my mother's, aunts, cousins. They kept talking about my wedding and how my mother wouldn't be there, as though there were a groom and a dress and now all I needed was a mom. But they were right: She wouldn't be there. And kids. If I have kids, it will be without her. How will I raise kids without her? And everything else: our gossipy phone calls, our shopping sprees, the hours we spent laughing over twenty-year-old jokes. My calls to her in the middle of the night: "How do I get rust stains off my countertop?" No more. I'll have to live with rust stains. And just when we had at last become friends. That was the worst part. It had taken us forever to be friends. We were finally there, finally able to appreciate each other, and now she was gone. I'd been wanting some time to myself for days. To think. To miss her. To feel sad. But there'd been no peace in the rush of ritual. There were people everywhere and pressure, perversely, to entertain. I hadn't lived in her house in years, but my father didn't know where she kept the big coffeemaker. Poor Dad. He hadn't bought his own groceries in decades, let alone lived by himself. We were both indulging in substance abuse. Lots of it. And laughter, distraction. Were we horrible people for laughing all the way to the funeral home and from there to the cemetery? What were we laughing about? I had no idea. Whatever it was, it was funny. Or it seemed funny at the time. Or it served as a helpful buffer for what we didn't want to feel. Something like that.

None of us saw it coming. It just came. In the morning. I was hungover when I heard the news. I'd left the hospital the night before, depressed, and met Dave in the bar across the street. Unlike that morning when I'd clumsily greeted him, unsure if I even wanted him to be there, I walked up to him at the bar that night feeling like I'd reached a wide and shady ledge in the middle of a grueling rock climb, a refuge to forget for a moment that I was dangling in the middle of a granite cliff and still a long way from the summit. "You need to catch up," Dave told me, handing me a shot of bourbon. I sucked it back, and he gave me another. I drank that and felt much better. We kissed in the bar. "What are you guys? Newlyweds?" the guy on the next bar stool asked. "No," Dave answered. "She just got sprung from prison." I smiled at him. "Or Poland," I said. There might have been another shot after that. And a beer. I'd have been fine, I think, if I had had dinner. Instead, I actually got sick on the sidewalk in front of the bar. We stayed that night at my friend Becca's place because it was nearby.

The morning my mother died, I was up early, leaning over the toilet in Becca's bathroom, wondering about the nature of the toilet's yellow stains. Becca was in her living room, knitting and reading a medical book. She was in her fourth year of med school. I collapsed on the chair next to hers. "Rough night?" she asked. "Rough week," I answered. "The waiting is really getting to me." That was more or less the exact moment when the phone rang, like some sick kind of cue. I saw my dad's number on the cell phone display but heard no sound when I picked up. I tried to call him back, but his line was busy. I took a shower, then called again while getting dressed, a towel around my head, half into my jeans. "Erin?" Dad's voice was cracking, high and shrill. I knew something had gone terribly wrong.

I knew what death looked like. I'd spent two weeks in the ICU, and I'd seen it. We'd be in the waiting room, and there'd be another family in there, weeping. An older woman would come in and say to a younger man something to the effect of "Dad wants to see you now," and then the younger man would stand, wipe his eyes, steady himself, and walk out. You'd see the whole family embracing in the hallway at some point later and the next day they'd be gone, replaced by another family, another set of kids playing board games in the waiting room, accidentally paging the nursing station with the device that looked like a TV remote but wasn't one. We never got our tearful good-bye. Mom couldn't be bothered. Dad simply walked into her room, as on every other day, and found, for the first time, silence. No machines. Mom was gone.

I didn't know what would come of David, whether he and I would find a way to be together. But I knew he would forever be a part of my family folklore for his presence in our lives that day, sitting there quietly on the leather sofa, drinking a beer, while we felt sorry for him. "Imagine," my father kept saying, shaking his head and looking over at Dave. "You come to see a girl for the weekend and her mother dies." We all shook our heads in sympathy. "Tough luck." Dave claimed he didn't feel uncomfortable sitting there, watching me call Grandma Fela in Atlanta. Because of Mom's absolute insistence on privacy, a woman who once cradled her own sister as she died in her arms, who watched as close friends were shot in the back and as babies' skulls were crushed on the ground, had to learn that her daughter was dead without even knowing that she had been ill. "I didn't knooooww," she wailed into the phone, so heartbroken, so bewildered. We had sent her son, my uncle Harold, to her house that morning to break the news. "I'm sorry, Grandma. I'm sorry. She didn't want to worry you," I told her.

There were many people Mom hadn't wanted to worry, her friends, the people who loved her, who would have wanted to be there for her in illness, who didn't deserve to hear the startling news without any warning. It was Memorial Day. They returned from their picnics and boats to our messages. "But why didn't she tell me?" they asked. "I could have helped. I could have . . ." Years later, I would continue to hear from my mother's friends about how her silence had pained them, how they'd wondered what they'd done to lose her trust, how they'd blamed themselves for neglecting their dying friend. But this was what my mother had wanted. Just as her earliest days had always been a kind of secret, little known to the people around her, her last days were private, too. And so the task fell to us, to her husband, to her children. We broke the news, and we offered comfort to them.

And all the while there was David, perched on the sofa, just kind of watching, not really belonging, looking like he needed a project. "Here, Dave." My uncle Bob took pity on him and gave him a broom. "Go sweep the porch." My brother begged me to send him away. "You've got to get rid of that guy," he said. "Take him to the movies. Anything." I offered to drop Dave off at the movies, but he refused, said he wanted to be near me. I wasn't sure what I wanted, so I let him sit there feeling useless. "It can't be helped," I told my brother. It really couldn't be helped.

It was peaceful up on the roof. My little retreat. Mom had hated it when I climbed out my bedroom window onto the roof. She'd been scared I would fall. I think she banned me from the roof, but I didn't listen. I was fifteen and knew better. These years later, it was still a perfect sanctuary, me and the treetops. The house had changed a lot since I moved away. The rug in the family room was new. The hardwood floors hadn't been here when I lived in the house. Mom had made a lot of improvements for Derek's med school graduation party a few years earlier. But the roof hadn't changed at all. It was like it always had been, a tranquil sea of black beneath the open sky, my cozy seat against the chimney. This was the only place I knew I could hide in a houseful of people. It was warm and sunny here, the shingles beneath my legs were sticking to my skin, like they used to when it was her I was hiding from, back when I thought I didn't need her.

Tracing my mother's story had been my dream. It had never been hers. But with no possibility of reuniting a brother with his sister, I didn't see much of a point. I no longer wanted to go back to Poland. I wanted to stay with my dad, with my family, with the people who knew how much had been lost. But I knew that I couldn't stay in Detroit. I had no life there. I couldn't go back to Philadelphia, either, and return to my life and my job like nothing had happened. I didn't want to deal with David. There was a strangeness between us now. Whether it was fair or not, I felt like he had been tested, and though it was a test I couldn't imagine anyone passing, I resented him for failing. In the end, Poland seemed my only real choice. And so, on a balmy June day in a scene reminiscent of a colder one three months earlier, my father took me to the airport in Detroit for another flight bound, via Amsterdam, for Warsaw. I tried to ignore the memory of that earlier flight, of Dad and Mom and I going together to the airport, of checking in, of waiting with Mom in line while Dad parked the car, of Mom and me sobbing as we hugged good-bye. At the time our tears had seemed overly dramatic, but they made more sense in retrospect. It was, as fate would have it, our last real embrace. I could never quite reach her in the hospital bed. It was also the last time I would see her standing. There was hugging and crying at the airport this time, too. Only this time it was my father—the man whom, a month earlier, I had never seen cry. I wondered if I was wrong to leave him, if it made more sense to stay with the only parent I had left. But they say to pick up where you left off. And though it had been five weeks and a very long time, Poland was where I had left off. My father hugged me good-bye and promised to come see me in September, when Mom was supposed to come. I promised I'd call. Then I left his side and boarded the plane, this time traveling the Atlantic without any fears at all. This time my worst fear had already come true.

CHAPTER SEVEN

I T WAS STRANGE TO RETURN TO POLAND, TO MY ROOM WITH THE bright green walls, to the kitchen with the floor painted red, to Krakow with its carnival plazas and medieval charm. It was warmer, sunnier, busier, but it felt queerly unchanged. My room was just as I'd left it, untouched, as if my life were the same, as if everything was as it had been. I told Krys on my first day back that I'd be smoking a lot more hash with him now. We were sitting on a shady bench in the Planty park around the old city, near the university, looking up at a bronze statue of Copernicus. This was Krys's favorite bench from his college days, right outside the history department, tucked far enough into the bushes that he could smoke anything he wanted and no one would bother him. I told him this. He nodded. "Okay," he said.

I spent the next day doing nothing. The day after that, too, lolling stoned by the side of the river in the shadow of the castle, watching the bikers and joggers out enjoying the weather, not quite sure what to do with myself, not sure if I'd ever be able to do anything again. It was the first time I'd been away from my family since my mother died. I was confused, grieving, and dreading the thing I needed to do.

Just over a hundred miles from here was a man to whom I'd promised a sister. His mother was gone, his father, his younger brothers. I had arrived out of nowhere and—like magic—brought his long-lost sister back to life. And now another blink and she was gone. "Don't tell him, Krys," I pleaded a week later when I finally felt ready to contact Wiesław. "Tell him I'm back in the country, that I'd like to come for a visit, but don't elaborate. *Please?*" Krys eyed me skeptically but nodded in agreement. He made an appointment for the following day, thinking he'd be able to go with me as an interpreter, but at the last minute, he learned he had to work. Magda was my next best option, but she had been acting strangely. Sometime in the weeks of my absence, she'd acquired a new cell phone and had begun receiving constant calls. When the phone rang, she'd get up from the table, go to her room, and close the door.

"How long has this been going on?" I asked Krys.

"Couple weeks. I don't know." He shrugged. "She hasn't told me anything." I pressed for details, but Krys said Magda would tell us when she was ready. He urged me to drop the issue. I knew he was right, but I was worried. Magda had barely said hello to me when I returned. She muttered something like "Sorry about your mother," then went back to her room and her phone calls. She had been a blur on the edge of my consciousness, this other sadness out there that I hadn't had time for. I missed the friendship we'd had and needed it now more than ever, but I wasn't sure how to approach her. I had low expectations when I knocked on Magda's door and asked if she'd come with me to Będzin. I fully expected her to refuse. But when I requested her help, she graciously agreed. "I'd be happy to," she said. I instantly felt sorry for doubting her, but I could tell that something was different with her now, something unsettling.

It was warm at the end of June, cheerful and summery. A soft breeze hugged the tracks as we sat on the platform, awaiting our train. The train station was filled with backpackers and families on trips to the mountains. It had changed sharply from the windy night a few months back when Magda and I first met here, eyeing each other across the platform. We, too, had changed, I thought. Both of us. "You want a strawberry?" I offered. We had arrived early for our train and settled on a bench. I opened the basket of fruit I'd bought at the market on the way to the station. The market was alive with color in summer, bursting with cherries and raspberries and luscious vegetables. There were more people shopping there than in the early spring, old ladies pushing their way among the card tables to find the sweetest fruits, to haggle a better price for tomatoes. I'd gazed with wonder at the market when I first arrived and it was even livelier now, but now I didn't have the heart to appreciate it.

Magda picked a dripping berry from the basket and took a tiny bite off the tip. We had walked to the station all but wordlessly. I had promised myself that I wouldn't push, that I would let Magda confide in me at her own pace, but I was weary of the distance between us, unsure what was behind it, and shortly after we sat down, I couldn't help myself. I asked about the man—I presumed it was a man—who kept calling on her new phone. "Oh, that," she said, blushing. "We're just friends." His name was Natan, she told me. He was Israeli but lived in New York. She had met him when he was visiting Krakow with friends. Natan and his friends had come into the bookshop where Magda worked as a tour guide, and she had shown them around, then joined them for dinner. "And you're not dating him?" I asked, attempting to believe her when she insisted she was not. Natan had sent her presents and was calling nearly every night, sometimes twice a night. But Magda was adamant that she was still with Ted, her boyfriend in London, that there was nothing romantic between her and Natan. "It's just, it's complicated," she said. "He's . . . well, he's helping me. I learn a lot from talking to him." I couldn't imagine how Natan was helping her. The biggest issue in her life had been her thesis, which she was already over a year late in finishing. Was he offering research assistance? Was it maybe something more serious? Was Magda pregnant? I asked more questions but she squirmed like she didn't want to answer. I regretted broaching the subject, but now I was worried. Was it something I could maybe help her with? I asked as we found our seats on the train. "No," she said. She didn't think I could help. I asked the same question in a few different ways as the train hurtled through the industrial outskirts of Krakow. When Magda finally relented and agreed to tell me what was going on, there was a strain in her voice that made me instantly regret my persistence. Krys had been right. It wasn't my business. I feared I'd made things worse between us. "Natan is helping me," she said, turning to look out the train window and then turning back to me. She pressed her lips together as she searched for words. "He's helping me to become a Jew."

I could feel my jaw fall slack as I searched for a response to her news. I had imagined everything from money problems to alcohol addiction, but religious conversion had never seemed like even a vague possibility. Was it for this man, I asked, this Natan? But Magda recoiled at the notion. "It has nothing to do with him!" she said. "I've been wanting to do this for years. He just helped me remember why." I stammered out an apology; at least I hope I did. The precise details of that conversation would later elude me, but I remember trying not to sound incredulous as Magda told me that her conversion—in order to be accepted by everyone—would have to be of the highest, most religious order. She would have to move to New York or Jerusalem. She would have to join an Orthodox community and follow strict rules about modesty and diet. I remember staring at her, telling myself to keep my judgment to myself, to try to seem like a supportive friend, to be happy for her, but the notion of Magda transforming herself into an observant Jewish woman seemed absurd to me. I suppose it shouldn't have. She'd had an interest in Judaism since long before I'd met her, and though she had told me her interest was cultural, not religious, this move wasn't completely out of context.

I wondered if I didn't want her to change or if I was upset that she might be moving. Or maybe it just seemed too sudden, like she had been one person when I left for home, and now I was back, my mother was gone, and Magda, in a way, was too, replaced by this other girl who wanted to be a religious Jew. I wondered also if my discomfort stemmed from something larger, if it had to do with Poles and Jews and Jews and Poles and my mom, who was a Jew but had to pose as a Pole, and Poles I'd met who were all but posing as Jews. And now Magda, this woman to whom I'd felt connected in ways that transcended religion and culture, was seeming to draw attention to the very things that were our differences. She was, in fact, creating a new difference by approaching a level of Jewish observance that I, as a secular Jew, could neither understand nor desire. And as much as I wanted to support her, to encourage her to follow the rainbow of her dreams, I wondered if this was the right dream for her, if this rainbow would lead to the pot of gold she imagined. Neither of us spoke much for the rest of the train ride. I watched the deep green fields blur past the windows and counted the seconds it took to zip through tiny, rusty towns in the train's path. Magda sat beside me, flipping through a Polish fashion magazine, her body all but screaming her aggravation. I had let her down, and I regretted that, but I still felt very bothered by her news.

In Będzin, there was none of the anxiety of our last visit. In May, as my heart raced with nervous energy, my eyes devoured the details of the place where my mother was born. Now every detail was another thing that she would never see. I felt no nervousness this time as we approached the front walkway of the three-story town house at 20 Małachowskiego Street. Gone, too, was the apprehension of our first shaky encounter with Wiesław Skowroński. This time there were hugs for me and for Magda. There were warm greetings not only from my mother's onetime brother but also from a buzzing cluster of people whom we took to be members of Wiesław's family. We were led to the living room by a half-dozen jumpy kids of various ages and a bunch of adults, mostly women, who proceeded over the next couple of hours to come and go, moving back and forth between the living room and the kitchen. They were curious about me and, I hoped, about the story I represented, the moment in time when the narrative of their family intersected with the narrative of mine. They introduced themselves. One was a niece, one a daughter, one a friend. They kissed our cheeks—right cheek, left cheek, right cheek—and then some sat down on the sofa and some hovered near the door. Someone put a cake on the table. We were asked if we took coffee or tea. "We're so happy you've come!" someone said.

I tried to make myself look friendly, like a long-lost relative. I pulled a stack of snapshots from my bag, including a host of old pictures that had been taken by my mother's cousins in this very house. I handed Wiesław a copy of the photo I'd shown him on my previous visit: of his mother with my mother and grandfather. "You can keep this," I said as Magda translated. Wiesław sat down in a chair beside the table and, holding the picture gingerly in both hands, brought it close to his face, which took on a tender sadness. He looked over at a shy-looking blond boy of about five who was squeezed into a wedge of space on the sofa. "Marek, come here," he said, reaching for the boy and seating him on his lap. "This is your great grandmother," he said as the boy tugged on his grandfather's ear. The other kids crowded around to get a look. They were jabbering in high-pitched squeals that I didn't understand. The progress I'd made with the language in the spring had vanished in my weeks at home. I was back to only basic sentences.

A plump woman with short gray hair whom I took to be Wiesław's wife came over to see the photo. As she peered over her husband's shoulder, she started laughing and said something that prompted Wiesław to laugh, too. "*Tak! tak! tak!*" he said through his laughter. Yes! Yes! Yes!

"They're saying that your grandfather wanted to take his mother, Mrs. Skowrońska, with him to America," Magda translated. "He wanted to marry her, but she refused because she had three kids of her own." They all got a hearty laugh out of this and seemed to be talking about how their lives would be different if she had accepted his offer. I couldn't imagine that what they were saying was true. I didn't remember much about my grandfather—I was nine when he died—but I knew he had been single-minded on the subject of intermarriage. According to him, Jews didn't marry gentiles. There were no exceptions. Then again, the war changed many things. "Are they sure about that?" I asked. Magda shrugged. "That's what they're saying," she said. "His mother said later that she wished she'd gone with him, that she was sorry she gave up your mother."

I smiled to be polite and considered asking more questions. Instead, I made a note to return to the subject later and, for now, tried to focus on the person who was really on my mind. In the rush of our arrival, the people, the hugs, the photos, Magda and I had not yet broken the sad news. But as I tried to prepare myself, I knew I couldn't go through with it. They had been so happy to see me, I didn't want to ruin their day—or mine. Silly as it was, I wanted to pretend for a moment that maybe the news wasn't true, that maybe it was still possible Wiesław would someday be reunited with his sister. "You know what, Magda," I said, hoping no one else in the room could speak English, "don't tell them today. We'll do it next time. I just really want to talk to him today without any distractions." Magda looked confused. She opened her mouth to object but then closed it again, nodding her understanding. "Okay," she said. "If that's what you want."

I suggested that we pose Wiesław some questions. "Ask him what he remembers about my mother," I said. Magda nodded, tapped Wiesław on the arm, and repeated my question to him in Polish. Wiesław smiled, set the boy from his lap on the floor, and started to speak. But before Magda could translate, more people came into the room, and there

were more greetings. I'd brought a tape recorder and had been hoping
to interview Wiesław, but there were too many people all talking at
once. The short plump woman who I'd decided earlier was Wiesław's
wife sat down next to Magda and started talking to her, speaking
quickly and gesturing. Magda tried to interrupt so she could translate,
but the woman kept grabbing Magda's shoulder to finish a point. I
tried to interject, to explain that I didn't speak Polish, that I needed
Magda to translate for me, but the lady kept talking. Magda signaled
that she'd tell me about it later. Then, as if things weren't confusing
enough, she was joined by a second, younger woman, one of Wiesław's
daughters, and now they were tag-teaming Magda, each of them talking into each of her ears. Magda could do little more than shoot me
apologetic glances. I had no idea what these ladies were saying, but
whatever it was, they were energized about it. They spoke quickly, vigorously, for what seemed like ten or fifteen minutes without a word of
translation. I was becoming increasingly annoyed. "Magda!" I reached
across the table to tap her shoulder. "I'll tell you about it later," she said,
a tone of stress in her voice. "It's complicated."

They were still talking, but now Wiesław, who had said very little
as he continued to study the picture I had given him, was trying to say
something. As he rubbed his thumb against the edge of the photo, a single tear crawled down his right cheek. He wiped it away, then touched
me on the arm and muttered something not quite under his breath but
not exactly out loud. "*Proszę?*" I said, thinking maybe I could speak to
him in Polish. "I'm sorry, but I didn't hear you." He repeated his mum-
bled remark in a low and gentle voice, but I still didn't understand. "I'm
sorry," I said in Polish. "Wait a minute." I tried to get Magda's attention, but she couldn't seem to pull free from the women, who were now
showing her a stack of documents that the younger woman had run to
the next room to retrieve. There were other conversations going on in
the room, too. The kids were jumping up and down, running from the
sofa to the kitchen and back to the sofa. Their mothers were yelling at

them. "*Magda!*" I reached across the table again, hoping she could say something to establish order. She again tried to stop the women from talking, but they kept at it. Only now we had an ally. Wiesław tried to intervene with his wife and daughter, but when that failed, he slammed his fist down on the table. "*CISZA!*" he barked, demanding silence as the table shook. "I'm speaking."

The women slumped down in their chairs. "Sorry, Tato," the younger one said. The older woman had a snarl on her face—she wasn't pleased—but she did stop talking. Even the squirming children went quiet, as did the women in the doorway. In the momentary still, we heard a car with no muffler *vrrrrumming* past the open window. Then the room was quiet, and Wiesław began to speak in a voice so low it was barely audible.

"He says he remembers her, your mother, that he took care of her." There was relief in Magda's voice as she translated this clean and easy sentence. "They would hide her in cupboards and in the cellar." A woman who'd gone to boil water came back with two coffees in small juice glasses. She set them noiselessly on the table, then sat on the arm of the sofa to listen. "There were three boys, Wiesław and his brothers. He was twelve, the oldest. His mother came home one day with a baby in a blanket. She set her on the floor and said: 'This is your sister. If anybody asks you who this is, you tell them that this is your sister.'" Another tear chased the first one down Wiesław's cheek. He blotted it with his sleeve. "He says this is very moving for him," Magda said.

"Does he know how his mother met my grandfather?" I asked. Magda transmitted my question and waited for his answer.

"He says his mother was a trader on the— What do you call it in English? Black market? Sometimes she traded goods in the ghetto. He doesn't know for sure, but that's probably how she met your grandfather. She must have traded with him. He doesn't really know. He says his mother went with a friend of hers to get the babies, your mother and another baby, a boy, only the boy didn't make it home. The woman left him on the streetcar."

I bolted upright in my chair. "The baby on the streetcar!" I said. "I know that story!"

"His mother told him that when they were coming back from the ghetto with the babies, the Germans got on the tram. They were getting people out and sending them to Germany to do slave labor. His mother said she grabbed your mother and ran away. She got off the car. She was very alarmed later when she realized that her friend was empty-handed. She didn't have her baby anymore. She left him on the seat. She got scared or something. Or forgot the baby."

It was fascinating to hear a slice of my family folklore told here, in translation, from a man I barely knew, but with key details changed. In my family's version, the baby was a girl named Gitte, and the woman was Honorata's sister. "I always heard the baby was a girl," I said. "No," Magda said after running this by Wiesław. "He says it was definitely a boy. He was circumcised. That's why the woman was afraid she would be caught." I agreed that this made sense and asked if Wiesław remembered the name of the woman who left the baby on the train. He said he did not know her name, but he was certain she was not his mother's sister.

Wiesław launched into a string of memories that covered the years before and after the war. He told us stories, snapshots, in no particular order. He repeated some of the things he'd told us on our first visit, about getting up early to milk the goat so the baby would have fresh milk, about making her pancakes, about her following him around because he was the oldest and she was his pet. He called her Zosia, he told us, because that was the name on the fake baptismal paper that his mother managed to acquire. Wiesław was fifteen when suddenly, in 1945, the little sister he cared for disappeared from his life forever. He couldn't remember if he cried that day, but he remembered that his mother did. He remembered that the girl's father had shown up one day without any notice and taken her away. He remembered that he missed her.

His mother at the time was running a small café on Kołłątaja Street in Będzin around the corner from where we were sitting now. Somehow my grandfather had found them. Wiesław remembered that Zosia was terrified. She didn't recognize this man who had come for her, and she screamed when he arrived. She didn't want to leave with him. He was going to put her in an orphanage, and Wiesław's mother didn't want her to go. She thought the girl should stay until her father was ready to take her, but her father was insistent. Wiesław wasn't sure why. He remembered that his mother had to accompany Zosia to the orphanage because she wouldn't go alone with her father. Later, he recalled visiting his sister in the orphanage with his mother. It was the last time he saw her. The orphanage staff asked Honorata and her son not to visit again because the girl was too upset after their first visit. Eventually, the Skowrońskis heard that the girl had left for Sweden and later for the United States. They figured she'd get back in touch with them one day, and they were sad when they realized that she never would. "His mother was always saying, 'I shouldn't have given Irenka away,'" Magda translated. "She had a daughter later, and when that daughter died of cancer, she cried that now she had lost two daughters." It was a sad story.

"He wants to know why your mother never came to visit," Magda said. I thought of all the reasons why Mom never came and the much more significant reason why she wouldn't come now. "Tell him—I don't know—that I wish she had come while his mother was alive." Magda passed this on to Wiesław, who smiled as he responded. "He says that, uh—" Magda looked down at the table and then back at me. "He says that when your mother comes, he'll take her to visit his mother's grave. His mother will be happy that her daughter finally came. Do you want me to tell him that—"

"No! Don't! Please? Be vague, will you?" I wasn't sure why it was so important to me to keep my mother's death a secret, but I wasn't ready to break the news. Magda tried to reason with me. "Erin, I think you should—" But I begged her: "Tell him I'm looking forward to him meeting my mother," I said. "Tell him!" Magda frowned her disapproval but then lied for me. She told him we didn't know when my mother would come, that we were still working out the details.

The first time I met Wiesław, I was so overwhelmed by the emotions of the encounter that I never stopped to look around my family home or to consider that I was standing on the very floor that my mother may have explored as a baby. I took the chance on this longer visit to take in the place, to try to wonder how it must have looked then, when the name on the bell outside said Frydrych, not Skowroński. Wiesław's living room, the largest room in the apartment, was big and open. It had weathered brown wood floors and white walls tinged yellow by dirt and nicotine. There was a drawing in black crayon on the wall above the lumpy striped sofa. Some of the adults were seated around the table with us on a jumble of metal and wooden chairs; others hovered in the doorway or leaned against the wall. The table, near the center of the room, was a small rectangular thing covered with a cotton floral cloth. I wondered if any of these things were here before the war, used by my family. Maybe the lace curtains over the two big windows were ours, filtering light from the sun and billowing in the summer breeze. The shiny brown cube of smooth ceramic that dominated one corner of the room was clearly here from the beginning. On winter nights, someone in my family might have opened the small iron door on the side of the cube, filled it with coal, and lit a fire inside to keep the apartment warm.

We stayed at the Skowrońskis' over two hours. We drank coffee, ate cake, and thirstily consumed Wiesław's memories. Then, as we were preparing to leave, he surprised us by sending one of the kids to fetch a round brass medal on a colorful ribbon that he stored in a flat wooden box in his bedroom. From the box, he also pulled a certificate written in French and Hebrew that he proudly set on the table. "Oh, wow!" Magda said as she picked up the medal, brushing its surface with her fingers. "I've never seen one of these!" "What is it?" I asked.

"It's the medal," she said. "From Yad Vashem, the Righteous Gentile award. This is really special."

I reached for the certificate. "Let me see that," I said. "She got this for saving my mom?"

Magda looked confused. "You didn't know?" she asked. I shook my head. Magda pondered this, then leaned over and asked Wiesław who had nominated his mother for the award. He shrugged as he answered. "He says he thinks she nominated herself," Magda told me. "I didn't know you could do that."

I didn't know that, either, and wasn't sure how I felt about it. I was glad that Honorata had been awarded the medal. She had saved my mother. But it was strange that no one had thought to tell my family she had been honored on our behalf.

When it was time to leave, we asked if we could come back in a couple of weeks. I told the family through Magda that I was a writer, that I worked for a newspaper, and that I wanted to interview them one at a time. They seemed interested, and we promised to return as soon as we could. Then two of the women and five of the children walked us back down the street and to the bus that would take us to the train station. As we found our seats, I put my hand on Magda's shoulder. "Thanks for that," I said. "I couldn't have gone through that without you." I meant what I was saying, but I was also trying to make up for earlier. I resolved to bring up her conversion again soon and this time to be more enthusiastic about it. I remained skeptical, but if this was what she wanted, then it wasn't for me to judge. Magda thanked me and seemed to understand the multiple levels of my gesture. She told me she had enjoyed herself at the Skowrońskis' and was glad she'd been able to help.

"So what in the world were those ladies going on about for so long?"

I asked. Magda had managed to tell me only that it had to do with the house, something about its ownership. "They're not worried that I'm going to take the house, are they?" I asked.

"No," Magda said. "That's not it." She looked as though she was still trying to process what she'd heard. "It was kind of confusing, but it's more like they're trying to get rid of it. Or they want you to fix some problem they're having . . ."

I couldn't understand. "Is it like the plumbing?"

"No." Magda laughed. "Some paper they want your mother to sign? I don't know. It was puzzling. Something about people who need to pay and don't pay. They kept explaining it to me, but they were interrupting each other, and there were all those kids. I could barely understand it in Polish, let alone translate it to English. Next time it'll be easier. They probably won't invite the whole family. We'll be able to straighten it out."

"Okay," I said. "We'll figure it out next time."

Flashes of the day strobed around me like the jumpy kids jostling for space on the sofa. Between Magda's surprise announcement, Wiesław's stories, and the new mystery issue with the house, I'd barely had time all day to remember my grief. And now I felt a surge of guilt, like I was neglecting my mom. I pictured Honorata Skowrońska on her deathbed, pining for her lost daughter, trying to nominate herself for an award she thought she deserved, an award for which she presumably thought we should have nominated her. I had conceived this project with my mom in mind, thinking how meaningful it would be for her to reconnect with her past. It had never occurred to me that there was a past out there waiting to reconnect with her. Magda told me about a Jewish archive in Warsaw that might have records related to the Righteous medal. I said I would also contact the museum in Israel to see what they had in their files.

As we switched from the bus to the train in the city of Katowice, we talked about the other mysteries that had emerged that day: Was the baby left on the streetcar a boy or a girl? Had my grandfather really considered marrying Honorata? There was also a new, fascinating question about my grandmother and the real story behind how she died. The question had arisen late in our visit. Wiesław's wife had been chatting with Magda, passing on things Honorata had said to her over the years. I was zoning out, discouraged by how little I understood, when Magda became suddenly animated. "*Na prawdę?*" she said, alarmed. "Is that true?"

"What is it, Magda?" I asked.

"You're not going to believe this!" she said, her eyes wide. Then she translated a Skowroński recollection that called into question the greatest, most dramatic moment of my family folklore: my grandfather's heroic solo leap from the train. In my family's version of the story, my grandparents had been together on the train most likely en route to Auschwitz. When I imagined the story, I pictured a dramatic exchange, my grandfather turning to his wife, theatrically begging her to escape with him: "There's a window, darling, come with me," he pleads. "Irena's in danger. We can't just leave her." My grandmother is terror-stricken and refuses to go. "It's too dangerous," she says. "We're young. We can work." She is twenty-two. He is thirty-three. But my grandfather disagrees. He kisses his wife, pries open a window, and slides himself out, hurling his body from the moving train and sailing through a hail of bullets until landing hard on the embankment. That's when he feels a sharp pain in his leg. He's been shot. He hobbles into the woods, bandages the flesh wound with his Jude armband, and starts to run. He runs until he reaches the ghetto, finds his daughter, and holds the girl in his arms. Next he gets in touch with Honorata. He plies her with money and promises, then, choking back tears, he hands her his only child, not sure if he'll ever see Irena again.

Only this is where the plot just thickened, because according to Honorata's son and daughter-in-law, when my grandfather found Honorata and plied her with money and promises, he also told her what had just happened to him. And as she would later recall the story for her family, my grandfather told her that he and his wife had jumped together from the train and that his wife had been shot, that he had watched her crumple when she hit the ground. He told Honorata that he didn't start running when he hit the woods. Instead, he turned back, hoping to save his wife, but found she was already dead. This was what had Magda jolting up in her seat and now had me mesmerized. It wasn't that I doubted my grandfather's version of events. He was the only one who really could have known what happened. Wiesław and his wife were repeating a story they'd heard secondhand decades earlier. But the very existence of their story cast doubt on my grandfather's. It wasn't that I thought he'd lied about so vivid a memory, but I did wonder if he'd chosen to pass down a less painful version to his daughter. It was possible that he'd told a false story to Honorata, thinking she'd take better care of a child whose mother was already dead. Or maybe the version he'd told to his family had been reconstructed in his mind as a protection against so wrenching a memory. I'd heard that it was common for survivors of extreme trauma to remember events differently, to change them over time.

It was a lesson I learned during an unpleasant encounter with a historian at the U.S. Holocaust Memorial Museum. I had just come from interviewing Grandma Fela in Atlanta and related to the historian my grandmother's harrowing tale of near death in the gas chamber at Auschwitz. The door had slammed shut on the chamber, Grandma Fela said, and she and her sister knew that death was seconds away. Then a miracle: The phone rang. Workers were needed. The women in the chamber were herded out to the sunlight and, at least for a moment, spared. It was a haunting story. But the historian harshly shook her finger at me. "That didn't happen," she said.

"What do you mean it didn't happen?" I asked. "My grandmother told me that story yesterday."

"And I'm sure that's how she remembers it," the historian said. "But

I've been interviewing survivors for thirty years, and I've never heard of anyone going into the gas chamber and then getting out. They had trainloads of people arriving every day. Why would they need that specific group at that specific time? Why not just wait for the next train? Your grandmother saw that scene in *Schindler's List*. After the movie came out, I started hearing that story all the time. Suddenly, everyone had a phone call in the gas chamber. The people who tell it remember it vividly. They believe it happened. The movie was very real. It brought a lot of things back for these people. They were reliving a lot of things, and the movie itself became part of their memory."

I was put off by her suggestion that my grandmother couldn't separate reality from film, but I'd been unable to forget the poignant reminder: Memory was not the same as truth. My grandfather's firsthand version of the train story was not necessarily more accurate than the second- or thirdhand version the Skowrońskis were telling. Honorata would have heard my grandfather's story when it was fresh, within days of the events in question. Who knew how accurately she remembered it or how accurately she retold it to her children? The only thing clear was that all of these versions contained some glimmer of truth. Was the child left on the streetcar a boy or a girl? Did my grandmother leap from the train or ride it to its deadly destination? I didn't know if I could prove any of these things, but it felt good to wonder about them. They were the first complex thoughts I'd had in weeks that weren't specifically about death or loss. The dream I came to Poland to pursue was dead, buried with my mother. But now I wondered if I could assemble another dream from the ruins of the first.

As the belching train sputtered back across the bright summer fields, I wondered how hard it would be to fact-check my family folklore. It wouldn't quite measure up to traveling with my mother. There would be no promised prize at the end, no rewarding personal connection. But I might learn something, uncover curiosities. Then again, the story would be one I'd never be able to share with her. I tried to remind myself that my mom didn't care, that she never had, that this search had always been about me and not about her. But what good was information in my own personal vacuum? Did it matter how someone died if, either way, she was dead?

"I'd rather be the granddaughter of the one who jumped," Magda said, as if hearing my thoughts.

"Well, sure," I said. "But you know where she was headed. If you had no idea about Auschwitz, don't you think it would have been stupid to jump?"

"Maybe so." Magda nodded. "But I still think I'd rather be the one who jumped."

CHAPTER EIGHT

T HE DOORBELL OUTSIDE STALOWE MAGNOLIE ASSURED SELECT
admission. The members-only back room featured velvet-covered
beds instead of tables. The cocktails were expensive, the clientele chic,
and the music lavishly rich. I was drinking vodka, my friend Ron was
drinking beer, and we were watching a dark-eyed lounge singer turn
out lush ballads one after another. That was when Ron came face-to-
face with the jarring disconnect of twenty-first-century Poland. Since
arriving in this country, I had come to appreciate the space between its
horrid past and its sometimes surreal present. But the first confronta-
tion with this time warp can be a harsh one. It can leave you wondering if what you're seeing is real or if somehow you've fallen asleep and
awakened, confoundingly, on the set of *The Producers*.

Ron and his wife, Carol, were in town from Philadelphia. They visited their college-aged son, who was studying in Prague. They stopped
in the small Moravian village that had been home, before the war, to
a Torah scroll that later found its way to Ron and Carol's Philadelphia
synagogue. Then they arrived in Krakow, where, like many of the city's

tourists, they spent their first day at Auschwitz. Now it was late. Carol had gone to bed, and Ron had asked me to show him the city's night. I led him to this dark and smoky club, a cavernous room decked with red and gold light and Klimptian swirls, where the woman on the microphone was singing in a deep and sultry voice. As hipsters at lounge tables sipped their drinks, she sang "Guantanamera." She turned out a few jazz standards like "When the Saints Go Marching In." And then, to Ron's amusement, she broke into a rendition of "Sunrise, Sunset": *Is that the little girl I saaaang to?* He recognized the tune from *Fiddler on the Roof* and started to laugh. *Is that the little boy at plaaay?*

"This is great!" he shouted in my ear above the music. "It's a Broadway take on the old country, right here in the old country!" *I don't remember growing olll-der. Whennn. Diiiid. Theeeey?* Ron was even more tickled when the slow, sweet "Sunrise" paused on a note, twirled on the whisk of a snare drum, and sprinted into a faster, poppier *Fiddler* tune: *If I were a rich man, di, de, de, de, de, di, gedingy dingy dingy dum. All day long I'd biddy biddy bum . . . If I were a wealthy man!* But when the girls at the next table jumped up and yelled, "Hey!," Ron looked a little stunned. "This must be a big musical here!" Ron said, grinning doubtfully as a table of young couples joined in to belt out the lyrics. More people came in from the next room and rocked their hips as they sang along to the ambitions of Tevye the Milkman. Then, as the band extended a note, slowly winding down this familiar tune to ease into the first unmistakable notes of the next, the "isn't it cool" expression on Ron's face began to shift into something more like distress. Around us, men in leather pants were leaping to their feet. Women in belly shirts were squealing in anticipation. The upright bass on the stage joined the piano, followed by the drums, followed by the woman at the microphone, who smiled broadly and launched enthusiastically into her evening's finale: *Havah,* she sang as the audience shrieked. *Nagilah Havah . . .* There were cries of joy and coos of delight. *Nagilah Havah, Nagilah venism'chah . . .* Now everyone was on their feet and dancing. *Havah, na-ra-na-na, Havah, na-ra-na-na* . . . Ron looked at me, slack-jawed. The pace of the music quickened. The skinny blonde next to us swirled the jewelry in her navel with dramatic gyrating motions. A young couple clutched each other and started to lambada. The band raced faster, stoking the crowd, spinning them into a frenzied gallop toward the final note. Everyone was moving, singing, loving the music—*Uru ura achim b'lev sameach, Uru uru achim b'lev sameach*—everyone in the entire club seemed to be up and dancing. *Uru uru achiiiiiiiiiiiiiiim* . . . *Uru achiiiiiiiiiiiiiiim* . . . Everyone, that is, except Ron and me. *B'lev sameeeeeeee-aaaaccch* . . . I was looking sympathetically over at him as he slumped against the wall, his hand on his forehead.

"*Dziękujemy bardzo!*" the singer shouted as the crowd cheered. "Thank you! Good night!" The band members put away their instruments. The bartender replaced the new silence with a hip-hop song from the radio. The people who were singing and dancing went back to their drinks and their conversations. But Ron leaned against the wall, shaking his head. "I'm sorry," he said after a stretch of minutes. "But where was I six hours ago?" I smiled a look of understanding. "Yep," I said, and went off to buy him another beer. It was all I could do. Six hours earlier, the where he'd been was Auschwitz. Like most Jews who visited Poland, he'd come for the past, to pay tribute to murder and memory. He and Carol had spent the day seeing what you see at the death camp: the hair, the shoes, the suitcases, the candles burning quietly in the ovens. They had stewed in the anger that fouls the air of the camp, and they may have blamed not only the Germans but the Poles who bore witness. They knew the stories about Polish hatred of Jews. They may have feared, as I once had, that Poland was a country of anti-Semites, rejoicing in our absence. And now here they were—the present—members of the Polish beauty class, dark lipstick, constant cigarettes, swirling their bellies in grateful rhythm to a song synonymous with Jewish celebration.

"Havah Nagilah" is the theme song of the Jewish wedding. The sound of its joyous notes prompt guests to hoist the bride and groom high onto chairs and dance around them in a Horah, shouting, Mazel tov! It is a song sung to a Hasidic melody rooted in this part of the world, which, in point of fact, belonged here much more than the Jay-Z song now playing through the lounge stereo system. But to hear it so gleefully celebrated an hour's drive from the former death camp, in a trendy corner of twenty-first-century Krakow—not a Jewish-theme café, not a Jewish tourist trap, but a popular, mainstream after-hours lounge where the Jewish partiers that night most likely numbered two (Ron and me)—was to slam headlong into the contradictions of Poland today. This was a country at once coursing with Jewish life and more or less devoid of it.

This was the kind of paradox that could turn a fun night's entertainment into an evening of questions without answers: Were they making fun of us? Paying tribute? Did they have any idea at all? Before my mother died, I spent hours considering these questions, but when I returned to Poland, drained from weeks of sorrow at home, these concepts were part of a landscape I no longer had the energy to explore. The theme cafés, the ubiquitous references to *Fiddler on the Roof,* even the roommate who talked elatedly of her impending conversion, were all things I could see beyond the screen that grief had put between me and the world. But unlike before, when I saw Poland with curious eyes, I now had neither the ability nor the interest to give the subject more than a passing acknowledgment. So when Ron asked me to explain the crowd's adulation for "Havah Nagilah," all I could do was admit that these were questions I had stopped asking. I told him about Magda and her possible conversion, about the people I'd met in cafés who had queried me on Jewish culture and faith. But I could shed no light on his questions.

The truth was, I no longer cared. If young Poles were into *Fiddler on the Roof,* that was their business. But I also knew that Ron wouldn't be the last to ask and that I needed some viable answers. And so, with more than a hint of reluctance, as soon as my friends departed for the Slovakian leg of their vacation, I applied for a press pass to cover Krakow's annual Jewish cultural festival. Magda had been buzzing for days about the festival. She insisted I'd be blown away by the final concert in Kazimierz, when thousands of people would converge on the central plaza of the Jewish quarter for an enormous outdoor klezmer-palooza. I had told her that I didn't think I would go; I didn't have the energy for a campy week of Jewish kitsch like the one I imagined. But though the premise of a Jewish cultural festival in Krakow seemed laughable to me, I was here as a student of this culture and knew I couldn't justify missing the festival. So on the night of the opening concert, I slipped in to the back row of an old, restored synagogue and listened as cantorial music soared high into the rafters. With the microphone I last used to interview my mother and grandmother at their respective kitchen tables, I pulled people aside at the concert to ask why they had such an interest in the music of cantors.

I asked similar questions over the next ten days in exhibits of Jewish photography, in a meticulous demonstration of Jewish paper cutting, and in a Yiddish class that drew nearly sixty people every day for a week. I did interviews in a Hasidic dance class that crammed nearly two hundred people, silly and sweating, into two giant dancing circles in a school gym, and at a series of Jewish cooking demonstrations that were so popular, they were standing-room-only. I even tried to ask these questions at the uproarious closing concert on the final night, which, true to Magda's promise, did absolutely amaze me, though maybe not for the reasons she anticipated. The final concert drew ten thousand young and screaming klezmer fans to the cobblestones of the central plaza of Kazimierz. They thronged the space between the theme cafés as TV cameras, broadcasting the event to every corner of Poland, shone brilliant lights out across the night sky to illuminate the dancing fans. Kielbasa sizzled on grills at each end of the plaza, filling the air with the succulent smell of hot pork as Jewish musicians from New York and Berlin rocked the night with bows that raced across strings, lips that whistled through trumpets, and voices that sang stories in Yiddish.

The festival impressed me, both because of its remarkable size and because, unexpectedly, I enjoyed myself. With a few notable exceptions, my fears about mocking kitsch were unfounded. There was no one in costume and very few caricatures. When I let myself relax and experience the festival, I was actually rather moved by the sound of Jewish music played so vibrantly and skillfully in this place where it so intensely belonged. Some of the Jewish musicians and artists who came from abroad to perform had been playing the festival for as many as ten years. They came here, they told me, because the music and art needed to be here even now—especially now. And that was when I started to get it, to see the point of it all. That was when I stopped seeing the crowd at the festival as culture stealers and started seeing them more as preservationists—people invigorating a culture that otherwise would be nearly dead here.

The people I interviewed offered a range of answers about what had brought them to the festival. Some liked the music. Some of the women in the cooking class said they were there to learn new recipes. But most of the festivalgoers professed an admiration for Jewish tradition. "I just love to be close to this festival, this atmosphere!" said Ksenia, a pretty young grad student I met at an art exhibit. "It is something beautiful!" Ksenia told me she was writing her thesis on Reconstructionist Judaism in the United States. There were curiosity seekers: "Jews are so exotic!" gushed a teenage girl named Marta whom I interviewed on a break from a Jewish dance class. "It's really exciting that these people lived so many years next to us and we don't know them. Jewish culture is totally different from Polish culture." This girl was one of the few whom I challenged. I told her that I had been living in Poland and had been struck by how similar our cultures were, from our food to our mannerisms. I told her that I'd come to see how, in centuries of coexistence, our cultures had become almost mirrors of each other. But Marta disagreed. "Jewish culture is much more interesting," she said.

I was amassing a decent picture of the nature and breadth of Polish interest in Jewish culture, but no matter how many interviews I did, I still struggled to find anyone who could explain why it was happening. It wasn't until after the festival was over, as I was going back through my notes, that I began to approach an answer to why, but the answer wasn't in the words that people used. It was in their voices. Take Ewa, a twenty-nine-year-old professional translator whom I met outside a photography exhibit. As she spoke, she closed her eyes. "There is a strong feeling of regret whenever I roam along the streets of Kazimierz, of this former Jewish district," she said. "I can realize how many people were crowding the streets, how many small shops were opened. It was a thriving culture, and my grandmother's sister told me about the festivals, especially about Shabbat on Saturday. She can recall the whole thing, how she could see the lit windows in which there were candlesticks, and they started singing all the Jewish songs. Even for the Catholics, it was incredible to feel and experience the different culture which was next to them, but then everything perished. Everything disappeared." There was a romance in her voice as she summoned the image, the candles in the windows, the sweet songs in Hebrew. Playing this recording later, I chuckled, thinking about how she would have reacted if I'd pointed out that many of her countrymen hadn't seen this Jewish life so romantically, that many had felt threatened by it. I thought I should have told her that when her grandmother's sister was her age, many people in Poland were voting for anti-Semitic parties whose platforms included the mass deportation of Jews and wide-scale boycotts of Jewish businesses. But to this woman, Jews were lovely and charming. She felt a connection to the culture that she could still sense whispering through the streets.

It was not a coincidence that the Jewish fad in Krakow did not take off in earnest until just after *Schindler's List* was released in Polish the-

aters. Before the movie, there had been a single theme café in Kazimierz, a novelty created as a gesture to the neighborhood's past. Kazimierz
in the early 1990s was so run-down, the movie's ghetto scenes were
filmed there, the neighborhood's decrepit storefronts standing in for
wartorn facades. But as soon as the movie opened, tourists and curiosity seekers began to arrive. They came to see where the movie was made
and where the people it depicted had lived. More cafés opened to feed
their interest, followed by bars and hotels. Within two years, an entire
industry had grown up around a collective fascination with tragedy.

"My grandmother lived next door to Jewish people. They were
neighbors," said Agnieszka, the twentysomething bar manager who was
Krys's boss at the Eden Hotel. She was a tour guide at the same Jewish
bookshop where Krys and Magda worked and was writing her master's
thesis on Isaac Bashevis Singer. She told me she felt cheated because,
unlike her grandmother, who grew up in a Poland where nearly every
Pole knew someone who was Jewish, she didn't have the same chance
to experience another culture. The Communist history books of her
childhood had largely omitted Jews, she said. "The books said one word
about the King Kazimierz the Great who invited Jews to Poland in
the fourteenth-century, and then *biiiiig* nothing"—she drew the abyss
with her hands, holding them wide apart—"and then the holocaust.
You would suddenly wonder why there were three and a half million
Jews living in Poland." After Agnieszka identified this gap in her edu-
cation, she started making up for it, reading stories by Jewish writers,
attending synagogue services, trying to understand why married Jewish
women covered their hair. "This wasn't a separate country," she said. "I
would like to learn about it."

Agnieszka made it seem very natural, like Jewish culture really was
a part of the air that Polish people breathed. She and I discussed how
many of her friends had grown up in cities and villages that still had
Jewish cemeteries, untouched, on the fringes of town. These cities were
dotted with abandoned synagogues, old Jewish schools, buildings that

had letters carved above their doors that, to a passing child, seemed like a secret code. I could see how shocking it would be to discover at some point in your teens or twenties that your country once had an ethnic population of three and a half million people that was now almost entirely depleted, and how upsetting it would be to learn that your grandparents knew many of these people while you had never met one. You really would feel a loss, as though you'd discovered a sister who died before you were born. But as I replayed this and other conversations later, in the quiet of my green-walled bedroom on Ulica Staszica, I finally understood that the reasons behind their fascination were also the reasons it troubled me: The Jewish culture they were admiring was one that never existed. They were in love with a wistful culture of candles in windows and of songs sung on a sabbath night. They felt a kinship with an ancient tribe, expelled from Jerusalem, who wandered the earth in search of a home until finding one in Poland—in this very city—for a thousand years, only to be tragically destroyed. They were conjuring the dead sister who gazed sweetly from a photo on the wall, a sister who could do no wrong.

Lost in that reverie is the fact that in real life, sisters fight. In real life, they become jealous of each other. They may love each other, but they also know each other's flaws and despise them. And just like that sister—the real one—most of the three and a half million Jews in early-twentieth-century Poland were not quaintly fulfilling the commandments against the pressures of the modern world. Most looked nothing like the wooden "Jew dolls" for sale in the markets here, and most had little in common with the people whose sad faces were featured in one of the festival's photo exhibits—aging, pious men in dark hats superimposed like hovering ghosts in the doorways of Kazimierz today. Most of the Jews of the 1930s were assimilated. They competed with Poles for jobs, for business, for slots in the university. They were mixed up in politics, supporting labor and socialist movements or Zionist parties. They were fully integrated in a society ripe with life and conflict. And while many Jews and Poles were friends, and many also were lovers, the two groups historically held each other at a distance. In fact, the years just before World War II were marked by some of the lowest points in the history of Polish-Jewish relations. Europe's dismal economy in the 1930s and the rise of nationalism generally triggered waves of pogroms. There were efforts to ban kosher slaughter and laws that targeted Jews. In 1937, the Jewish students who could still gain admission to universities—far fewer than in prior years—were ordered to occupy a special "ghetto bench" in the classroom. But all of this was missing from the soft-focus art exhibits. It was missing from the tours of "old Kazimierz." And it was missing from the pictures in antique frames that hung in the Jewish theme cafés. The Jews whom the concertgoers described were quaint and old. They were wonderfully, pleasantly nonthreatening.

I had more or less successfully removed the chip that weighed so heavily on my shoulder when I first arrived. When I saw my mother's cousins at her shivah, I spent hours defending Poles to them, explaining the larger context. But now I found myself retreating back to my initial cynicism, seeing it all as a very big fraud. And then I thought of Magda. Unlike most of the people at the festival, she knew a lot of actual Jews. She had traveled to Israel and New York and had a much better sense of reality than most of her peers. Still, part of me wondered if she was at least partly driven by an extreme extension of this dewey-eyed Jewishness, if she was not only adoring the sister who could do no wrong, but actually trying to become her. She had the same self-doubt and insecurity that trouble many young women at some point in our lives. And she wasn't the first to try a radical change in lifestyle in an effort to become someone new, maybe somebody better. All of Poland, in a way, was striving to redefine itself as a free and independent nation after decades of occupation. I wondered if Magda was doing the same thing on a personal level, establishing herself as someone unique and worldly and different from other young Poles, as if by entering a *mikveh* and immersing herself during her conversion ceremony, she could cleanse herself of every flaw she detested in the self that she was and emerge a new person, a better person, someone she had always wanted to become.

I knew that I wasn't being fair, passing judgment on those around me, questioning their motives, even as I knew that I had done much the same thing at another point in my life. I had all but majored in Latin American studies and had spent my college years traveling through Guatemala, Nicaragua, and Costa Rica. I'd tattooed a bird of iridescent feathers on the side of my leg—a resplendent quetzal, the endangered national bird of Guatemala. And wasn't I doing the same thing? Couldn't the people of those countries have questioned my motives? Couldn't they have noted the irony of a woman from a country that was partly responsible for Central America's problems going down there to marvel at the precious beauty of their lives, how well they'd maintained their culture despite colonial and imperialist rule? I was sincere, at least I think I was. I had enormous respect for those cultures. But culture is a delicate and personal matter, drawn of lines both shaky and thin. Sometimes we cross those lines even when we set out to honor them.

Poland was an independent country for only a minuscule portion of the last three centuries. It was occupied by Russians, by Germans, by Austro-Hungarians. And the people around me at the festival were becoming adults at the same time their nation was finally breaking free, about to join the European Union and become an official part of the West. It made sense that they would want to sample new cultures. The Poland that existed in their grandparents' time was a diverse place. It was home to Ukrainians, Belarusians, Germans, Lithuanians, and in almost every town, it was home to Jews. But the people I was meeting had known only a bland 95 percent Polish-Catholic, monolingual Poland. From World War II until 1989, their country was constrained by Soviet laws and shortages that dictated everything from home design to paint colors. I asked Krys once what his favorite ice-cream flavor had been when he was a child, and he answered: "When I was a child, there was only one flavor." But now Poland had more flavors than it knew what to do with. The stylish beauties hanging out in the market square were reading *Cosmo* and talking on cell phones. They were eating in brick-oven-pizza shops and buying lamb sliced into pita by Arab merchants. Whether or not visiting Jews were comfortable with this dynamic, ours was one of the more popular flavors that had flooded this country in the years since the Iron Curtain lifted like a dam, drenching a homogeneous culture with waters from around the world. Whether these flavors were authentic was another question. But that was the reality.

Most of the Jewish tourists I encountered at the festival—there were a handful, including some who said they came to Krakow specifically for the event—said they were happy, even thrilled, to see Jewish culture celebrated here rather than maligned. But almost all of them also sounded a note of caution. One of the best interviews I did was with Lea Gleitman, who was born in the city of Oświęcim sixteen years before the Germans changed the city's name to Auschwitz. She lived now in Sweden. At seventy-eight, she had come for the festival with her daughter. "My feelings are very mixed," she told me in a thick Yiddish accent that reminded me of Grandma Fela's. "I am born in Poland, and I know what they did to us . . . I know stories about Polish who take the kids and they promise to save them. They did terrible things with the kids and took the money from the family." I asked her what she thought of the festival, and she stopped a minute before answering. "I hope they are honest," she said. "I don't know. Everything is so mixed in my soul, in my heart. Maybe if they are honest, it can be better on the earth now."

CHAPTER NINE

MAGDA PICKED UP THE LETTER TO READ A SECOND TIME. "IT'S just so sad," she said, dabbing moisture from her eyes with her sleeve. I could sense a lump forming in my throat, as though the letter were directed at me, the blame for its torment mine. "You think he ever wrote back?" she asked. I bit my lip, knowing the answer but not wanting to say. "I wonder," I said. We were reading through the documents I'd wrested from my grandmother the previous winter in Atlanta. Now, in the lazy calm of late July, as a subtle breeze slipped through the open window of our sunny kitchen, my grandfather's records were fanned out across the pale pine of our kitchen table like tarot cards about to reveal their secrets. Magda was sitting cross-legged in the sunken red chair beside the table. I was taking notes and handing her one page after another. Slowly, we ventured down a paper trail that spanned fifty years, two continents, and a salad of languages.

We started with the oldest record—a single-page declaration from 1945 that seemed hastily drafted on a piece of scrap paper. It was penned in a formal legal tone, Magda said, and signed by my grandfather: "'I, Berek Frydrych,'" Magda translated, "'hereby authorize Honorata Skowrońska, who resides at Kołłątaja 45 in Będzin to administer and manage in broad terms . . . the property at Małachowskiego 20 in Będzin.'" The declaration went on to describe the rights Honorata would have over the house, from collecting rent from the tenants to suing them if they refused to pay. "She basically had every right over the house except to sell it," Magda said. I berated myself for waiting so long to translate a document that seemed so crucial to my family story. I quickly wrote down Magda's translation and started to record the date at the bottom of the declaration—November 28, 1945—but stopped to consider it. The war had been over since May of that year. Had it taken my grandfather six months to come home to Będzin? I made a note to ask Wicsław if he remembered whether Beresh had returned in the summer or the fall.

The declaration must have been the formalization of the promise my grandfather made to Honorata two years earlier in the ghetto, when he vowed that if his daughter survived through the war, he would repay Honorata with his home. Two years later, he moved her into his three-story building in the center of town. It was hard to know whether her family and mine were satisfied with this arrangement, but it seemed like it would have been beneficial to both, like this would have been the next stage in a relationship that, in some form or another, would last for the rest of their lives. I had never been entirely clear on what it was that put my grandfather and Honorata out of touch, what kind of rift had divided two families who came together so dramatically. Then Magda read me the letter that put the lump in my throat and tears in the edges of our eyes. It was a handwritten note on two pages of notebook paper, penned in a tidy Polish cursive that ran to the margins of the page. It was signed Skowrońska and dated May 22, 1962—sixteen years after my grandfather collected his daughter and left Poland forever.

In 1962 my mom was twenty and living in student housing at Wayne State University in Detroit. It was two years after she refused to move with her parents to Atlanta. She'd already purged her memory of almost everything connected with her childhood, including, she claimed, everything about Honorata Skowrońska. At that time my grandfather was running a small store in Atlanta with his brother Laybish. Members of the Frydrych family—now Fredericks or Friedricks or Friedrichs—began moving south from Detroit to Atlanta when Laybish's granddaughter Marcy contracted polio. Marcy's parents, Lillian and Lou, moved south to be near the legendary treatment center at Warm Springs, Georgia, that had treated President Roosevelt. They were followed by their parents, an aunt, an uncle, some cousins. My grandfather had had difficulty keeping a job in Detroit. As a tool and die maker trained in his family's Będzin brass factory, he should have been employable in industrial Detroit, but the beatings he took on the head from an Auschwitz guard had left him with epilepsy. A seizure at an auto plant in those days meant an instant firing, and my grandfather struggled to find and keep work. When Laybish invited him to go into the grocery business in Atlanta, he accepted. He and Grandma Fela took their son, Harold—then eight—and moved south, leaving my mom to start college in Detroit. My grandfather would have been living in Atlanta when he received this letter from Poland in 1962:

Dear Mr. Frydrych,

I am writing to you after such a long time because we haven't been corresponding, because you are a man of honor. I have been waiting for your letter and maybe you have been waiting for mine. Now I'm writing to you that I am sorry. You may be angry at me because of the letters I wrote to you. I also was offended because of the way you wrote to me but let's forget about that. I was happy to have someone abroad and I felt you were my brother. And you are so cold to me. I don't want much. All I want is us to live in peace because life is so short. We should be kind to each other.

Mr. Frydrych, let's forget about it. I'm just curious how you are doing. Is Irenka married? Does she have a family? Is she doing all right? Are you in good health? How is your family? Are you still close with your brothers and your sister?

As for me, I'm a little bit sick. I have rheumatism. I don't trade anymore because they don't give permission or license for that anymore. I still have three children with me. They attend school. My son is 16 years old. The second one is 12 years old and my daughter is 14 so you must know that I have to work because the children get only 590 złoty in a pension from their father. You can imagine that it's enough only for milk and it's really hard to live.

Regarding the house, Mr. Frydrych, I will write everything about it. There are eight tenants and they pay 40 złoty each per month with all the utilities. As for the factory, some storage space and offices have located there. They pay rent with a check straight to the municipality and it covers the taxes, renovations and some real estate taxes because this is the law in Poland. If you don't believe that I am able to manage your property, you can ask anybody or the municipality. I've just carried out a renovation but the money goes to the municipality so I have nothing left.

At least the house is kept in order and is well maintained. Mr. Frydrych, maybe you could come and see your property. You could see its condition. I would be very happy to see you here with Irenka. I would like to see my daughter. I would be very honored to see her. And if you cannot come to Poland, maybe I could visit you and then I would see how the world looks. Maybe I will write some more in the next letter. Best regards to you, to Irenka, and to your family.

Skowrońska

I await your letter

"Oh *God!* It's just so *sad*," Magda said, dabbing her eyes. "Look, she refers to your mother as *my daughter*. She uses *swoja*, the pronoun for *my very own. My very own daughter.* What do you think they were fighting about? *You are so cold to me.* It gives me chills."

I, too, was affected by the letter, but to me, the subject of the fight was perfectly clear. "It was the house," I said. "He must have thought she wasn't taking care of it. She sounds defensive about it."

"But to be so callous with the woman who saved his daughter?" Magda asked.

"It does seem extreme," I agreed. "But I don't know. Maybe she hurt him in other ways. My mom used to tell me that Mrs. Skowrońska once wrote to ask for a Chevrolet."

"A Chevrolet?" Magda laughed. "You're kidding!"

"He was in Detroit," I offered. "I guess she knew that's where Chevrolets come from."

Magda shook her head as she reread the letter. "It's so tragic," she said. "That must be what this was about: *I was happy to have someone abroad and I felt you were my brother.*" My grandfather must have written to Honorata at some point and told her off. Meanwhile, she thought he was rich and that he was selfishly refusing to share his riches with her. "It's the classic misunderstanding between Poles and Jews after the war," Magda said. "Your grandfather didn't understand property ownership under communism. He thought she was lying about the house. And she just assumed that he was a rich Jew in America and should help her. She writes to him, asks him for money . . ."

I saw where Magda was going and finished her sentence. "And they're both fulfilling each other's stereotypes."

Magda put the letter down on the table, still shaking her head. "She comes out like the greedy Pole, trying to get something out of him. And he looks like the selfish American, the ungrateful Jew."

"She saves his daughter," I added. "And he can't even send her a car when he has so many. No wonder he never came to visit."

"No wonder she had to nominate herself for the Yad Vashem medal," Magda said. "You don't think he ever wrote back?" I sifted through the letters on the table, but this one, dated 1962, was the latest of those that seemed personal. I said we could ask the Skowrońskis if they had

Honorata Skowrońska, Irena Frydrych, Beresh Frydrych, 1945

Pełnomocnictwo

Ja niżej podpisany Berek Frydrych niniejszym upoważniam Skowrońską Honoratę zam w. Będzinie ul. Kołłątaja 45. do administrowania i zarządzania w najszerszym zakresie. t. j. do pobierania czynszów zawierania i rozwiązania umów najmu występowania na drogę sądową o czynsz rozwiązywanie umów najmu osobiście lub przez pełnomocnika nieruchomością położoną w Będzinie przy ul. Małachowskiego 20 oznaczoną № hip. 585. w posiadanie której to nieruchomości wprowadzony zostałem z mocy postanowienia Sądu Grodzkiego w Będzinie w dniu 28/XI 1945 r.

∞

Power of attorney, November 28, 1945. Beresh Frydrych authorizes Honorata Skowrońska to manage his family property at 20 Małachowskiego in Będzin.

20 Małachowskiego, Będzin, Poland

Courtyard behind 20
Małachowskiego and
former brass factory
(right)

Erin (third from right) with Skowroński family including Helen (far left)
and Wiesław (far right), 2001

Sura Leah Rozenblum,
ghetto ID photo

Brian, Irene, Erin, and Derek Einhorn, November 2000

Frydrych family with Faygl's in-laws, the Weindlings, 1934.
Back row: Shmil Biber, Duvid Oyzer, Faygl, Chaim, Beresh, Chaya
Weindling Ferenz, Moyshe Ferenz, Yankl, Heltsha, Chamil Fernsi;
Middle row: Liba, Zisl, Yisruel, Pesl Weindling, Shaya Weindling,
Rivka Weindling Biber, Mendel Biber;
Front row: Gloria, Kiva Paserman, Jane

Erin with Fannie Adolffson, Stockholm, 2001

Fannie, Benjamin, and Shprinsa Keijler with Irena,
Stockholm, 1949 or 1950

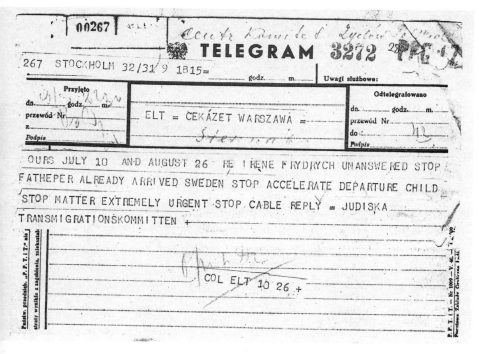

TELEGRAM 3272

267 STOCKHOLM 32/31 9 1815=

godz. m. Uwagi służbowe:

Przyjęto

dn. godz. m.
przewód Nr
z.
Podpis

ELT = CEKAZET WARSZAWA =

Odtelegrafowano

dn. godz. m.
przewód Nr
do
Podpis

OURS JULY 10 AND AUGUST 26 RE IRENE FRYDRYCH UNANSWERED STOP
FATHEPER ALREADY ARRIVED SWEDEN STOP ACCELERATE DEPARTURE CHILD
STOP MATTER EXTREMELY URGENT STOP CABLE REPLY = JUDISKA
TRANSMIGRATIONSKOMMITTEN +

COL ELT 10 26 +

Telegram, 1946

RESIDENT ALIEN'S BORDER
CROSSING IDENTIFICATION CARD

A. R. No. **7 923 777**

NAME **FRYDRYCH: IRENA**

ADDRESS **3734 GlynnCt.**

AT TIME OF ISSUE **Detroit, Michigan**

DATE OF BIRTH **Feb. 20, 1942**

PLACE OF BIRTH **Bendrin, Poland**

SEX **Female** NATIONALITY **Poland**

HEIGHT: FT **4** IN. — WEIGHT **70** LBS.

COMP. **Fair** HAIR **Red** EYES **Blue**

VISIBLE MARKS OR PECULIARITIES **None**

No. **755716**

CARD VALID TO

FEB **1 9 1952**

REVALIDATED TO
AT
INSPECTOR

REVALIDATED TO
AT
INSPECTOR

REVALIDATED TO
AT
INSPECTOR

REVALIDATED TO
AT
INSPECTOR

REVALIDATED TO
AT
INSPECTOR

REVALIDATED TO
AT
INSPECTOR

No. **755716**

Resident Alien's Border Crossing ID, issued by U.S. Immigration
and Naturalization Service, August 20, 1951, Detroit

any letters, but I knew my grandfather had never written back. I took the letter from Magda and examined Honorata's tidy handwriting. "He did keep the letter, though," I said. "That must mean something."

After Magda left for a Kazimierz tour, I gathered the untranslated papers from the table and carried them to the bar where Krys was working. He had been busy lately, working long hours, trying to make money for a trip to Italy. He was preparing for an exam to become a certified translator but needed to be able to translate Polish into both English and another language to qualify. He had studied Latin in school and figured that if he spent a few weeks at a language school in Florence, he could learn enough Italian to pass. He'd been coming home late after closing the bar and was often still sleeping when I left for the day. To see him, I had to track him down in the basement pub of the Eden Hotel, Ye Olde Goat. There were rarely any customers, just Krys behind the bar, lighting one cigarette after another. He smiled when I walked in and poured me a *piwo z sokiem,* beer with heavy currant juice that sinks to the bottom of the glass. We gossiped and caught up in the basement's cool dank, then I handed him a document and asked him to rattle off a quick translation. He obliged and began to fill in the story of what had happened between the best intentions of 1945 and the enmity of 1962.

Krys read me a letter dated September 1949 that my grandfather, then living as a refugee in Stockholm, received from his attorney in Poland—a Jozef Ursztajn at 2 Sądowa Street in Sosnowiec, Poland, the next town over from Będzin. "*Answering your letter, sir,*" Krys recited, a formal tone in his voice. "*I would like to inform you that your enterprise is doing really badly. Actually . . .*' Oh, *Boże*! This is hilarious!" Krys was giggling and holding one of his long, thin hands to his forehead.

"What does it say?" I asked.

"It's terrible!" he said, snickering. "Listen to this: *I am not interested in it much because I don't want to waste my time on it. The person who rented it lost a lot of money and now the enterprise is almost liquidated.*

Some parts of it are turned into flats, let by Skowrońska. It seems that she is the only one who makes good money on the whole thing. I can't deal with your business because if I got any money, I would have to pay them on a special, blocked bank account, which brings more losses than income.'" When he reached the end of the letter, Krys was still laughing. "That's so rude!" he said.

My grandfather's papers didn't seem to contain any correspondence from the early 1950s, but the narrative picked up again with a flurry of anxious letters at the end of the decade. My grandfather kept a copy of a letter he sent on January 9, 1959, to an attorney in Poland in which he begged for help with his property: *I have been informed that Skowrońska doesn't pay the taxes and that she got into debt because the city took the factory buildings away and turned them into a school that doesn't pay rent. All of this happened without my knowledge.* Another letter, addressed to my grandfather from someone in Będzin in July 1959, slammed Honorata as a *boorish person* who *administrates your property in a very "robbing" way.* Neither Krys nor I could make out the signature on the letter, so we weren't sure who had authored it, but whoever he was, he had nothing kind to say about Honorata Skowrońska. *She scrounges all that she can out of the house without investing anything. She doesn't maintain it well, doesn't care about renovations and even doesn't want to have it renovated from municipal funds,* he wrote. This 1959 letter was a densely typed, single-spaced diatribe that ranted on for four pages: *I don't like prying into other people's affairs, especially as I have some disagreements with Skowrońska, caused by her,* he wrote. *[But] I find it necessary to inform you about the situation because I wouldn't like you to lose your house.* The house was *messy and run-down,* he wrote. Honorata was raising pigs in the cellar. *Worse,* he wrote, *Skowrońska doesn't pay the taxes. She doesn't pay the municipality the money she collects from the tenants (for water etc.) . . . She deals with trading and is out all the time. She has constant problems with police and is facing charges in court. Recently, she was facing very serious charges for*

abusing her children. She may even go to prison and then the house will be
abandoned completely.

Krys and I got a chuckle out of this letter because it was so nasty and pointed. But even as we laughed, I was starting to understand why my grandfather, even if he had been wealthy, would not have been inclined to send Honorata her desired Chevrolet. Magda may have been correct that my grandfather didn't understand the nature of Communist property law, but the writer of this letter probably did. I could only imagine how my grandfather reacted to this letter, thousands of miles from the home he loved. Maybe he had an emotional attachment to the place and a desire to know that a piece of his past was still standing on Będzin soil. And maybe he thought if he could keep the house from falling apart, he'd have a claim to the financial security he'd known before the war. But there he was, a struggling immigrant in the United States, a holocaust survivor with head injuries that kept him out of the trade he learned from his father, and now he was discovering that someone he once trusted with his own child was destroying his home. The writer of the diatribe warned my grandfather that under the law of the time, an ill-maintained house could be seized and the owner would be powerless to stop it. And on top of that, Honorata was writing to ask for money and gifts, for American cars.

When I called Atlanta a few weeks after my mother's funeral to check on Grandma Fela, I asked her about Honorata. What happened between them? Grandma Fela was indignant. "I don't want to hear about this Mrs. Skowrońska!" she said, her accent thicker in anger than in kindness. "Such *tsuras* she gave us!" *Tsuras* was the Yiddish word for trouble. "What kind of *tsuras*?" I asked. "The worst kind!" she said. "I don't want to talk about her. I don't even want to hear her name." The fight obviously had been ugly, with both sides emerging deeply resentful. But it was hard for me to doubt the sincerity of Honorata's apologetic letter a few years later: *Mr. Frydrych, let's forget about it . . . I felt you were my brother . . . All I want is us to live in peace.* It was hard for me to escape the tug of her words, not to believe she genuinely wished my family well. I felt she sincerely dreamed of one day seeing her *very own daughter* again. So what if she was raising pigs in the cellar? Krys said that sort of thing was a common form of supplemental income during communism. Maybe she was neglecting the house, and maybe she did squeeze every last drop of value out of the place, but the truth remained that one and a half million children were killed in the holocaust, and whatever else happened later, my mother was not among them. I wanted to go back in time and plead with him: *Forgive her, Grandpa. Just send a kind word.* But even if time travel were possible, my grandfather likely would not have been willing to forgive. In fact, the only documents in his files produced after 1965 were letters to various government authorities asserting his claim to the property, trying to repossess it from Honorata Skowrońska. After my grandfather died, Grandma Fela took up his cause and, into the 1990s, wrote letters to Poland, to Germany, and to the U.S. government, hoping to reclaim her husband's land.

In Warsaw, I located the Polish satellite office of the Yad Vashem holocaust museum, requested its file on Honorata Skowrońska, then found translators to help with the Hebrew, Yiddish, and Polish contents of the file. Reading through these papers was like reading the next chapter in the same heartbreaking tale—a chapter that began twenty years after the terrible fight between Honorata and my grandfather. It was May 5, 1982. As far as I knew, my grandfather had had no contact with Honorata in decades. He was nearly seventy-two, retired in Atlanta, recovering from a debilitating stroke that had robbed him of much of his cognitive function. His son with Grandma Fela, my uncle Harold, was thirty at the time and training to become a radiologist. My mom was forty, living in a suburb of Detroit with her family. I was nine. My brother was eleven. It was the year Mom started entering us in junior tennis tournaments. Honorata Skowrońska, at seventy-one, was still managing my family property in Będzin, collecting rent from the tenants, paying the taxes. Or who knew? Not paying them. She, too, had had a stroke and had been left paralyzed on one side of her body. Bound to a wheelchair, she was embarrassed to leave her house, her children said. She spent most of her time at home, in her second-floor apartment at 20 Małachowskiego, watching television and reminiscing. Poland was under martial law. Six months earlier, in December 1981, the Soviet-backed Polish government had responded to the budding Solidarity movement by dramatically curtailing civil liberties. Protestors were killed, thousands of activists arrested. The country's borders were sealed. Tensions in Poland were at their highest levels since World War II, but Honorata wasn't inclined to go outside anyway.

Dear sirs, she addressed a short handwritten note to the Jewish Historical Institute in Warsaw where Yad Vashem had its office. *I would like to ask your institute to present my affair to the relevant institutions in Israel in order to reward me with the medal for saving a life. During the war and occupation, I hid a Jewish child, Mr. Bernard Frydrych's daughter. I lived, then as now, in Będzin. I don't have to describe all I went through during the time from July 1943 until the end of the war when I kept the child. I had to run away many times risking the lives of the child and of my family. In 1945, the child's father came back and they left for the USA. After some time, he stopped writing to me.* With her note, she included an address for my grandfather in Atlanta that proved to be obsolete and wrote that she was attaching several letters from him that she hoped would serve as proof of her claim.

This application took fifteen months to process. Except for a confirmation that it had been received, Honorata heard nothing about the medal until August 1983, when she received a letter from Yad Vashem informing her that *without evidence from the rescued person,* her request could not be processed. This was what I'd thought, that testimony from someone who'd been saved was necessary to receive the prestigious Righteous Among the Nations medal, the same medal bestowed on famous heroes like Raoul Wallenberg and Oskar Schindler. To win the medal, Honorata needed to find my family, but in letters to Yad Vashem, she claimed she had already tried and failed. The file contained copies of requests she'd sent in 1978 to the Red Cross and to the Polish consulate in the United States, trying to locate my grandfather. *I hereby kindly request information about the citizen Bernard Frydrych who lives in the USA,* she wrote in her letter to the consulate. *I have received back the letter I sent with a note that he moved to Atlanta, Ga. This was in 1966. During the occupation, I kept his daughter. Initially, he used to write to me. Now I've lost contact. I'd like to see this girl who was miraculously saved from the Nazis. She was two years old and of Jewish nationality. I risked my life and my family's life hiding the child during the occupation.*

Her search for my grandfather had turned up nothing, but, undeterred, she sought assistance from Marian Szwarc, the man believed to be the last Jew in Będzin in 1983. Szwarc had been a leader in the Jewish community immediately after the war and claimed to have been present when my grandfather reunited with his daughter. He knew what Honorata had done and offered to take up her cause. According to the documents in the file, he encouraged her to write to a Jewish newspaper in Warsaw called *Folks-shtime,* which she did:

> The case concerns the help I gave to a Jewish child under the German occupation in Poland. Bernard Frydrych and his one-and-a-half-year-old daughter, Irena, lived in Będzin, 20 Małachowskiego Street. His wife was taken away to the ghetto. I took his daughter, Irena. At the very beginning, I kept her in my home until I was accused of doing that. Then, I had to take the child and escape to Miechow, where my family lives. I spent about two months there but then had to escape to Jędrzejow because the inhabitants of Miechow suspected me of hiding a Jewish child. I

stayed in Jędrzejow with my family in the place where my parents used to live (they were already deceased). I lived in the village Borszowice by the river Nida with Irena until 1945. During my stay in Borszowice, I prepared a birth certificate for Irena with my family name. I carried the child on my back through the border while escaping from Dąmbrowa to Miechow and, so that people wouldn't find out that she was Jewish, I used to dye her hair.

In November, 1945, Mr. Frydrych came to get Irena back. She was four years old and I gave her back to him in the presence of two witnesses: Mr. Szwarc of Będzin, the former president of the Jewish committee in the years 1945–50, and Dr. Szeftel from Będzin. I went with Mr. Frydrych to take Irena to the orphanage in Chorzów because she was crying very loudly. She didn't know her father and she was more attached to me than him. She was crying and was calling me: "Mommy, take me home with you." During her stay in Chorzów, I visited her once only because she cried and she missed me a lot. The caregivers at the orphanage didn't allow me to visit her because they didn't want to upset the child.

We made a photo of me, Mr. Frydrych and the child as a souvenir when I was giving the child to Mr. Frydrych. I don't have this picture now because I've lost it. When they were about to depart, Mr. Frydrych promised to pay me back and told me that until the end of my life, I would be all right and he would never forget about me. I used to correspond with Mr. Frydrych until the 1950s but since that time, Mr. Frydrych hasn't responded. Mr. Szwarc got an address from the Landsmanschaft and I have been writing to that address but there hasn't been a response.

Right now, I am in a grave situation. I am paralyzed. I can't walk. All I want is to live until the moment when Mr. Frydrych will thank me. I would like to ask you, the editors, to print my letter and maybe Mr. Frydrych will change his mind. The Jewish Historical Institute in Warsaw has all my data but I need to have the confirmation from Mr. Frydrych that I kept his daughter during the occupation.

This letter appeared in *Folks-shtime* on September 7, 1983, exactly one year from the date of my grandfather's death. Having had another stroke, Beresh Frydrych died four months after Honorata first contacted Yad Vashem. My mom broke the news to my brother and me as we sat in the living room watching television. "You should know that your grandfather died," Mom said unemotionally, without touching the volume on the TV. My brother and I barely knew him. We'd met him only a handful of times on our occasional visits to Atlanta or his occasional visits to Detroit. He was quiet and didn't say much. My most vivid memory of him was his telling me once when we were in Atlanta and I had a stomachache that I should lie on my stomach; he had heard on the news that it was good to lie on your stomach when it hurt. It was advice I would follow, decades later. I still lie flat on my stomach when it hurts.

When I was nine and learned that my grandfather was dead, I wondered if I was supposed to cry. When I asked Derek about this recently, he had no memory of the day. My parents went to Atlanta without us for the funeral.

A year later, Honorata Skowrońska and Marian Szwarc, having no idea my grandfather was dead, were still trying to find him—or at least to demonstrate to Yad Vashem that they were making the effort.

Szwarc sent a letter in Hebrew to Yad Vashem and sent his own note, in Yiddish, to the newspaper. He verified Honorata's story and added that before Beresh Frydrych left for America, *he promised that he would never forget the gentle, polite, courteous, kind Polish woman who had saved his daughter. In the beginning, he wrote letters to her, full of assurance that he would remember,* Szwarc wrote in his Yiddish account in *Folks-shtime. To his great regret, he forgot his promise. He moved to another area and does not write anymore. The woman, Skowrońska, is already elderly. She is 70 years old and says that while she is still alive, she would like to see the child that she saved . . . When she saw on television that Yad Vashem was giving thanks to the polite, gentle, courteous Polish people who saved Jewish families, she burst into tears and cried for a long time, for the thought that she does not even hear a good word from the Frydrych family.*

My family had no idea this exchange was taking place. I'm not sure how my grandfather would have responded had he learned of Honorata's application before his stroke. He might have supported her efforts and given his testimony, but that might actually have harmed her application because he would have testified that he paid Honorata to save his daughter. Yad Vashem's official Righteous Gentile criteria at the time specified that applicants prove they had risked their lives "without exacting advance monetary compensation." Without my grandfather's testimony, there was no mention of compensation in Honorata's file.

As far as I was concerned, Honorata deserved the medal. Paid or not, she put her life and the lives of her children at risk and could just as easily have pocketed the cash and abandoned my mother, as her friend had done with the other baby. I was saddened by what had happened later between her and my grandfather, but I also resented the tone of her letters. Maybe my grandfather did turn his back on her, but she and Szwarc gave him no credit for having had his reasons. As I read this now, twenty years after my grandfather's death, six years after Honorata's, and a couple of months after my mother's, my gratitude for this woman was hampered by her trampling of the truth. In her dogged determination to win a medal despite him, she had denied my grandfather his say and smeared my family's name in the process.

After reading Marian Szwarc's letter, the committee that administers the prestigious Righteous Among the Nations medal voted on March 5, 1984, to award the medal to Honorata Skowrońska. In August 1985 Honorata traveled in her wheelchair to Warsaw with her sister and granddaughter to attend a ceremony at the Israeli embassy. Wiesław told me there was a nice reception that she enjoyed. The following year Yad Vashem arranged for her to start collecting a pension from the Jewish Foundation for Christian Rescuers, which, at the time, was a division of the Anti-Defamation League in New York. For the last decade of her life, she received payments of thirty dollars a month—paid quarterly—plus an occasional Christmas bonus. It wasn't a Chevrolet. It wasn't the visit she desired from her "daughter." But perhaps to her, it was a hint of the recognition she thought she deserved.

Knowing this previously hidden back story complicated my next trip to Będzin. I didn't want to take sides in a forty-year-old dispute involving people no longer alive, but I knew now what the Skowrońskis had been thinking about us all these years. They held a certain warmth for my mother, the little girl they'd nurtured, but there was a hint of resentment there, too. Perhaps they saw me as an agent of reconciliation, here to do the honorable thing that my grandfather had not, but I wanted no part of that. I wouldn't indict my grandfather for any crime; nor would I suffer his sentence or shame. I wouldn't apologize for choices made years before I was born, made in their own context. Nor was I particularly hell-bent on avenging the way Honorata and Marian Szwarc had slammed my grandfather as a heartless, ungrateful abandoner in the annals of one of the world's most significant memorial institutions. I'd come looking for their story, maybe their friendship. A part of me believed the past existed here like a book on a shelf I could check out and take home, show to my family. I hadn't considered that the past may have lived on here, its characters still angry, its plots unresolved.

Walking up the increasingly familiar stairs of Małachowskiego 20 on my next visit, I thought of the sleeping dogs I'd awakened and now needed to feed. When I rang the buzzer under the tag that said SKOWROŃSKA, HONORATA, I was intensely aware as I hadn't been before of the hurt stirred beyond the door. Wiesław welcomed me with a hug and told me again that he looked forward to seeing my mother. "I hope you will soon," I told him, my Polish sufficient for simple truths and easy lies. I'd warned the friend I'd brought with me to interpret that I wasn't yet ready to tell Wiesław about my mother, and she had agreed to keep my secret.

Magda couldn't join me this time. She had selected the day for this meeting and even called the Skowrońskis to reschedule when she had a conflict with an earlier date. But then her Israeli friend suddenly offered to fly her to New York for the weekend. Her friend had made an appointment for her with a rabbi in Brooklyn who had agreed to perform her conversion, and she had boarded a plane that morning. Since Krys had to work, I scrambled to get in touch with a woman named Ania whom I'd met at the gym in May, a few days before my abrupt departure. I'd approached her in the locker room after an aerobics class to ask if she could speak English and, if so, whether she would decode the sign above the sink. She told me it warned against drinking the water, and we struck up a conversation about her impending plans for graduate school in Indiana. (She wondered if she'd be able to ski there.) When I called to ask if she would join me in Będzin, she happily agreed and even volunteered her car for the trip.

There was no big crowd this time, only Wiesław and the two women I knew now to be his wife, Helen, and his daughter, Marta. It was more manageable, but it was a desperately hot day, and the two living room windows offered scant ventilation. We settled into chairs around the room and sat looking at one another for an uncomfortable few minutes until I decided to start. "Why don't we do the interview first," I suggested, reaching into my bag for my recorder and microphone. "Can you tell him that I'm going to ask him some—" But before I could go on, Helen jumped up from the sofa and approached Ania with a stream of Polish too swift for me to follow. She was apparently picking up with Ania where she had left off with Magda on our previous visit. She was hovering over Ania's shoulder and pushing a stack of papers into her hands. A little stunned by the assault, Ania sifted through the papers. I had warned her that the confusing real estate problem would come up again, but I'd thought maybe we would ease into it. No such luck.

"So it seems they have a problem with the property," Ania translated as Helen continued to speak. "She's saying that, uh . . ." Ania was trying to stop Helen from talking so she could translate, but Helen continued, delivering what seemed to be a long and rapid speech. My Polish was getting much stronger. I had been taking private lessons a few days a week. But I could barely catch anything Helen was saying. She punctuated her words with fat pokes of her finger. She was a bulky woman with dark gray hair, cut short in the back and layered on top. Unlike her husband, who seemed gentle and kind, and who was saying nothing, just sitting in a soft chair near the table and smoking a cigarette through a thin glass pipe, Helen was speaking forcefully and raising her voice. I didn't bother trying to stop her. I just hoped Ania was taking it in. Her English was excellent—she had translated English-language novels into Polish—but even for her, this was difficult. "So, uh . . ." Ania had convinced Helen to stop for a minute so she could translate. "It seems that when his mother died," she said, gesturing at Wiesław, "the people stopped paying the rent."

"The people?" I asked.

"The tenants in the other flats. These tenants say that Mr. Skowroński and his wife don't have the authority to collect the rent."

"But they do," I said. "I have a copy of my grandfather's declaration that gave authority to his mother. Did they go to the police or anything?"

Ania nodded. "They did. They went to the municipality. But the people there looked at their legal papers and asked: 'Who is this Frydrych? The house is owned by Frydrych.' They tried to explain, but the city says these people aren't the owners. They won't help. And it's even worse. The government says they have to pay the taxes, and it's a lot of money."

"Wait." I stopped her. "If they're not owners, why would they have to pay taxes?"

"See, that's the problem," Ania said. "The government can't find the Frydrychs, so these people pay the taxes." I tried to argue that this was irrational and that Ania must have misunderstood, but Helen was talking again, saying how much she paid in taxes and how she'd been having all of these problems and how the family had even considered moving but couldn't because they would still have to pay the taxes. None of it made any sense.

"And the tenants don't pay anything?" I asked. "They live for free?"

"That's the worst part," Ania said. "These people are paying for everyone. It sounds like a real problem."

It took us an hour to clarify the details, and when we were done, I still wasn't sure what was going on, but according to Helen, the government considered the Skowrońskis owners for the purposes of taxation but not for the purposes of collecting the rent. The problem had been going on for years, since Honorata's death in 1995. Since then, the family had been hoping that my mother would come to Poland to set things right. Now, Ania said, they wanted me to have my mother go to the Polish embassy in Washington to sign a document declaring that her father had given this family his property. As Ania told me this, she put on a sympathetic face. "Do you want me to tell them that your mother—"

"No!" I said. "I'll tell them. I will. Just not now." I looked at Wiesław, who hadn't said much today. I really should tell him, I thought. Instead, I looked down at the floor. "Tell them they don't need a signature from my mother because I have a document from my grandfather that says they have every right of ownership here. Tell them I'll bring them this document the next time I come." Ania passed it on, but Helen seemed unconvinced. She told Ania that she still thought my mother should go to the embassy.

My head was starting to throb. The room was hot and stuffy. The windows were open, but heat clung to the motionless air. Smoke from Wiesław's cigarette collected in my throat. I wondered if I needed a lawyer, if I was in over my head. I wondered if they were being truthful or if this was a scheme to distract the tax collectors and send them after me. Eventually, Helen was satisfied by my promise to look into the matter, and she let me interview her husband, but I had trouble focusing. I kept forgetting to listen to Wiesław's answers, forgetting my next question. I was thinking about the property, wondering if the documents I'd copied from Grandma Fela would be enough of a solution. I wondered what would happen when I returned to Będzin without the sworn testimony they needed from my mother. I wondered how they'd react when they found out I'd been lying about my mom. I was building up to come clean about my lies. I told Wiesław on this visit that my mother was sick, that I was worried about her. "The doctors think it might be cancer," I said. His eyes creased with concern. "Maybe it isn't cancer," he said. "You know, doctors are often wrong." I smiled. "I hope you're right," I said. His words felt encouraging, and I briefly forgot the truth myself. "I'll tell her you wish her a speedy recovery," I said as Ania begrudgingly translated. I should have told the truth from the beginning. But for the moment it was nice to know that here, in the place where my mother was born, she was still alive. Here, she might not even have cancer. But now Wiesław was counting on me to produce her, and not just for emotional reasons. Now he needed her legal signature.

CHAPTER TEN

THE BORDERLAND REGION OF ZAGŁĘBIE (ZAG-WEM-BEE-EII), which included the sister cites of Będzin, Sosnowiec, and Dąbrowa Górnicza would be known in the mid-to-late twentieth century as Czerwone Zagłębie—red Zagłębie—for its support for the latest occupation by the latest iteration of Russians. But in 1911, when Honorata Kłys was born here—the eldest daughter and the third of seven children born to Jan and Karolina Kłys—the Russians in charge were the old Russians, the ones who reported to the czar and who at that particular moment in time were kicking and screaming their way through the waning days of an empire. The Zagłębie where Honorata was born three years before the start of World War I was rammed against the old Russia's border with Germany and Austria-Hungary at the far western tip of the czar's sprawling reach. Poland as a country had been erased from the maps of Europe since 1795. It had been swallowed, first in piece and then in whole, by its three formidable neighbors. And those three empires slammed together here, in Zagłębie.

It seemed fitting somehow that Honorata—who, after her death, would be remembered as a fighter and a scratcher, as a worker who would take no guff and would never stop working until her body could work no more—would be born in a time and place as turbulent as the life she would have. It seemed fitting, too, that she would be born in the same year and in the same town as a man who would also have a turbulent life and who would one day ask a favor of her that would forever change the fortunes of his family and hers. But she wouldn't meet my grandfather until later, until Poland had returned to the map, then found itself essentially erased again. She wouldn't meet my grandfather until the Germans had become the ones in charge.

Honorata spent the early years of her life in Dąbrowa Górnicza, a fast-industrializing but still-rural town in a busy region that coursed with international trade. After World War I, when Poland won its independence for the first time in 123 years, there would be new options for people with initiative and energy. Jan Kłys, Honorata's father, had his share of both. He was a man of ambition who took advantage of his region's location on what had become the border of three independent countries. He would cross into Germany to the west or into the new Czechoslovakia to the south, returning with goods that could be sold in the newly independent Poland. Soon he built a thriving business in horse trading. He traveled the region, buying and selling horses and cows, becoming successful enough to buy a plot of land in Dąbrowa Górnicza and build a two-room house there with a garden of potatoes and greens. Like her siblings, Honorata attended school through the fourth grade. Schooling beyond then would have cost money that her family didn't have. At that young age, she went to work for her father, learning his business, crossing into Germany or Czechoslovakia, buying what was for sale, selling what she had to sell. As she grew older, she developed her own routes and contacts that would be helpful to her later, when she needed to keep moving and to depend on a network of friends. "She was a natural-born trader," her son would tell me decades later. "She had very good skills for trading, for making money. She would take any opportunity to gain some money. She would buy some clothes and then go to the village and sell them and then buy spices and sell them in town and then smuggle something through the border." She also took occasional steady employment, including a job in her late teens at a butcher shop on the campus of a coal mine near her parents' house in Dąbrowa Górnicza. It was in this butcher shop, her son told me, where she met her husband, Jan Skowroński, a coal miner, who came into the shop to buy meat. They married in the late 1920s, and Jan Skowroński moved into the crowded Kłys family home. The couple would have six children, three before the war, and three after it was over. Honorata kept on trading even when her children were young, sometimes strapping a baby to her back as she went, sometimes leaving the kids with her mother, a devout Catholic, who stayed at home to look after the house.

I asked Wiesław if his mother had interests other than work, whether she went to church or played cards. He laughed. "She was too tired," he said. "She was a workaholic. Whenever she came back home, she would give the kids dinner and go to sleep." Part of this was necessity, he said, but it was also her nature—a hardened ethic of constant work that she learned from her father. This was what sustained her after the Germans invaded in 1939, after her husband and her sister, along with thousands of other Poles, were forced into slave labor in Germany. It was what saved her when the job of supporting the family fell solely to her. Black-market trades were riskier under the Nazis than they had been in free Poland, but Honorata continued to engage in even the riskiest trades: in the closed Jewish ghettos. According to my family folklore, my grandfather gave her raw metal that he smuggled out of his brass factory in exchange for food. Precise details of these transactions died with them—whether they met before the war or during it; whether my grandfather, in looking for a place to hide his daughter, approached other people before Honorata; whether she refused him first before agreeing to help. I wondered if Honorata's decision was rooted in morality, or if my mother was simply another loaf of bread to barter. All Wiesław could recall of the transaction his mother made in the year when he was twelve was that she came home one day with a baby in a blanket. But when I inquired about her motives—what it was that convinced her to accept the risk—he could tell me only what she had told him: "She wanted to have a daughter," he said. "She had three sons. This was her chance to have a daughter."

My grandfather had also promised her property, so that sweetened the deal. "She used to say that if the Germans don't kill all of us, we will survive," Wiesław said. I told him that this made sense, but I asked if there wasn't something more—something about her character that made her willing to take in a stranger's child when everyone else was either not interested in helping Jews or too scared to take the risk? He thought about this. "She had a lot of trading contacts," he said. "That helped. Whenever she was in dangerous situations, she would take the girl to the places she knew from trading. She would pay people to keep the child. She'd say, 'It's my cousin' or 'My family' or 'My niece.' Because at the time, if they learned that this was a Jewish child, they wouldn't keep her. People were afraid of, you know . . ." Yes, I said, I knew. But why was she not afraid when everyone else was? Wiesław stopped again to think. I rarely had the chance to talk to him alone. Sometimes his wife answered for him, or his daughter, or whoever else was in the room. Often they all talked at once, and I was never sure whose words, precisely, were being translated for me. But in this case, I was certain that Wiesław alone was speaking. "She had a very strong personality," he said. "She was a very strong woman. She could even beat people with a stick. She was not afraid." I asked if people were afraid of her. Wiesław laughed, and so did his wife. "Yes," he said. "People had respect for her." Helen chimed in that when Honorata managed the house, the tenants were never late with their rent. "She didn't even have to go around and collect the money. They would bring it around by themselves," she said.

I was trying to remember how I had pictured Honorata before I met her family. I think I'd assumed she was religious, a kind and caring mother who took in a stray and loved her like her own. But the woman Wiesław described barely had time for her own children, let alone someone else's. There probably were "righteous gentiles" who fit my stereotype of God-fearing folk, motivated to do good in the face of evil. But in many cases, I was starting to understand, these heroes weren't selected for their noble deeds because of righteous hearts or exceptional decency. Some became heroes because they were the ones with the skills and connections to actually hide a human being from the omnipresent eyes of an oppressive regime. This required living, perhaps, outside the mainstream. It was a call uniquely suited to people like Honorata, who were movers and talkers and black marketeers. They could doctor a baptismal certificate. They could convince a farmer that the girl in their arms was their sister's child, not the daughter of a Jew. They could disappear across a border. They could hide among thieves. It made sense when I put it together. Honorata was not a wimp to be pushed around by nosy neighbors. She wouldn't be cowed by their threats to turn her in. Just like, years later, she wouldn't give up a medal and its promised pension because she couldn't find the man whose child she had saved.

The last years of Honorata's life were the least pleasant. After her stroke in 1980, her family said she sat around, angry at my grandfather, angry at the world. Her daughter, Ela, born after the war, died of cancer in 1985 at the age of thirty-seven—a piercing loss that compounded another. Honorata had had two daughters in her life. Now she had none. After Ela died, Wiesław, who was an electrician in a steel mill before he retired, moved in with his mother on Małachowskiego Street, along with Helen, his second wife, and their kids. As she grew frail, Honorata talked about the Jewish man who had asked her to marry him and who had wanted to take her with him to America. She talked about his daughter, whom she had risked her life to save. And she spoke of how the Jewish man had promised her wealth and a home if she could keep the girl safe. She lamented that he broke his promise, that he moved away and never returned, that he had stopped writing.

In 1945 my grandfather named Honorata to manage his property, but according to Honorata's family, he also promised that he would return to Poland and transfer the property into her name. The house and the brass-making workshop behind it would all be hers. The fact that my grandfather never did come back, never did make good on his promise, infuriated her. Grandma Fela insisted my grandfather never made any such promise. On the contrary, the only documents in my grandfather's files after the *you are so cold to me* appeal of 1962 were letters addressed to government agencies in various countries asserting my grandfather's claim to his home.

On my next trip to Będzin, I presented Helen with the document I'd promised that named Honorata as manager of the house. Helen thanked me but said she still needed a signature from my mother. This time, I questioned her: "Why my mother? Why not anyone else in my family?" Helen seemed puzzled. "Because she's her father's next of kin," she said. Technically, Grandma Fela was my grandfather's next of kin, but as far as I could tell, that didn't matter. What did matter, I told Helen, was that my grandfather never owned the house.

Helen, Wiesław, and their daughter, Marta, all immediately contradicted me. "Of course he owned the house," Helen said. "He gave it to Honorata." She added that my grandfather was listed on the deed to the property as the owner, but on this point, I had to disagree. The deed was one of the documents Helen had given me to copy on an earlier visit, and it was clear to me that the names on the deed belonged to my mother's grandparents, not to her parents. "See?" I said, producing my copy of the deed and pointing to the top of the page. The owners were listed as Izrael syn Szmula, Izrael, son of Szmul, and his wife, Zysla Frydrych z Pasermanow. These were the Polish names of my great-grandparents, Yisruel and Zisl. Wiesław, Helen, and Marta crowded

around to look at the deed, then all started talking in an angry, combative tone. Even Wiesław, who was usually passive, was saying something
very quickly and pointedly. I turned to Basia, my interpreter, but her
face took on a wash of angst as she struggled to follow three simultaneous Polish monologues and figure out how to convert them into
English. I'd met Basia through Jarek, the Będzin historian. He had told
me she was fluent in English, but I hadn't spoken to her long enough
on the phone to confirm this. Now it was clear that she was flailing.
She was a sweet girl, an English teacher at a local school, and trying
her best, but the Skowrońskis were making her job extremely difficult.
I wished I had one of my friends with me, someone with stronger English, but Krys and Ania were working, and Magda was still in New
York. Her weekend trip had stretched to a week when a toothache led
to the removal of her wisdom teeth. I was floundering.

I wondered how much English Basia actually understood and how
well she had conveyed my words to the Skowrońskis. I wondered if they
had understood anything I'd said. Finally, I decided to try Polish. "*Dom
nie była dziadek dom. Była pra-dziadek dom*," I said, messing up the
grammar. House was not grandfather house. It was great-grandfather
house. This only further agitated Wiesław. He responded loudly, faster
than usual. Then Helen interrupted her husband, and he became annoyed and barked at her. They were both arguing, with each other and
with me, cutting each other off until at last they were done. "They
say you're wrong," Basia said. I turned back to Wiesław and Helen
and answered them in Polish: "But I'm not wrong. Look." I pointed
to the deed again. "*Izrael jest moj PRA-dziadek*," I said, my GREAT-
grandfather. "My grandfather was *Beresh*, Izrael's son." Helen shook
her head. "*Nie, nie, nie, nie, NIE!*" she said. The Polish word for *no* is
pronounced *n'yeh*. Until now I hadn't realized how much it sounded
like the noise a child makes when he doesn't like his food.

I rested my head in my hands, not sure what to do. My great-
grandparents had eight children. Four of them died in the war, along

with their children and spouses. Three of them moved to the United States before the war. With my grandfather, that left four surviving heirs, all of whom had children and grandchildren. I pictured the massive family tree on the wall at the reunion that one of my cousins organized in Detroit a decade earlier, each name on a different paper plate, each plate connected to the others with bits of colored yarn. Would each of those shiny plates have a claim to this house? Would any of the plates actually want to keep the house? Could I just give the Skowrońskis a document saying they owned the house when I was only one of an entire wall of shiny paper plates? This house and its issues were much larger than me or my mom. I wondered how my grandfather had even claimed the authority in 1945 to name Honorata as manager.

Every time I'd visited Będzin lately, I'd returned to Krakow feeling tired and upset. The three hours of travel by train and bus in each direction seemed endless. I always arrived home feeling dusty, dry, and nauseated from reading on the slow-moving train. I felt weak when I dragged myself back to Ulica Staszica at night and attempted the three flights of stairs to our flat. I opened the door with its old-fashioned key, jiggling it in its old-fashioned keyhole, and went straight to my room. I swallowed a couple of Advil and crashed on my bed, feeling the sweat and dirt on my face mingle on the pillow with the first of what would become a wave of exhausted tears.

A day or so after that tense encounter with the Skowrońskis, I picked up a ringing phone in the apartment to the sound of an angry, antagonistic voice. "How do you know my uncles' names?" the voice demanded. The female speaker had an accent in English—thick and harsh—that I couldn't quite place. I could tell she wasn't Polish, and I was both confused and alarmed by the call. "I'm sorry," I apologized, "your uncle's names?" I had no idea what this woman was saying. "My name is Hannah Baytner," she said. "I am calling from Israel. You sent me a letter." Then it was clear.

A few weeks earlier, Helen Skowrońska had given me a tour of the
Będzin property, revealing that the land was much larger than I had originally known. In addition to the main three-story building that fronted
Małachowskiego Street, the property included a long, low building that
ran along the left side of the courtyard behind the main house. That
building had been my family's brass factory, the *meshingiser*. It had been
converted more recently into apartments, including one that was occupied by Wiesław's daughter Marta. The Frydrych property also included
a narrow three-story house attached at the end of the factory building
and, at the far rear of the lot, a row of small wooden storage sheds and
another, even narrower freestanding two-story house beyond that. But
my family, I learned, was not the only owner of 20 Małachowskiego.
There was a second long, low building—also a former factory—that
extended along the right side of the courtyard, so that the two factories
and the main house formed the letter U around the courtyard. That
second workshop and the right half of the main house were owned before the war by a family named Baytner who now lived in Israel. Helen
had met a woman named Hannah Baytner who had come to Poland a
decade earlier and left an address. I had a friend in Israel verify the address, then sent Hannah a letter asking her to call.

In the letter, I took the names of men I now understood to be Hannah's uncles from one of Helen's real estate documents and wrote that
I was looking for the Hannah Baytner who was related to Hersz Lejb
Baytner, Wolf Baytner, Iser Moszek Baytner, Josek Aron Baytner, and
Lejzor-Lipa Baytner of Będzin, Poland. Now I imagined how Hannah,
in Israel, must have received a letter from Poland with a list of relatives
who had most likely been killed. She'd called to find out what kind of
scam I was running.

"It's nothing like that," I assured her. "Honestly, I'm doing research
about my family. I'm American." Then I added, "I'm Jewish." I contemplated reciting the blessing over the wine as proof, but Hannah agreed
to hear me out. "I thought maybe someone in your family might re-

member mine," I said. "The Frydrychs? They lived next door to your family?" I thought the name might ring a distant bell, but to Hannah, the name was anything but distant. The line grew suddenly quiet until she started to speak:

"All my life I hear about Frydrych," she said. "How they gave a baby to be hiding in a family in Poland and they paid a very lot of money to hide her."

"Yes! Exactly!" I said. "The baby was my mother!" I was eager to hear what else Hannah knew, what other aspects of the story she'd heard, but she said she had very few details. I asked more questions, but she had little interest in the subject.

"My parents, they are old people." She sighed. "I don't want to upset them and ask about these things. I know only that my mother told me that she was very sorry that she hasn't give money to hide her child like Frydrych did." Then I understood why her voice held none of the joy that mine did.

"Her child was killed?" I asked.

"Of course," Hannah said. "She had two children. One was born in 1942."

I told her that this was the same year my mother was born, but she already knew. "My mother tell me this," she said. "This is why she was so sorry."

It was eerie to again hear a slice of my family history spoken by someone I'd never met, by a voice on a phone in another time zone that belonged to someone who had never known my family. But here, my mother's story, the tale of her good fortune, was another mother's tragedy. "I met this old woman who hid this baby, your mother," Hannah said. "She lives now in Będzin, where my family lived."

"You met Honorata Skowrońska?"

"I don't remember her name, because I don't like the goyim," Hannah said. "But my parents told me that they give her a lot of money to hide her—your mother—and after, your family give her to live there without paying. She was very old, I remember, when I meet her. I think it was 1994 I was there." I felt a pang of jealousy, wishing I had come to Będzin in 1994. "I talked with her—this old woman in Będzin," Hannah said. "But she wants money, so I leave."

"She asked you for money?"

"Of course she asked for money," Hannah said. "What do they want from Jews but money?" I stumbled for something to say, to argue on behalf of the good Poles I knew, people like Krys, who wouldn't even let me tip him when I drank at his bar.

"I mean they might want . . ." I wasn't sure what exactly to say, so in midsentence, I changed course. "Did you give her money?"

Hannah made a sucking noise with her teeth. "I give her something. I don't remember. She was an ugly woman. Very, very old. I remember. It was a very dirty house. Dirty and in bad condition. There were a lot of children—like cats. She did not say very much. She had a look on her face like a scowl. She said nothing until she asked for money, and she ask me, 'Where is Frydrych?'"

"She asked you that?"

"Yes. I tell her I do not know this family, Frydrych. It was very sad for me when I meet her. I keep thinking about my mother. All the time, she say, why hasn't she paid a lot of money to make her child be hidden? So that her child could survive like this Frydrych child? And then after that, I leave."

Hannah had a video she made on her trip to Będzin that she said she would show me if I ever came to Israel. She had visited Poland with a group of Jews who had roots in the Zagłębie region. They came, among other reasons, to install a marble memorial on the grassy hill beside the Będzin castle where the synagogue once stood, then burned. She laughed when I told her that I'd assumed the Polish government had installed that memorial. "No," Hannah said. "The goyim, they don't do for Jews. You listen. I know what I say. The goyim, from Jews, they want only money."

CHAPTER ELEVEN

TOMASZ BORCZ INSPECTED THE DOCUMENT AND BRUSQUELY shook his head. "This," he said, "is an interesting piece of history, but in the court, it is garbage." I'd had high hopes when I found an English-speaking lawyer and handed him my grandfather's 1945 declaration. As far as I could tell, the document clearly named Honorata Skowrońska as the manager of the house, and I was certain its existence would enable the Skowrońskis to again collect rent from their tenants. But Borcz swiftly rejected this notion. "This is a power of attorney," he said, handing the document back to me. "Your grandfather—you tell me he is dead, yes?" I nodded. "And he gave authority to this Skowrońska, who you say, correct, also is dead?" "That's right," I said, "they're both dead." Then this paper is as dead as they, he said. "It was garbage when one died. Now they are both dead. It is double garbage." "Oh," I said, trying to disguise my disappointment. I looked down at the cigarette burns in the varnish of Borcz's conference table. I really had thought the declaration was a kind of Rosetta stone for the Będzin house that explained everything anyone needed to know. I felt a flash of dread, picturing my next trip to Będzin, breaking the news that I was worthless. I couldn't produce my mother—I would have to tell them eventually—and I couldn't help collect the rent. "Isn't there anything I can do?" I asked, almost whining. "I told them I would help." Borcz looked sweetly at me as though I were a puppy trying to eat his shoe. "If I am you," he said, "I walk away from this. This too much trouble."

Borcz was a large man with a dark, trim mustache and an easy laugh whose name and number I'd found on the American consulate's list of English-speaking attorneys. I'd initially thought the consulate might help with the house, but a perky blonde with a Texas drawl apologized behind bulletproof glass and told me through a sugary smile that the consulate couldn't involve itself in private property matters. "You understand," she drawled as she slid a piece of paper toward me through a slot in the glass. "You'll need an attorney." I glanced down at the list of names on the printed page and asked if these were people the consulate recommended. "I'm sorry," she cooed. "We can take no responsibility." I was more than a little leery when Borcz invited me and my pile of documents to his office on the second floor of a medieval-looking building in the old city. I told him the story, from the woman who had taken a stranger's child into her home in the summer of 1943 to the headaches her son was having half a century later. Then I turned to Borcz for guidance.

"You can give them money," he suggested. "That would help them." But I insisted I wanted to fix what was broken and implored him for answers: Why, I asked, if the family didn't have the authority to collect the rent, did they still have to pay taxes? I asked about the other tenants: Was there no way to force them to pay? Borcz seemed determined to dissuade me from getting involved, but at my insistence, he eventually agreed to describe the legal maneuvers necessary to truly set things right. For one thing, he said, the Skowrońskis had no legal obligation to pay the taxes. "They could stop paying," Borcz said, "but if they do, the government can come and say: 'You don't pay taxes. You are no one.

You leave.' Then where do they go? If you want to help these people, you tell them to keep paying taxes." As for the other tenants, he said, they wouldn't pay until they had to. Why would they? But the only way to compel them to pay was to formally change the deed on the property—a process that could take years.

The good news, Borcz said, was that 20 Małachowskiego did not have the typical quandary that made Jewish property so controversial in Poland. The properties that sparked fury in towns across the country were typically those that went unclaimed after the war and were nationalized by the postwar regime for use as schools, post offices, or affordable housing. Many were still government buildings. Others had been sold in recent years to private investors. Either way, it was no surprise that tempers flared when families appeared abruptly after decades away and demanded cash for a home or tried to take a school from a neighborhood. Jews were not the only people coming back with claims. There were Polish families, displaced by the war or its aftermath, Germans, Ukrainians, Byelorussians, Lithuanians. Jewish claims were not even the most common, but they were the ones most embittered by history.

The situation at 20 Małachowskiego was actually much simpler, Borcz said. Because my grandfather had named Honorata to manage the building, it was never nationalized. If the government ever came for it, Honorata was always there, always acting as its owner. She had an apparently valid document from my grandfather that gave her authority to collect the rent. And as long as she paid the taxes, the government left her alone. That was why the deed still listed Izrael and Zysla Frydrych as homeowners. This seemed like promising news, like it might be easy for my family to again bestow management rights on the Skowrońskis, but Borcz shook his head.

"You don't own the house, either," he said. He lifted the deed from the table and pointed to my great-grandparents' names. "These people," he said. "Izrael and Zysla Frydrych. They own the house. Only they can give anyone anything. You would have to inherit the house from them."

"So I'll do that," I said.

Borcz smiled and lifted his eyebrows high up into his pink and shiny forehead. "Tell me," he said. "How do you know they are dead?"

I was stunned by his question and answered perhaps too harshly. "My great-grandparents were holocaust victims," I said. "Believe me, they're dead."

Borcz swatted my indignation with a sweep of his hand. "I know, I know," he said. "I know they were killed, but can you prove it? See, here is your problem: Unless you can prove that these two are dead, they are alive and still own this property. Before you can inherit anything from them, you must prove they are dead."

"Wait a minute," I said, sifting through my files to find my great-grandparents' birthdates. I located a copy somebody had given me of my family's page in the 1939 Będzin census. It showed that Izrael, who we called Yisruel, was born in 1868 and Zysla, our Zisl, in 1870. "They're obviously dead," I said.

Borcz shrugged. "In Poland they are alive," he said.

"They're a hundred and thirty!" I protested.

Borcz grinned wildly. "They must eat very well," he said.

That was when I started to wonder if he was making this up, playing a joke on me. "You're saying my great-grandparents somehow survived the holocaust and reasonable human life expectancy to—"

"Ah, ah, ah!" Borcz wagged his finger at me. "You are thinking logically, and you are in the wrong country for that."

I was fuming on my side of the table as Borcz took a cell phone out of his pocket. "See, Poland today is confusing," he said, flipping the phone open and setting it down on the table. "Here is what confuses. You see this phone. Everyone in Poland has this phone. We send instant message. We pick up phone, we call friend, we say, 'Meet in pub,' and friend comes to pub. And we think, Good system, modern country, Western country! But it is easy to make a phone system," he said, flipping the phone shut and putting it back in his pocket. "And much harder to change thinking." Borcz seemed pleased to pass on pearls of wisdom to a neophyte foreigner, but I was starting to wonder if he was even a lawyer, if he'd maybe put his name on the consulate's list just for yuks, to make fun of foreigners. But as we talked, Borcz began to grow on me. He was born in Poland, he told me, but spent twenty years practicing law in Washington. He moved back to Krakow after 1989, thinking he could ride the wave of Poland's new economy, take advantage of its new opportunities, but the courts were as corrupt as they had always been, the system even more convoluted. Cases like mine, layered with history and contradiction, were far too common. He'd had to adjust to what he saw as Poland's failure to modernize quickly. It was a source of grief for him, and he saw himself as something of a pundit. I knew I'd have to confirm his advice with other attorneys, but the more he explained the process to me, the more I believed him. He did seem to know what he was talking about, even if he was showing off. He told me that despite the absurdity of proving the death of someone born in 1868, it was not difficult. The process involved placing an ad in the Będzin newspaper, asking if the citizens of Będzin had seen a nice old couple in their hundred and thirties answering to the name of Frydrych. According to the law, if nobody came forward with verifiable information about my great-grandparents' whereabouts within six months, we would get a pair of death certificates. Then we could start the inheritance process, which would be mostly paperwork.

"It is easy enough as long as you are the only heir," Borcz told me.

I shook my head and produced a hand-drawn copy of my family tree. "See, here's Yisruel and Zisl, may they soon rest in peace," I said, pointing to the top of the diagram. "And these people—" I drew my finger across the next line down, "are their eight children. This lady lived, and this guy and this guy. They were all in the States before the war. And here's my grandfather. See, here's me. So all these people under them"—I circled four clusters of names with my finger—"are alive. And these four—Shloyme, Yankl, Duvid Oyzer, Liba—they were all killed, along with their children." I circled four more blobs of names on the tree. As I did this, I realized what this big family could mean. "We're not going to have to prove them all dead, are we?" I asked.

Borcz looked at the chart and put his hand on his forehead. "No." he said, shaking his head. "Here is why." He picked up a pen and gestured toward the family tree. "May I?" he asked.

"Sure," I said.

With his pen, he drew big X's across huge swaths of the tree. "For our purposes," he said, "these people, they do not exist. Don't exist. Don't exist. Don't exist." He drew more X's. "Unless you want to spend ten years and thousands of dollars, your grandfather was the only survivor." He circled my grandfather. "He had one child, your mother. She had one child, you." He drew two more circles, around my mother and me, then slid the chart back across the table.

I looked down at a page of X's and three lonely O's. "My brother can't even exist?" I asked.

"No," he said.

I glanced down at the chart and tried to tabulate how many people he'd just erased. "I have a feeling you're going to laugh at me again," I said sheepishly. "But if I say that I'm the only heir, wouldn't that be, like, fraud?"

Borcz lifted his shoulders to his chin and bobbed his head back and forth as if keeping time to music. He made a skirting gesture with his hand, as though trying to unstick an imaginary piece of gum, then answered, "It's not *fraud* so much. It is, well, *fixing* the problem. You don't want to lie, I know. This is very noble. But let me tell you what happens if you tell the truth."

For me alone to inherit the property, Borcz said, I would need my grandfather's birth and death certificates and my mother's birth, marriage, and death certificates. I might also need my mother's immigration documents to explain why her name went from Frydrych to Frederick and from Irena to Irene. And then I would need my birth certificate. Everything would need to be original copies with raised seals. Then every document issued in the United States would need to be sent to a Polish consulate for verification—and not just any Polish consulate. Different consulates verified records from different states, so my birth certificate from Michigan would have to go to the consulate in Chicago, while my grandfather's death certificate from Georgia would have to go to the one in Washington. Each verifying stamp would cost thirty-five dollars—certified checks only—and after each paper had been stamped and returned, each would be sent to a certified translator in Poland who would type the translations onto special translator paper, charge another fee, and affix another stamp. Then these documents could be submitted, and we would wait to see if the court had any questions. Multiplying the process by nine grandchildren, twenty-two great-grands, seventeen great-greats, and two great-great-greats would magnify the hassle by a factor of fifty. "You can do all the heirs if you want," Borcz said. "But you would be very foolish. If we do only you, no one will know."

"Would I have to lie on the stand?" I asked.

"Would that be a problem?" Borcz asked.

I pressed my face into my hands. "Wouldn't it be easier just to buy the house?" I asked. "You know, start over?"

Borcz smiled his pandering smile and asked from whom I hoped to buy this house. "Well," I suggested, "if my great-grandparents are alive, won't they sell it to me?"

This set Borcz into another of his grab-the-belly guffaws. "Maybe if you ask them nicely," he said through his laughter. "I like you. You are funny girl."

I was glad I could provide amusement to a Polish lawyer, but as we discussed the house's murky status, I started to see the problem in the larger context. I pictured Będzin, its dingy streets, its sidewalks full of loitering men laid off from the mines. This was a city that needed developers to buy up downtrodden tracts and revitalize them, but if our property couldn't be sold or cleared, what did that mean for Będzin in general? Ours couldn't be the only house with an ambiguous status. "What if a developer came to town and wanted to do something to help the city, you know, create jobs?" I asked. "Is there no way someone could buy this house?"

Borcz shook his head. "Not legally," he said. "This is a real problem for Poland." No one wanted to buy property here because no one knew what lurked in a deed. It was easier to buy somewhere else. I pictured our house, in the center of Będzin's main commercial street, and wondered aloud if I might be doing the city a favor by clearing this up. "Maybe the city will even help us," I suggested.

Borcz laughed. "What did I tell you about thinking logically?" he said. "You have to stop doing that."

"Oh, right," I said. "Sorry."

As I returned to the heat of a muggy summer day, my head swarmed with notions of ads in the paper, second deaths for the dead and vanished lives for the living. I wondered whether the end of helping the Skowrońskis justified the means of fraud and perjury. I wondered if I could afford the legal and court fees and the expensive prospect of capital gains and inheritance taxes. Borcz said my costs could run as high as twenty or thirty thousand dollars. I could reduce the taxes by using my mother's birth certificate to become a Polish citizen, and I could possibly make the money back by selling off units in the building, maybe all of them except the ones where the Skowrońskis lived. Another option would be selling the property and using the money to buy the Skowrońskis a new home, but before I could sell anything, I would have to come up with the twenty or thirty thousand. To do that, I'd have to mortgage my house. And for what? For nostalgia? To make good on a promise that my grandfather would deny ever making? And what if there were no buyers? The house was in terrible condition. Even if it were pristine, Będzin's economy was suffering. It was hard to know if anyone had money to buy it. I could be stuck with debts I couldn't pay.

I knew the effort wasn't worth it, that it was too big a risk, but a part of me wanted fiercely to see it through. Inheriting my family home had a sense of adventure, but it also seemed like the right thing to do. As intimidating as the process seemed, I thrilled at the notion of doing something exciting in a city that needed some attention. I thought about Yisruel and Zisl and how, when people die, their children or loved ones are supposed to tend to their affairs. I watched my dad for weeks, processing the papers for Mom, writing to her credit-card companies, to social security. It was part of the ritual of death. But sixty years after their demise, my great-grandparents weren't even allowed to be dead in this country. Three of their sons and one of their daughters had been murdered, along with their spouses and children. Two other sons and a daughter were an ocean away. The son who was both alive and nearby—my grandfather—did as well as he could. He named someone to look after the family home, then spent the rest of his life trying to save it from her. But two generations later, I was the only heir both near and alive, and I, more than anything, needed a purpose, a mission. I was on a yearlong quest that, until this moment, had been largely rudderless. In Borcz's office, I started to see how I could spend the next few months or even the next few years. I knew the decision was foolish. I knew with some certainty that I would come to regret it. But, eyes open, I waded in.

Two days later, Jarek Krajniewski, the town historian, agreed to meet me outside of Będzin's city hall. Borcz had given me a list of documents I needed in order to inherit my great-grandparents' home, and Jarek said that everything from the twentieth century would be on file in the city's main archive. I had never understood the merits of genealogy or why anyone would spend months or years plumbing aging records

for signs of ancestors long dead. But I had a specific assignment and
was curious to see how much I could find. Jarek led me down a narrow passageway on the first floor of the municipal building to an office
marked BUREAU OF CIVIL RECORDS. He watched as I wrote the Polish
spellings of my grandparents' names and birthdates on a piece of notebook paper: BEREK BRYDRYCH, 8 VI 1910 and SURA LEJA ROZENBLUM, 2
II 1921. I tore the page from the notebook and handed it to the clerk,
but Jarek stopped me. "You should write your mother's name, too," he
said. "She was born here, wasn't she?"

"She was," I answered. "But she was born in . . ." I wanted to say
secret but didn't know the Polish word. "If anyone knew of her birth,
they would . . ." I drew my finger across my throat.

Jarek nodded. "I understand."

The clerk took the page with my grandparents' birthdates and
crossed the hall to the file room, returning minutes later with a stack
of index cards in her left hand, waving two in her right. "They're here,"
she said, dropping the cards on the counter. I was stunned by the ef-
ficiency of it. It was no particular surprise that two people born in
Będzin in the twentieth century would have birth records on file in the
town hall, but I didn't expect them to appear minutes after I'd walked
through the door. I'd pictured myself scavenging basement records, but
these two finds surfaced as easily as a lost autumn rake on the lawn
after a winter under the snow. My mom had spent a lifetime wondering
what her mother looked like, not knowing even basic facts about her.
The answers, meanwhile, were here all along, waiting for the rotating
planet to move closer to the sun so that spring could reveal lost treasures. Before this year, the only thing we knew about Sura Leah was a
possibly mythical story about her decision to stay on the train when
her husband jumped to safety. Now we had a picture of her. A friend
in Israel had trekked to Yad Vashem for me to acquire a quality photo
from the museum's digital archive. And now I had a document that
introduced me to her parents. Her father—my great-grandfather—was

Judka Rozenblum, a merchant from the village of Zarzerze. Sura Leah's mother was Chana Rozenblum z Rozenblumow, which meant her married name was the same as her maiden name. I decided to hope that this was coincidence, though most likely it was not.

My grandfather's birth record was also instructive. While his wife's record from 1921 was written in Polish because she was born in the brief period of Polish independence between the wars, my grandfather's birth record from 1910, in the late days of the Russian empire, was recorded in a slanted handwritten Cyrillic with two birth dates: one from the Russian Julian calendar, the other from the Roman Gregorian:

> It happened in the city of Będzin on the 26th of May / 8th of June, 1910, at 10 a.m. Izrael Frydrych appeared. He was 42 and an inhabitant of the city of Będzin. He brought two witnesses, Jankel Woszebrot, 42, and Nutan Swimer, 56. They brought a male child who was born the 19th of May / 1st of June at 6 a.m. in the town of Będzin on Ulica Modrzejowska, number 7 from the mother Zysla Paserman, who was 38. The child was given the name Berek. This document was signed by Izrael Frydrych, Jankel Woszebrot and Nutan Swimer.

Izrael Frydrych's signature at the bottom was awkward, written with a shaky hand in the Roman letters of the Polish alphabet, not the Cyrillic letters of the Russian. It looked almost as though he had signed from right to left, as though he couldn't break his hand from the language—Hebrew—he'd been trained to write. I had no idea why he wrote in Polish letters instead of Cyrillic. It was a confusing clue, but one that spoke to the complicated ethnic and linguistic legacies of a city of Jews, Poles, and Germans, controlled at the time by Russians and eternally plagued by change.

The clerk made copies of the records for me and directed me to a room down the hall where I could buy stamps to pay for the documents, but as I turned to walk away, she called to me. She'd been sorting her index cards into alphabetical order when she stopped to ask for my mother's name. I told her not to bother, that she wouldn't find my mom, but the clerk persisted. "Her name was Irena," I told her. "Irena Frydrych." The clerk shook her head and wagged a finger. "Irena is a Polish name," she said. "What was her *Jewish* name?" Her Jewish name was Irena, I said. "She was a Jew. It was her name." It seemed obvious to me, but the clerk again shook her head. "Irena is a Polish name," Jarek confirmed, setting his hand on my shoulder. "Jews had Jewish names." I looked at him and then back at the clerk. I didn't like what they were suggesting. Until she moved to the United States and became Irene, she didn't have any other name except . . . well. "Do you mean her *Hebrew* name?" I asked. "*Po hebrajsku?*"

"*Tak, tak, taaaak!*" the clerk smiled. "Exactly. What *was* her Hebrew name?" What *was* her Hebrew name? I knew the answer. I'd known it at the funeral home. There were all these questions to answer the day after my mother died about where she was born, who her parents had been. The funeral director had asked for Mom's Hebrew name, the name she'd used for Jewish rituals. My father and brother had looked at me blankly. I'd looked blankly at them. And then somehow I'd known. I hadn't known I knew, but I opened my mouth, and out it came: "Yehudith!" I said. "Her Hebrew name was Yehudith."

"That's it!" The clerk grinned in victory as she waved a card at me. "Yehudith. It's here."

I was dumbstruck. I tried to argue, to point out that this couldn't be true, but there it was on the card, my mother's Hebrew name and the names of her parents. *I was born in secret,* Mom told me. *If anyone knew of my birth, I would have been killed.* But my mother's birth, it seemed, was not a secret. It was recorded in the town hall and written not in Polish, like her mother's birth record, or in Russian, like

her father's, but in German. It was stamped with the swastika of the
ruling government of 1942. My mom and her parents were all born
in the same city, but each on different points of the time line of Polish conquest. I was starting to understand the power of even the most
mundane historical record, to see how a narrative could emerge from
a few lines of text. My mother's birth record was the shortest of the
three, but its story spoke volumes about the time and place in which
it was written:

> Sura Laja Sara Rozenblum, single, a Jew, living in
> Bendsburg, Kattowitzerstrasse 20, gave birth to a girl
> on Feb. 24th, 1942 at 5 o'clock in Bendsburg, in her
> apartment. The child received the first names: Jehudt
> Sara. The above-mentioned child was recognized as
> his own by the father, Berek Israel Frydrich, a Jew, on
> the 29th May 1942, registered upon oral acknowl-
> edgment of the father.

In the record, Będzin was listed by its occupation name, Bendsburg.
My family's street—Małachowskiego—was listed by its wartime name,
Kattowitzerstrasse, and everyone named in the record was listed by required Jewish names. Jewish women in this part of occupied Poland had
to add the name Sara as a suffix to their given names. Even my grandmother, whose first name was Sura, was listed on the record as Sura
Laja Sara. All Jewish men had to add the name Israel. I was surprised
to see my mother's birthday listed as February 24, since she always
celebrated her birthday on February 20, and I was even more surprised
to see the adjective listed immediately after my grandmother's name.
I wrote back to the friend at home who had translated the record for
me by e-mail. *Are you sure the record says SINGLE?* I asked. I consulted
the original record. The word was *ledig. Could this word mean anything
else?* I found it very difficult to believe that my grandparents hadn't

been married when my mother was born, but my friend wrote back decisively. *Ledig,* in this context, could only mean single, unmarried. *What a scandal!* she wrote. *Check other Jewish birth records. See if they all say* ledig. *Maybe Jewish weddings were illegal.* This was a possibility. It was, after all, a Nazi record. Then again, it was wartime, and as the story goes, my grandparents were in love. This could explain why the clerk at the town hall found no marriage record for my grandparents in her stacks of filing cards.

Genealogy no longer seemed like a waste of time. After discovering these few records, I could see how elaborately a single document could expound on a much larger truth. I was determined to find more. I noticed when I studied my grandmother's birth record that her mother, Chana, was thirty-nine years old when Sura Leah was born and that Judka Rozenblum was forty-one. That meant there were probably older siblings, but the only sibling I could find for my grandmother was a sister named Chaja who was only two years older. I was certain there were more, but where were they? Had there been sisters who married and changed their names? Were there brothers who had moved to another town? There were puzzles to solve on my grandfather's side as well. Tomasz Borcz wanted me to find birth records for my great-grandparents, Yisruel Frydrych and Zisl Paserman, but I would soon discover that the regional archive that stored the Będzin records from the eighteenth and nineteenth centuries had no record of either surname. My family clearly had come from somewhere else—a smaller shtetl, most likely, but which one? Genealogy groups had been working on collecting enough data to someday make questions like mine as easy to answer as typing a name into a database. Someday it might even be possible to pull digital images of entire Polish record books up on a computer screen. But in the summer of 2001, the Internet offered little more than lists of towns where certain surnames had been spotted. It fell to me to see if those Frydrychs or Rozenblums were mine.

I spent the next few weeks waking up early and plotting new routes to old archives, but my early success in Będzin was little more than a false promise. The impressive card catalog at the Będzin city hall quickly proved more exception than rule. In most towns, if I was granted access at all, the only way to find anything was to sift through endless processions of dust-caked, moldy pages. It was August in Poland, and the entire country, it seemed, had gone on vacation. Borcz had gone on holiday with his family to the mountains. So, apparently, had all the other lawyers in Krakow with whom I had hoped to consult. Krys was in Silesia, visiting his parents. Magda, it seemed, was making no plans to come back to Poland. After her emergency oral surgery, she needed another week in New York, then another. Almost a month had passed, and a number of flights she claimed she'd be on had landed without her. With everyone gone, genealogy became my only companion.

I spent my days coughing my way through heavy volumes of nineteenth-century records, scanning page after page of birth, marriage, and death records in search of the combination of Cyrillic letters that spelled Frydrych or Paserman. I suffered in hot, airless rooms as my neck throbbed and my throat clogged with dust. Polish records from the time were recorded in massive books—three feet tall, two feet wide, and bound in red or faded brown. Each book contained the annals of a single year in a single town. Most books had indexes for births, marriages, and deaths, but some were incomplete, some nonexistent. Sometimes the only way to know whether my family appeared in a book was to turn each of its hundreds of pages. It was tedious work. I photocopied every page that seemed promising, including many records for Rozenblums. But it was such a common name that I doubted my weeks of wearisome page-turning had produced anything at all.

Sometimes, the clerks who stood between me and the records were helpful. They would smile and tell me proudly, since I had asked for the Jewish records, that this was a Jewish town once. And I would smile at them and say, "That's why I came." And they would shake their head and cluck and say, "So sad what happened to the Jews." And I would nod and say, "Yes, it was sad." Sometimes, these nice clerks would help me. There were other clerks who were not helpful. They would stand, arms crossed, in front of the books. They were nervous when foreigners arrived. They would check my ID and tell me about the personal-property law in Poland that prevented them from opening the books to me. If they showed me something I wasn't allowed to see, they'd tell me, they could go to jail. This wasn't true, I'd tell them. I had looked into this law and knew I was allowed to see records that pertained to my family. But they didn't want to get in trouble. "No," they would say. One lady called her boss in a fluster when I walked in: "Come help me," she pleaded into the phone. "This woman is from abroad!"

I wondered if I was supposed to bribe them. That would have been the method under communism, when most of these people got their jobs. But what was an appropriate bribe? Should I offer money or vodka? I didn't know the rules, so I begged. *Won't you help me? Please?* There was almost never anyone else in these offices, so I tried to be nice. I would tell them I had come a long way. I'd apologize for my muddled Polish. *Please excuse me.* But often they wouldn't budge, and I would go away without answers, often in tears. Even after days with the nice clerks, I might cry on the way home, not really sure why, exhaustion, maybe. Ambient sadness. More of the same. I had a car now. It belonged to my friend Ania, who had left in early August for graduate school in Indiana. She told me she would need a car when she got there, and I told her she could have mine if she could get to Detroit, where it was parked in my father's driveway, and if she would leave her car with me. But as convenient as it was—and as much as the car enabled me to access towns that would have been difficult to reach by bus or train—my solitary daily drives seemed only to compound a sadness that was mounting with every failed journey to every distant archive. The glee of my early success—the three records in a single day—faded quickly into a droning monotony of dusty books and a deepening longing for home.

In the stagnant, motionless days of humid August, I found myself, for the first time since my mother died, completely alone. I had no family here, no close friends. The apartment seemed vast with no one in it but me: three bedrooms, a spacious kitchen, high vacant ceilings. I listened to the sound of my bare feet sticking to the floor as I walked to the bathroom. I heard the clang of the dishes as I put them away and the shushing of the broom as I swept dust from the floor. Every noise echoed off the walls, against the windows, around the upper reaches of the ceiling, inside my head. It was too quiet. Tears started coming too easily, to the point where, in late August, I had a kind of hysterical public breakdown in the regional archive of the city of Częstochowa. They had some Rozenblum records that I asked them to copy, but when they did, they handed me a bill for ninety dollars. "What's this?" I asked, insisting that the clerk must be mistaken, that I needed only one copy of each record. But the lady pulled out her price sheet and pointed to a number. It was the foreigners' rate, listed in U.S. currency at ten dollars per page. This was compared to the locals' rate, listed in złoty, at roughly a dollar per page.

"No," I said, or tried to say in my faltering Polish. "The foreigners' rate is for people who write from abroad to request information. It includes the price of having someone do the research and mailing it. It doesn't apply to someone who is standing here, having done her own research."

The lady crossed her arms over her chest. "These are the rules. It's ten dollars per page. If you want your copies, you'll pay."

"This is *dyskryminacja!*" I shouted, discrimination, because it was one of the few Polish words I knew would suit the situation. "Don't you want justice?" My simple vocabulary robbed me of subtlety. I could make a better argument in my own language, but here, I was helpless, stupid. They looked at me like my language skills reflected my intelligence. "I want to speak to the boss!" I said. And in the heat of battle, I lost control. I started to gag on accumulated rage in my throat, to engage in the kind of full-body weeping that actually makes a noise, like hyperventilating. Mucus dripped from my nose in stringy lines of defeat as tears of humiliation collected on the table.

I was completely overreacting, hiccupping, and they were staring at me, horrified, like I might turn on them, my tears feeding my fury and—who knew?—pull out a gun and shoot them. "I am not a foreigner," I whined through my tears. "I shouldn't have to pay the—*hiccup*—foreign rate. See? *Hic.* My mother's birth certificate. She was born in Poland. I'm almost as Polish as you." But it was no use. If I could have spoken the language better, and if I hadn't been so upset, I could have kept going, could have said what I was really thinking, what was really burning me, like: "Do we really need to explore why I'm not Polish now, why my family had to leave, what your people helped do to mine? And do we need to wonder why I need these papers in the first place? Why I've been cut off this way from my family's past? Why the chain was broken?"

As tears blurred my vision, everything I'd learned about Poles and Jews, and the deeper understanding I'd acquired about Polish responsibility, and how, despite everything, Poles, too, were victims, was completely forgotten, drowned in my anger at them and my shame in my own outburst. I was the victim here. They were the perpetrators. They were the reason my grandmother had been killed, taking with her all knowledge of her family, making my job so much more difficult. I knew that they honestly thought they were doing their jobs, enforcing the rules. They were no different from any other bureaucrat anywhere in the world. But they were standing between me and my mother's family, and I hated them for it. And while I was at it, I hated their country. I hated Poland and Poles. I hated their obnoxious fees, their obsession with putting stamps on documents, their petty bureaucratic ways. I hated their personal-property law and the little annoying things they seemed to do just to make things more difficult. I hated them for their role in making me feel that much farther away from my mom and her family and her past and the future that she wouldn't have. I hated them so much that after paying their shakedown money—I had to go to an ATM for cash—I threw my photocopies down on the passenger seat of Ania's car and steered directly to the first fast-food restaurant I saw. It was a Kentucky Fried Chicken. I ordered a finger-lickin' special of chicken and fries. I'd sworn years earlier that I would never eat American fast food on non-U.S. soil. The markup for processed American fast food was shocking. It was offensive the way the Colonel ripped people off here for food that looked good on TV and came with plastic toys. But I wiped the grease from my mouth with pride that day, happy that American corporate imperialism was giving Poles a taste of their own rip-off medicine. I, too, had paid too much for the food, but it tasted great to me: chicken, fries, and the savory salt of revenge.

It was all very depressing. I returned to Krakow to collapse on the floor of my room. I sprawled in the center of the smooth, worn wood where I could lie low beneath the summer heat and try to relax, let the day slide out, collect in my throat, dampen my face. Weeks had passed since I'd had anyone to talk to, and grief subsumed the space where my friends had been. It slithered up beside me as I slumped through the market, and it clutched at my gut as I tried to eat. I escaped to the movies, to the bars, but it tailed me. Three months had never passed in my life without a single conversation with my mom, and now I sensed the infinite emptiness of her absence in everything. My mom was gone and I was miserably alone.

CHAPTER TWELVE

AFTER MY HYSTERICAL EPISODE IN THE CZĘSTOCHOWA ARCHIVE, I decided I needed a break from genealogy and drove the next day to Będzin. I had initially planned to visit the Skowrońskis, but when I arrived in the city where my mother was born, I steered away from Małachowskiego Street. I still wasn't ready to break the news about my mother's death, and the lies I'd been telling had begun to gnaw at my conscience. Instead, I parked in the shadow of the Będzin castle and walked slowly around its perimeter until I found the broken tombstones of the old Jewish cemetery, buried under roots and leaves in the woods that sloped down the back of the castle hill. I recalled the quaint vow I'd made when I first came to Poland, how I wouldn't spend my time here focused on death. But now, with fate having rendered that vow both useless and lame, I found myself increasingly drawn to the holes in the landscape, taking advantage in this land of what's missing to marinate in the salt of what's lost.

It wasn't that Poland had no Jewish life. The community in Warsaw had been steadily growing for years and boasted a Jewish school, a Yiddish theater, a kosher kitchen. Smaller cities like Krakow and Wrocław had clusters of elderly survivors and younger people getting in touch with their roots. But these last few weeks had taken me to countless little villages, tucked into the lush, rolling hills of Poland's fertile south, where the Jewish life that once thrived in this country was survived exclusively by relics. There were broken headstones in overgrown cemeteries. There were burned-out shells where synagogues had stood. There were faded Hebrew letters etched into weather-worn walls. I may have mocked the Jewish Disneyland in Krakow and marveled at the hipster Poles and their ersatz dances to "Havah Nagilah," but there was little comparative comfort in the vast miles of Polish farming fields and industrial burgs, where the problem was not a Jewish life contrived of plastic and schmaltz but, rather, one known only by archaeology.

In Będzin, a city once home to twenty-seven thousand Jewish souls—45 percent of the city's official population in 1939—you could find many such vestiges if you knew where to look. If you walked from the ruins of the cemetery around the base of the hill, you could stand on a grassy clearing near the Czarna Przemsza River and read the inscription on the marble cube that recalled the night of September 8, 1939, when two hundred people burned to death here, locked inside the Synagoga Wielka, the great synagogue. If you continued around the circumference of the castle, you could see the sign on the wall of the church that honored the city's war-era priest for opening his gate the night of the fire to allow a few escapes. But you could not find a minyan, real or pretend. The last Jew of Będzin, Marian Szwarc, had been gone for several years. And though I could not say for sure, I'd have been surprised if anyone in Będzin in 2001 knew the lyrics to "Havah Nagilah."

I wandered around the castle until I found one of my own family's relics: the address—7 Modrzejowska Street—where a 1920s phone directory and my grandfather's birth record listed the Frydrych home and *meshingiser*. This was the house where my great-grandparents lived before growing their brass business enough to afford the bigger house on Małachowskiego with help from their daughter and sons in Detroit. But like so much else here, the old house was gone. The lot where it stood was now a vegetable garden beside a mural of Disneylike ducks in a rowboat. I wondered if the house had burned the night of the synagogue fire. Fifty-six homes were destroyed that night.

I had the feeling sometimes, on solitary walks like these, that my mom could see through my eyes, that what I could see, she could, too, that if I walked slowly enough and thought enough about her, she would be with me, as she would have been if things had turned out differently, if we'd had a little more luck or she a little less cancer. And so I talked to her silently in my head, describing what I saw. *This is the park where you would have played, Mom. Here's the castle you might have visited.* It was odd to see a castle in a soot-covered traffic jam like Będzin. But here it was: a cluster of three narrow towers built of stone—one round, one square, one with a conical roof—that are filled today with medieval armory, ancient shields, and other whatsits from the town museum. The small fortress was not much larger than many of the houses in town, but it sat regally up on the top of the hill, looking out over the noisy city.

Będzin today looked gray and gloomy, polluted and poor, but the exhibit in the castle museum told of a city dating back to the eleventh century, when the castle was a wooden fortress. Będzin was a major stop on trading routes from west to east, and it prospered through the glory years of Polish-Lithuanian commonwealth in the fifteenth and sixteenth centuries, when the country was the largest in Europe. Będzin struggled later, when, like the rest of Poland, it found itself under attack by Swedes, then Russians and Germans. Napoleon's troops came marauding through on their way to invade Moscow, only to return in retreat a few months later, marauding again, followed by the czar's troops, who piled on the destruction. The castle stood watching, powerless to protect, just as today it watches the city's decline.

As I ascended the stone spiral stairs of the castle's tallest tower to reach the turreted platform on top, I considered how much of the town's history could have been seen from this high perch. From 1795 until World War I, in the years when Poland had vanished from the map, subsumed by its more powerful neighbors, you could have stood here and seen the point, twenty-one kilometers away, where three global empires collided: where Russia met Prussia met Austria-Hungary. In 1939 you could have watched to the west as German troops approached. Now, from the turreted platform, mostly what I saw in the haze of a humid and drizzly day was an ocean of gray. I put my camera into panoramic mode and snapped three wide photos of the city: one of the distant cooling towers of a coal-fired plant; another of the forest of drab concrete apartment blocks that flanked the hill beyond the city's main traffic circle. The third photo captured the dark rooftops of the old city, the corroded copper dome of the church, and a four-lane highway bisected by a streetcar line.

Będzin has a sadness to it that you don't see in Krakow, a kind of lethargic decay. The city's problems aren't unique. I've worked as a reporter in Detroit and Philadelphia; I've walked through many careworn neighborhoods. But Będzin's blight seems heavier somehow, darker. It can't be forgotten that the people who abandoned their buildings here, condemning them to neglect, didn't just flee to greener pastures in the suburbs.

During the rainy first week of September, I drove to Auschwitz in search of the story of my grandmother and the train from which she may have jumped. I thought the camp might have a record of her arrival, something that would reveal the truth of how she died. But the Auschwitz archives—stored in the first building on the left beyond the ARBEIT MACHT FREI gate—had no information on Sura Leah Rozenblum of Będzin. That could mean she never arrived, that maybe she made the courageous leap from the train. Or it could mean she was selected for immediate death and that her presence in the camp was never recorded. Either way, it meant my grandmother died an anonymous death—and she wasn't alone. I submitted the names of eighteen other family members to the archives that day. I thought the archivists would find at least one or two people. But all of them, it seemed—my grandmother's sister Chaja; her parents, Chana and Judka; my grandfathers' three brothers; his little sister; their spouses; their children—had all died silent, anonymous deaths.

I had heard it said over the years that the Nazis were so evil, it wasn't enough to kill people, they also wanted to document their triumph over the Jews. For my purposes, I wished that were more true. I wanted to honor the deaths of my great-aunts and -uncles. I wanted to know something about my cousins, like the two darling girls whom everyone called "big Gutsha" and "little Gutsha." Big Gutsha was probably eleven the year she was killed, along with her brother, Abramek, her mother, Heltsha, her father, Yankl. Little Gutsha was eight, the only child born to Liba, my grandfather's youngest sister. Liba was killed. Her husband, Shmil Biber, was killed. Little Gutsha was killed. But Auschwitz remembered none of them. I thought maybe if I held a piece of paper with their names on it, something confirming they had been here, had died here, that somehow it could bring me closer to them.

I tried to picture them in the last year before everything changed, tried to see, perhaps, the wedding of Duvid Oyzer Frydrych and Baltsha Gold. I knew about this wedding. I had interviewed my cousin Lillian about it at her house in Atlanta the previous winter. She'd told me that she traveled to Poland in 1938 to attend this wedding with her brother and parents. Lillian was eight; her brother, Bernie, was four. The groom, Duvid Oyzer, was the brother of my grandfather and of Lillian's father, Laybish. Baltsha, the bride, was the sister of Lillian's mother, Tillie Gold. The Frydrychs and the Golds were neighbors in Będzin, and now a second Frydrych brother was marrying a second Gold daughter. The engagement was announced at a formal reception held in the home of Baltsha's parents, Yankl and Rivka, at number 42 Kołłątaja Street. Lillian still had the invitation that her parents had received at their home in Detroit. The invitation announced, in Polish, that the engagement party would take place on October 16, 1937, at seven P.M. and that the wedding would come fourteen months later, on December 31, 1938. According to the Będzin archives, where a marriage certificate was still on file, the religious ceremony was preceded by three announcements in the synagogue on October 22, October 29, and November 5. *The newlyweds,* according to the marriage record, *declared that they made no pre-nuptial agreements.*

It was a joyous *simcha* of the highest order, both because of the marriage and because the wedding had brought the two sides of the family back together. The family had been fractured since 1913, when Faygl, the eldest Frydrych child, got married and left Poland with her new husband for a new life in Detroit. Faygl, eventually the mother of four girls, was followed to Detroit by her brothers, Moyshe and Laybish, who came together in 1921. In Detroit, Moyshe met and married a Russian-born woman named Minnie who gave him a daughter and a son. Laybish returned to Będzin in 1929 for a visit, where he met Tillie in her father's ice cream parlor. "I saw Tillie and I said I liked that girl," Laybish told my cousin Gloria when she taped an interview with him in 1984, a year before he died. "She served us ice cream. She was jolly and beautiful." The two were married that year in Będzin, then traveled together to Detroit. Like most new arrivals in Detroit at the time, the men worked first at the Ford Motor Company. When they'd saved enough money, they started dry-cleaning businesses and grocery stores. And as they entered the middle class, they dreamed that the rest of the family would join them someday in the United States, that they might all be together again, but there were too many reasons for the others to stay in Poland.

My great-grandparents, Yisruel and Zisl, I'd heard, told their children that America was *traif,* not kosher; meanwhile, they had prosperous lives in Będzin. The families of all Frydrych sons and daughters still in Poland had their own apartments in the spacious complex on

Małachowskiego Street. The eldest son in Poland, Shloyme, was a rabbi who lived with his wife, Rudl Ester, in an apartment above his parents. In the 1984 interview, Laybish said that Shloyme had studied in Berlin until Hitler came to power in 1933. It's not clear if he was ordered to leave or if he left because leaving seemed the safest choice. Either way, he returned to Będzin, to Małachowskiego Street. Rudl Ester was a *sheitelmacher*, a wig maker, Laybish said. His mother Zisl had chosen her to be Shloyme's bride because Shloyme needed a wife who could support him while he studied. When I interviewed Lillian about the six months she spent with her family on Małachowskiego Street in 1938 and 1939, she remembered that Shloyme spent his days studying and that Rudl Ester kept mostly to herself, that the other women didn't seem to like her, that Rudl Ester often had a runny nose.

The youngest of the Frydrych children was Liba, who married young and lived with her husband and little Gutsha in an apartment that Lillian recalled was on the Baytner side of the courtyard. And then there were the three Frydrych sons—Yankl, Duvid Oyzer, and Beresh—who worked with their father in the *meshingiser*, producing candlesticks, doorknobs, drawer pulls, and pressing irons. Laybish said the *meshingiser* was profitable in the years leading up to the war. It had sixty-eight employees and thrived, in part, because of Duvid Oyzer's sharp mind for business. "Duvid Oyzer was brilliant," Laybish said. "He was a very smart brother. He ran the whole factory. He straightened out a lot of things. He even went to Paris to find new materials to work with. . . . He made it very good and we got rich in that time." It was a contrast to when Laybish was young, he said, when the family was too poor to educate its oldest sons. The brothers worked long hours, Lillian remembered, then came upstairs for a meal around Zisl's table. They had flourishing lives in Poland and no need for the distant possibilities of the American dream. The two sides of the Frydrych family would reunite only for special occasions—like the wedding of Duvid Oyzer and Baltsha Gold.

I found it hard to think of this wedding now—hindsight being so much more powerful than foresight—in anything other than melancholy terms. It was difficult to imagine them on December 31, 1938, the last day of the last full year before the war—on War Year's Eve—and not see the celebrants as stupidly doomed, like climbers on the summit of Everest, oblivious to the storm below, laughing and snapping pictures. I wanted to reach back through the years and shout at them: *You fools! Stop dancing! Get out!* Historians frown on this kind of thinking. It's called back-shadowing, using what we know in the future to judge actions in the past. I knew I wasn't supposed to look back at my family and resent them for not having had crystal balls. But standing on this end of the time line, trying to see back through the decades, through the nineties, the eighties, the seventies, the sixties, the fifties, the fire and fury that scorched through the blistering forties, it was impossible to see them clearly beyond the smoke, beyond the blood and the horror. The view of them from here was irrevocably obscured. As with much of European Jewish history in general, it was difficult to look back at the joyous nuptials and not see them as tragic. On that joyous last day of December 1938, Hitler had been in power in Germany for five years. The German border was a matter of miles from Będzin. Lillian remembered crossing Germany on the train with her parents. She remembered the feel of money being shoved in her underpants as her mother told her that soldiers and thieves wouldn't search a child. These years later, Lillian still had her passport from the trip, stamped with two swastikas. One stamp came on her way through Germany to Poland at the start of the trip. The other came on her return home. She and her family left Poland a few months after the wedding, crossing back through Germany, back through France, and back toward the boat and the ocean that, heartbreakingly soon, would divide the family forever by geography and fate.

I thought if I could find some records, some clues, some documents, about the Polish half of my family left behind, that maybe, in my small way, I could bring the two halves of my family back together. But the only person in my family whose name could be found in the archives at Auschwitz was my grandfather, the sole adult survivor from the family's Polish half. He had arrived at the camp on August 6, 1943; his record stated: *FRYDRYCH, Berek, born June 1, 1910, Będzin, was deported to KL Auschwitz from Ghetto Będzin on August 6, 1943. He was registered in the camp under prisoner number 135823. He was on the list of transport, which contained prisoners transferred from KL Auschwitz to KL Buchenwald on January 26, 1945.*

I hadn't known that my grandfather was transferred to Buchenwald. My mom had only ever mentioned Auschwitz. I looked down at the official certificate that the Auschwitz archivist had typed up for me, and considered its three lines of text. A transfer from Auschwitz to Buchenwald in January 1945 was no ordinary move. It was a death march, a five-hundred-mile walk at gunpoint through the snow from Poland to Germany ahead of the approaching Russian front. I never knew that my grandfather was on a death march, but it wasn't the kind of information a granddaughter treasures. I looked around as I walked slowly back through ARBEIT MACHT FREI and back toward Ania's car. There was a group of Israeli teens literally wrapping themselves in Israeli flags as they toured the camp, loudly crunching on the gravel paths with heavy steps. I cringed, bothered by the sight of national symbols here, where the pride of nation had been so wretchedly perverted. There was a group of Polish high school kids hanging around by the gate, acting like what they were—kids on a field trip—laughing and teasing one another. Tourists with bags of memorial candles glared at them as they passed.

I wasn't sure why I had gone to the camp. As futile as my vow not to focus on death had been, I had made that promise for a reason. I really had come to Poland in search of something sweeter. A reunion? A better life in the future, one more informed by the past? I hadn't come to learn about transport trains or death marches. And now, even more

than before, this was news I couldn't handle. I'd been told that the re-
mains of the airplane factory where my grandfather worked as a slave
for the Siemens Corporation were still standing nine kilometers from
Birkenau in a town called Bobrek. The Jewish prisoners—engineers,
tool and die makers, skilled mechanics—built the plant from scratch
and ran it for years until the end of the war, producing a presumably
handsome profit for Siemens in exchange for their own lives. I had
planned to go to Bobrek after the archive this day, to find the plant and
ponder how it must have been for my grandfather there, to replay the
story he'd told about the call for men who knew the metal trade, how
he and Duvid Oyzer both volunteered in hopes of surviving, how he
had been selected and Duvid Oyzer, the brilliant businessman who had
gone to Paris for new materials, had not. I had planned to go to Bobrek, to curse the success of Siemens, which, I noticed, had produced
the hand dryers that hung now in the bathrooms of the Auschwitz
museum. But I couldn't handle it. Not now. Not anymore. When I
returned to Ania's car after the archive, I turned toward the road that
would take me back to Krakow. If I wanted to feel angry at Siemens, I
could stand in the Krakow market square and glower at the giant bill-
board shilling a cheerful collection of dancing Siemens cell phones. But
I'd had enough. If I could have handled it all when I began this trip,
now I could not. My grief was still fresh and becoming more so every
day. I needed to shift focus, to find something more uplifting to do. I
needed something to look forward to.

The only good thing on my horizon was my father's planned visit in
mid-September, so I called him when I returned to Krakow. I thought
we could talk about his visit, maybe plan a side trip to Budapest or
Prague. But when he answered the phone, something in his voice
sounded distorted. Everything was fine, he told me, but he was feeling down. Mom's doctors had called to say they had results from the
autopsy and had invited him to read them. Jewish law prohibits autop-
sies, but we had been so stunned by her seemingly sudden death, so

confused by how she'd gone from feeling better—from sitting up, from breathing on her own—to not doing anything at all. The game was over and we had lost, but we wanted to know. For the benefit of medical science, for peace of mind. They opened Mom up, took samples, then sat my father down to tell him the force that had killed my mother was none other than cancer. That was it—no weird diagnosis or crazy disease that could have been cured. Just the same old killer that kills so many. There were cancer cells everywhere—in her heart, in her lungs, in her brain—that overwhelmed her. "Oh," I said when he told this to me. "I guess that makes sense." He agreed that it did, but for reasons I couldn't explain, it really did not—not to me, not after months of muting my grief beneath a siren of outrage, taking at least a hint of solace in the injustice of it all, in how it must all have been a big mistake. I kept thinking that the days when she appeared to have beaten the illness were the days that portended her real fate, that her death was some kind of error. But no. She just wasn't meant to see sixty. The chemo, the nausea, the hair loss had been for nothing. It was only the false security that had let me leave her when she needed me most.

I hung up the phone, the familiar streak of tears on my cheeks, the wet spot on my sleeve where I'd wiped them, and sat by myself for an hour, quietly crying. My apartment was still vacuously empty, completely silent but for the noise of my grief. I sat feeling sorry for myself, feeling alone, feeling lost, and then I did something I hadn't done in months. I called David. We had barely spoken since the ruinous timing of his visit to Detroit. The playful e-mail banter we'd had in the spring never resumed when I returned to Poland. And though he had sent kind notes and made it clear that he was there for me in grief the way he'd been for me in worry, I'd distanced myself from him, ignored most of his e-mails. I knew it was unfair. I knew Dave didn't deserve to be treated as if he had done something wrong. But he had become so linked in my mind to the day of my mother's death that putting it behind me meant putting him behind me, too. Now, in an apartment so empty that the splash of a falling teardrop could be heard to echo as though through a canyon, his voice sounded to me like the footsteps of an approaching rescue squad, coming to guide me back to camp. He sounded surprised when he heard me on the phone, but he told me that he missed me. Then, before I even knew it was true, I told him I missed him, too.

CHAPTER THIRTEEN

I COULD HAVE VIEWED A VISIT BY MY FATHER AS A SAD SECOND BEST. I could have recalled that this was the trip Mom was supposed to take; that it was now, in September, when Mom was supposed to come, meet the Skowrońskis, tour Będzin, continue on with me to Sweden; that it was Mom I dreamed of bringing here, Mom I pictured greeting at the airport, and Mom I planned to install in Krakow's finest hotel. I could have spent the whole of my father's visit focused on what might have been, on whom we were missing. In fact, I may well have done that if my father's visit had been scheduled to occur in any other week of any other year. But it was September 2001, and history would dictate that the war I was living, fifty-six years after its end, would come to merge in my mind with the one about to begin.

I spent the night of September 11 in the basement of the Eden Hotel, watching the BBC with a group of blind Israeli teens. I was mesmerized by the TV, talking with Krys, feeling desolately far from home. That was when a girl approached me and tried to pick a fight. "I don't know why everybody thinks it's such a big deal," she said. I turned to look at her. She was about seventeen, chunky, and wore thick glasses and frosted pink lipstick. She was part of a tour group from an Israeli school for the blind that was staying at the hotel. Like hundreds of other Israeli high schools, hers ran annual trips to Poland to tour death camps. I had seen waves of these students in the spring, and now, in the fall, they were back, walking in large packs around Krakow, eyeing the Poles with disdain. This group had returned that day from a tour of Auschwitz and Birkenau and had come to the bar to decompress. It was there they heard the news from New York and Washington.

"Six thousand people were killed every day at Auschwitz," the girl told me with a sneer. "So your country loses a few thousand. It happens." I turned again to look at her, not sure how to answer. An odd consequence of living in Krakow as a foreigner, of hosting visitors and of passing my evenings in a hotel bar, was that I spent a great deal of time that year with people who had spent the day at Auschwitz. They returned to Krakow with a haze in their eyes and a view of a world that would never seem the same. It was tough luck for this girl that these were the eyes through which she was seeing this day. A part of me wanted to offer her some kind of comfort. Instead, I turned back to the TV, to the footage, to the plane gliding across the perfect blue sky. "I don't know why Americans are so pathetic about security," she continued, still trying to provoke me. "Nothing of this scale would happen in Israel." I wondered how much sight she had, whether she could see my face. I turned to answer her but had no words. Instead I asked Krys to turn up the volume on the TV. "Of course," he said, reaching for the remote. "You want another vodka?" I nodded. The girl picked up the tray of drinks she'd come to the bar to collect and carried it back to her table.

September 11 would be seen around the world as a day that changed everything. But my world had already changed that year, and the day just brought me back. It was May 28 again. I was watching my father lean over my mother's gaunt, lifeless body. There was something about this new grief that made my old grief feel raw, renewed, only worse, because now it wasn't just her. Now it was who knew how many thousands of others and who knew what kind of consequences, what kind of war would break out and be perhaps as horrid and sick as the war that was so much a part of my life here, the war whose ghosts I was constantly mourning. I was walking around in a daze again, sitting by the side of the river, getting stoned, not sure where to go, whom to talk to, what to do. My father's trip was basically scuttled. He had gone to Los Angeles on business on September 10, then couldn't get home. He was trapped. We were all trapped. I'd been telling myself all year that living abroad was no big deal, that I was never more than a day's flight away. But now that wasn't true. There were no transatlantic flights. U.S. airports were closed. I was as trapped in Europe as my aunts and uncles and cousins were in that other war. I worried that someone at home would get sick and I wouldn't be able to go.

"I really want you to come," I told my dad on the phone, knowing that I was whining, that there was nothing he could do.

"I know you do, Erin. I'm trying," he said. He was on his cell phone, in a rental car, driving east. He got as far as Denver on September 13, where he secured a seat on a plane to Detroit, returned his rental car, and actually boarded the plane. But while he was waiting on the runway, another security risk shut the airport down. By then the rental car was gone, and my dad was forced to spend the night in an airport hotel. His flight to Poland actually took off on schedule Saturday morning, September 15, but my father wasn't on it. At that hour, he was on a plane from Denver to Detroit, trying to finish his last trip before beginning his next. I, alone, was left to loll by the side of the river, doing nothing, feeling down, overwhelmed by how much I missed him and how much more I was missing her.

By the time my father found his way from Los Angeles to Denver, from Denver to Detroit, and from the airport to his house and back to the airport—this time with a repacked bag and a ticket for a plane that was scheduled to and, in fact, did fly across the Atlantic and speed toward me—I was so grateful to receive him, and so badly in need of his insight and jest, that nothing but his visit at this time could have seemed more ideal. I tried to clear my mind of the vision I'd had of Mom and me doing Europe together, enjoying ourselves one minute, then, in the next minute, fighting the old fights: *You know, Erin, you really could afford to lose a few pounds,* she'd say as I would take offense. *You know, Mom, you really could afford to BACK OFF!* We would bicker for an hour, then forget this fight and move on to something else. Among the many traits that Mom and I shared—an easy threshold for tears, pale skin that burned after seconds in the sun, and a body shape of all legs, no torso—we also shared short memories for anger. Soon enough, we'd be giggling and gossiping again, executing mutually sharp social critiques and assuring each other that we were both the wittiest women we knew. In the end, we would not have had a fun trip. Ours, more likely, would have fallen into the category of emotional journey, but given my druthers, that would have been my preference. Not Mom. She'd have chosen fun trip (*For what do I need such tumult?* she'd have said). But I wanted to push the boundaries of her memory, to see what, if anything, she was hiding behind her flip demeanor on matters of the past. I wanted to see if the girl whose tears had smudged a photo in the back of a car might still be in there somewhere, might still, after all these years, be able to find some comfort.

I would have felt guilty. I would have spent the entire time wondering if I was selfishly pushing her for the singular purpose of fulfilling my own curiosity. I would have doubted my intentions, wondered if I was helping or merely causing pain. And in the end, I would have been disappointed. Mom would not have played along. She would have maintained her careful distance, her appropriate nods, her casual offhanded remarks, and I would have become frustrated with her seeming indifference.

What are you hiding, Mom? I'd have challenged her. *All of this, coming back here. You must be feeling SOMEthing!*

And she would have answered me abruptly: *Yes, Erin, I'm feeling like you are being a pain!*

Eventually, I'd have doubted my every theory, wondered if maybe, all along, she hadn't been pretending, if she'd always rolled with it, as she claimed. But I wondered: Could Mom have surprised me? Could the effect of being here, of having survived cancer in order to be here, of being here with me, have triggered something? A memory? A feeling? Might she have been moved to tell me the kinds of things that mothers tell their daughters when the time is right? Might we have spoken frankly for the first time in our lives? The wondering was the greatest grief of all. I could have come achingly close this year to cracking the complicated code of my mother. Instead, I lived now with the knowledge that my mother's truths would remain forever unspoken.

My father was less of a puzzle, his story more ordinary. He grew up in the Jewish neighborhoods of northwest Detroit, ran track at a Detroit public high school, and earned a teaching degree from a state university in Michigan. He partied more than he admitted, enlisted in the Army Reserves, then went to law school at night while working as a high school teacher because a law degree would exempt him from Reserve duty. He became a litigator who liked to win, whether trying a case or playing tennis against his daughter. It didn't matter how long we'd been playing or whether my feet hurt or whether I was begging to be allowed to go home and eat lunch, no one could leave the court until he had won a set. He ran a marathon at age forty-five and injured his shins because he wouldn't stop running when they started to hurt. He believed in constant motion, in never stopping. It was the reason he refused to sit in the Los Angeles airport, waiting for it to reopen. My dad had given me ambition and my capacity for dreams. But while I had always wanted to impress him, to succeed for him, and while he, too, had high expectations for his children, he never had the pull over me that my mother had. He never judged me as harshly or resented me as pointedly when I managed to let him down.

Mom and I were too similar to be kind to each other. We thought alike, acted alike. And when she felt that I had failed her—when I earned a B that should have been an A or lost a tennis match that should have been a win—it offended her in a personal way, throbbing in her as though my solitary goal had been causing her pain, and it always ended with slamming doors and cinematic tears. I pined intensely for the lost opportunity of my mother's visit to Poland, but I knew also that my father's visit would be easier, especially now. Dad and I would not travel to Będzin or meet the Skowrońskis. We would not visit Auschwitz. We would hang out in Krakow, take the tour of the Polish royal castle, and go to the salt chapel at the Wieliczka salt mine, where everything from the floor tiles to the chandeliers to the relief of the Last Supper on the chapel wall was all carved in salt. We would go to Rosh Hashanah services in the little Krakow shul, then make fun of the Jewish theme cafés. Circumstances would rob us of a truly fun trip, but ours would at least be lighter than the one I would have had with the parent who knew me too well.

A few hours before my father was scheduled to arrive—and half a day before Rosh Hashanah was set to begin—I called Magda to check on her and to show my support for her conversion by wishing her a happy New Year. Things were strange in New York, she told me. It was as though no one was in a hurry anymore. "The city's in slow motion," she said. I asked if she knew when she would come home, but she still wasn't sure. She had met with a rabbi about doing her conversion and was thinking of staying until the process was complete. She had started reading the necessary books, she said, and had seen a laser technician about removing her tattoo. That seemed extreme, I told her. The conversion ceremony was supposed to simulate rebirth; you became a new person. "It'd be like having a birthmark," I offered, but Magda seemed determined. "If I'm going to be Jewish, I can't have a tattoo," she said. I wondered if she was trying to say something about the iridescent bird that had perched on my leg since I was twenty-two. I had had it burned into my flesh to remind myself of the things I believed at the time. The flamboyant quetzal meant freedom to me—and possibility. I never cared about religious prohibitions. Like many secular Jews, I had a nuanced relationship with the religious aspects of Judaism. I wanted them to be a part of my life—an important part, even—but only in ways that neither defined me nor interfered with my other objectives. That was partly why I couldn't comprehend Magda's transformation, why she would want to subject herself to relentless rules and restrictions. I regretted that I hadn't explored these issues with her while she was still in Poland, but I had been so wary of offending her with probing questions that I'd never asked them, and now it seemed too late. We talked for a few more minutes, then hung up the phone.

I still wasn't sure what it was about Magda's conversion that bothered me. It had something to do with Poles and Jews and the awkwardness of our mutual histories. But I was unsettled, too, I think, by the notion that she was taking something that didn't belong to her. I was connecting that year with a Jewish side of myself that I had barely acknowledged before, and I was starting to feel like I owned a piece of this magnificent story, like I had inherited a sprawling past that had flourished in this part of Europe for hundreds of years. But if anybody could claim a piece of that story by reading a few books and saying some prayers, it didn't seem quite as special. I knew I was being stingy, but I regretted having to share the one thing I'd gained that year that couldn't be taken away.

When I collected my father from the airport and took him to his hotel to change for services, he was disappointed to learn that we wouldn't be able to sit together in the synagogue—he wasn't sure he'd be able to follow along—but when we arrived at our separate sanctuaries, he fared much better in his than I ever had in mine. High holiday services at the Rema shul—founded in 1553 by the family of Rabbi Moses Isserles—had been conducted for years by a Brooklyn rabbi and a group

of Brooklyn yeshiva students who made it their personal annual mitz-
vah to see that Krakow had a proper service during the holidays. As I
settled into a front-row seat in the women's section, just behind the lace
curtain that hung in the window between the women's section and the
men's, I could see my dad leaning in to the sanctuary from the doorway, covering his head with his hand because there were no yarmulkes
available at the door. I watched as the local Krakow rabbi removed his
hat from his head, produced a yarmulke from underneath, handed it to
Dad, then welcomed him in with a handshake. Throughout the service,
I could see different men introducing themselves to my father. Someone gave him a book in English that Dad later told me explained the
different parts of the service. The next morning, when they read from
the Torah, they gave my father the honor of holding the scrolls as they
were prepared for the ritual, a privilege usually given to members of a
congregation on special occasions or to mark an important event.

I was actually rather jealous. I had been living in Krakow, attending services every couple of weeks for nearly six months, and had never
felt welcome in the shul the way my father was that night. I had a few
friends in the women's section, including an American who worked at
the consulate and a Polish nun who believed—and eventually was able
to prove—that her war-orphan father was really a Jew. But I always
resented having to sit in the back, away from the core of the service.
As I watched my father's warm welcome, I wondered if things might
have been different for me if I were a man, if maybe I would have
found more of a place for myself in Krakow, at least in the small Jewish community. But over the course of the year, I had also come to
appreciate the dark and quiet of the synagogue's rear sanctuary. There
was something rather sweet about sitting and listening to the murmur-
ing that floated through the lace-covered windows. This was even more
true on that quiet first night of Rosh Hashanah, just days after the
terrorist attacks, when the front of the room filled with singing voices.
It was not unusual to see ultra-orthodox Hasidim in Krakow, wearing

black hats and side curls. They came from London or New York or Jerusalem to pray at the graves of holy men who were buried in Poland. But on that night, as the men in the front began to mutter, then hum, then sing, and as the cozy stone shul—with a wrought-iron *bima* in its heart and an elaborate stone statuary around its ark—filled with a lofty melody, the room began to have a wholly different feel. It might have been the Yiddish the men were speaking as they filed into the synagogue. It could have been the full, rich voices that gave their songs a plush splendor, but I had an overwhelming sense as I sat there that night that I had been delivered back to an earlier time. At precisely the moment when I no longer wanted to live in my own time, these men in sixteenth-century costume, singing sixteenth-century melodies in a sixteenth-century shul, were inviting me back to a time before there were airplanes or people who wanted to hijack them.

I'd often thought about history while sitting in this shul, but usually, I thought only as far back as the war. I'd noted that the room had a single door, that its windows were covered with bars. I'd wondered if the bars had been there in 1939, when someone might have thrown a lock on the door and a fire through the window. This was yet another of the Shoah's disheartening effects. The tiny Rema synagogue had stood on this spot for 468 years, and in all of the time I'd spent there, I'd thought about only six of them. I'd never considered the rabbi's young wife in 1757, looking proudly through the curtain as her eldest son read the Torah for the first time, or tried to imagine the anger on a father's face in 1905 when he noticed that his son wasn't there, that he'd gone off to a political meeting. That night, though, I felt like I could smell the melting wax of candles in the chandelier. I felt like I could see the men who had built this shul, hunched over their books, davening like their fathers before them and like their sons in their wake, like the men I could see that day on the other side of the curtain, praying and singing and welcoming a man from the future, my father, who wasn't familiar with their ways.

My time-travel fantasy was lovely, but it was also false. On Yom Kippur I would meet one of the young yeshiva students from Brooklyn and would hear him boast that he and his friends were members of an Orthodox Jewish ambulance service and that they had been among the only first responders at the World Trade Center who hadn't sustained major injuries. "And why do you think that was?" I asked, suspecting that this was mainly because they hadn't gone inside. The young man seemed pleased that I'd asked; his face took on a satisfied smile. "You tell me," he said, lifting his eyebrows for effect. "We were all Orthodox Jews." I asked if that was why he thought his unit hadn't sustained casualties, and he responded defensively, "I'm not saying that. I'm just saying that God didn't want us to die. That's all." And that, roughly, was the moment when he produced a stack of glossy photos taken before and after the towers collapsed, complete with pictures of severed limbs and pools of blood. We had just finished breaking the Yom Kippur fast with huge trays of kosher Chinese food that the rabbi and his students had brought frozen with them from New York. It was a feast they sponsored every year for the entire community in the dining room of the Eden Hotel. I took one look at this man's photos and became sickened. I excused myself, left the room, and abandoned my time-travel fantasy forever.

My father had always existed in the considerable shadow that my mother had cast on my life. When we talked over the years, it was usually about her, usually because she and I were fighting and I was trying to convert my father to my point of view. But during his visit to Poland, in five days of visiting museums and hiking in the Tatras, the Polish Alps, I decided it was time for my father and me to have a new kind of relationship. I had always kept my personal life far from my parents, since I never trusted my mom enough to let either of them in, but things had been starting to change with my mom. I had actually told her about David. A few days before she died, when she was in the hospital, I told her that he was coming to visit me, that he was someone I was looking forward to seeing. And on this vacation with my father, I decided to let him in, too. I told him that Dave and I were in touch again, that we had found some cheap phone cards online and had been talking almost every day for several weeks, sometimes for as long as an hour. I told him that David had called me the minute he heard about the towers, and that this time he knew exactly what to say. And I told my father that I thought I was falling in love. "You're not in love," my father said. "You barely know that guy." That was true, I said, but I said I was trying to at least stay open to the possibility. I told him I regretted using grief as an excuse to push David away and that I wouldn't make that mistake again.

When my father asked about the Skowrońskis, I gave him a play-by-play of the kill-off-the-dead, inherit-the-house saga, then asked him the legal question that had been troubling me: "If I file a claim in which I state that I am the only heir, would that be fraud?" My father moved his head back and forth as he considered my question. His law practice had focused in recent years on defending judges facing disciplinary boards. He also handled legal malpractice cases and other matters that, over the years, had called for, well, squishy definitions of fraud.

"Look," he said. "You can't have fraud unless someone has been defrauded, so the question you need to ask yourself is: Who is the victim? You're not going to gain financially. Most likely you'll lose thousands of dollars and gain nothing, so the only victim here would be you."

This didn't seem like much of an answer. "So if it's victimless fraud, it's okay?" I asked.

Dad raised an eyebrow as he looked at me. "You mean morally? Is that really your question? What I'm saying is that if it's a victimless fraud, no one will complain."

Dad insisted I talk to at least two more lawyers before hiring Borcz, and when I took him to the airport, I told him I'd see to it immediately. He hugged me and told me not to stay in Poland longer than necessary.

"Just finish what you came here to do and come home," he said.

"Sure thing," I answered, wishing I knew what I had come to do.

Over the next few weeks, I followed my father's instructions and visited three more lawyers, but they all agreed with Borcz on the basic legal process needed to help the Skowrońskis. One lawyer—a formal professional in a pin-striped suit—was appalled when I asked if I needed to name all of my great-grandparents' heirs in my inheritance claim. "You could lie, miss," he told me in a haughty tone. "But you would need a different kind of lawyer." Another lawyer refused to take the case at all, saying it would be too much trouble. And the third lawyer took offense in the opposite direction of the first. She became insulted when I asked, after she suggested that I name only one heir per branch of the family, if this would constitute fraud. "It is not fraud!" she insisted. "Not fraud! It is how it is in Poland." She was so angry that she demanded I pay her immediately, even though she'd originally told me she wouldn't charge for an initial meeting. "You give me money for time," she said. "I do not work for free."

CHAPTER FOURTEEN

T HE FIRST DOZEN TIMES WE HAD THE DEBATE, I REMAINED PATIENT.
I explained, more or less calmly, that the process would take time,
that I was doing my best, that I was collecting documents and reaching
out to my family for help. But every time I visited the Skowrońskis,
things became increasingly querulous. Helen and Wiesław continued
to insist that my grandfather—not my great-grandfather—owned the
house and that the solution to their problems would come in the form
of a sworn statement from my mother. They had been discussing their
situation with me for months. I had brought Borcz to see them and to
explain the legal issues. I had talked them, step by step, through the
process I was planning to pursue. But they continued to disagree with
my methods, and now they seemed to be shifting a least a part of the
blame for their problems on to me. I tried to defend myself, to explain
that I was trying to help, but I could feel my composure dissolving
along with my greatest hopes that our families would again be friends
someday. "But the documents . . ." I argued, choking on my words.

I was sitting with Krys in Wiesław's living room one stressful evening in early October and could feel my frustration welling into tears. I bit down on my lip, forcing my eyelids into a vigorous blink. I looked at Krys with pleading eyes. I had brought him with me to translate, but I needed help with more than language. Krys had lived with me through these long, emotional months and could tell in a single glance that I was about to start crying. "Erin's under a lot of pressure," he announced to whoever was listening, "her mother is sick." As soon as Krys spoke, I could feel the weight easing off my neck. I wanted to smile at him, to thank him, but I followed his cue and stayed in character. "Remember, I told you she had cancer," I added in Polish. "The doctors aren't very positive." I looked over at Wiesław to see if this might soften his stance and watched as he nodded slowly and closed his eyes in a deliberate blink. "Irka may even have to go home to see her mother soon," Krys said, using his name for me in Polish. "It's true," I said. And then, though this wasn't necessary and our point had been made, I pushed still further. I told the Skowrońskis that my mother had been hospitalized in mid-September, that we feared she would die. I told them I had tried to go home to see her but had been stuck in Poland with American airports closed after September 11. Helen and her daughter Marta clucked and shook their heads as Wiesław looked sadly down at the table. "It was horrible," Krys said. "Irka was sobbing. She was scared that her mother would die without her."

"And how is she now?" Wiesław asked. I felt a stroke of guilt for enjoying his concern. "She's better," I said, pulling back a bit. "She's home from the hospital now." Then I took the charade another cruel step forward. "I need to go home soon because things are still uncertain with her," I said. "But I want to stay in Poland until this property matter is resolved. I want to be sure to leave your family in good hands." I regretted my words even as I spoke them. They were deceitful, used to take advantage of my fictionally sick mother in the worst, most manipulative way. But the words had left my lips before I could contain them and once they were out in the air, they couldn't be retracted. I wasn't even sure why I was still lying about my mom. At first I sincerely wanted to spare Wiesław the sting of bad news. Then I wanted to spare myself the burden of delivering that news. Eventually, I came to cherish the fact that here, in the place where my mother was born, she was still alive. But in real life, she had been dead for five months, and I couldn't find a way to surrender this indulgence.

"You think I went too far?" I asked Krys in the car on the way home. "No," he said. "They deserved it, these people. I don't like them." I suggested that Krys just didn't like that they talked at the same time and made it hard for him to translate, but while he acknowledged that he did hate that, his dislike of the Skowrońskis was larger. "Maybe you did go a little too far," he said. "But these people! They're so rude! They give Polish people a bad name. They're Silesian, too, which makes it worse for me. They speak the same dialect as my parents." He started to go off on the funny-sounding words in the Silesian dialect that his parents and the Skowrońskis all used, but I cut him off. "Krys," I said. "Don't you think I owe them something? I mean, they did save my mother."

He was smoking a cigarette and exhaled a large cloud of smoke. "*They* didn't save your mother. Honorata saved your mother. These people—that fat blabbermouth, Helen," he nearly spit her name. "She would have probably turned her mother-in-law in to the Gestapo." I objected that this wasn't fair. "Maybe not," he said. "But these people didn't do anything. And anyway, you *are* helping them. You talked to these lawyers. You're going to become a Polish citizen for them." He stabbed his cigarette out in the ashtray and laughed. "Actually, I like that part."

Krys didn't hate the Skowrońskis as intensely as the venom of his words suggested—at least I didn't think he did—but he'd been a good friend to me. For months he had patiently listened to my lamentations across the bar at the Eden Hotel. He'd heard my concerns about the property and the lawyers and the money and the complications, and when he saw the Skowrońskis doubting my efforts, he took offense on my behalf. Now, in the car, he was defending me from my own self-recriminations. But Krys's assurances aside, the Skowrońskis didn't deserve to be lied to. They had a legitimate problem that my family had played a role in creating. It was, after all, our house. And despite the broadly held Jewish position that Poland and Poles shared responsibility for the holocaust, the circumstances that resulted in our leaving the house had nothing to do with them. In fact, none of these problems would have existed at all if not for the bravery and sacrifice of Honorata Skowrońska. Whatever her motives, she had protected my mother from the fate of millions of others. She not only saved my mother, she also found resources to feed and care for her at a time of severe shortage. She had choices to make, and I owed her a debt of gratitude for having made the right ones. I really did want to help, but Helen's nagging and impatience had begun to wear on me. I now dreaded my trips to Będzin, hoping each time that my next visit would be better, but each time finding that the friction between us only became more pronounced.

That early-October visit with Krys had been particularly unpleasant, perhaps because it came at the end of a very long day. Krys and I were both exhausted. I had dragged him out on his day off to help me tour monasteries and convents in the area around Będzin. Knowing there were Catholic institutions that sheltered Jewish children during the war, I thought maybe I could find one with a record of a girl meeting the description of my mother's cousin who was abandoned on a streetcar. During one of my genealogy trips to Będzin, I had located her birth record. She was, in fact, a girl. Her name was Zilla—presumably Tsile in Yiddish—and she was born on March 19, 1943. That meant she was four months old when the Będzin ghetto was liquidated, and the odds of surviving were remote. The odds that she had both survived and somehow learned her true identity such that I could track her down were nearly impossible. But I wanted at least to make an attempt, to knock on a few doors and make a cursory effort.

Krys and I made three stops that day, all unsuccessful. Most institutions that hid Jewish children did not keep records, we were told. The existence of such records during the war would have implicated and imperiled the entire order. We did have one promising moment when a young nun—her convent's historian—heard what we were seeking and ran eagerly to collect a pile of research she had done on the subject. Her convent had saved a number of children during the war, she proudly told us, and had kept secret records. She brought us a black-and-white photo of a group of girls in school uniforms, each with a wooden cross around her neck. "This one," she said, grinning, her hand shaking with nervous energy as she pointed to a small girl in the front. "This little angel was abandoned on our doorstep." Krys looked at me as a remarkable possibility lofted in the air above us. We asked about the age of the girl, how old she had been when she arrived, but the nun checked her records and said the girl was about three when she appeared in 1943. "It wasn't her," I said, disappointed. The nun wouldn't give up easily. "Maybe our facts are wrong," she said. "Or maybe yours are." But no, I said. "I wish you were right, but this isn't her." There were many children left on doorsteps. There was no reason to believe that this girl, three years older than Zilla, was my mother's long-lost cousin. "It's okay," the nun said by way of comfort as we stood to leave. "I heard, anyway, that the girl died after the war, on a boat to Palestine."

Krys and I visited another convent and were truly dragging that evening when we pulled in after dark to the courtyard behind 20 Małachowskiego. We were irritable and probably should have skipped the visit, given the circumstances, but I had called ahead to tell the Skowrońskis that we would stop by and thought it would be rude to cancel. Our visit began pleasantly. The Skowrońskis, as always, greeted us warmly and served us coffee. I'd brought them a bag of French roast from Krakow, which they spooned into juice glasses for us and stirred with boiling water. This was called Turkish-style coffee in Poland. It meant unfiltered. We made small talk and shook our heads over the recent events in New York and Washington. I told them that the Jewish holidays had just taken place and that I had gone to religious services. This piqued their interest. Wiesław's daughter, Marta, asked about services and what happened in a synagogue. I told her, partly in my own Polish, partly through Krys, that men and women sat separately in the Krakow synagogue, that women dressed very modestly, and that men covered their heads. Krys modeled the yarmulke he carried in his bag for when he gave synagogue tours. Then the conversation took a disturbing turn.

"Do you eat anything at these ceremonies?" Helen asked. "Eat anything? No," I answered. Krys told her that Jews didn't take communion but did use wine for ceremony. Still, Helen persisted. "Aren't there cakes or something?" she asked. I was puzzled by this and wondered if maybe she was talking about Jewish apple cake, which you could still buy in Polish bakeries, but then Helen added something to clarify her question that I didn't quite catch. Whatever it was, it caused Krys's eyes to widen with alarm. He drew in a breath and quickly started talking: "*Nie, nie, nie, nie, nie!*" he said, waving his hands vigorously back and forth. "No, no, no, no, no! This is . . . it's nothing like that!" he said. He added something else very quickly in an urgent tone. Helen nodded, seeming unfazed. "That's interesting," she said, bobbing her head with comprehension. I turned anxiously to Krys for translation, but he shook his head. "I'll tell you later," he muttered. "You can't tell me now?" I asked. He looked over at me, trying to decide whether to tell me or to wait. "What is it?" I asked. Krys squirmed for a minute before letting out an uncomfortable sigh. Helen, he said, had asked about cakes with blood in them. She'd heard that Jews ate "some kind of blood-filled cake."

I wasn't nearly as alarmed by this as Krys was. I felt quite certain that Helen was innocently inquiring about something she'd heard once, probably decades earlier, completely oblivious to the fact that she was casually repeating the oldest and most virulent lie in the global history of anti-Semitism—that Jews used the blood of Christian babies to make Passover matzo. Krys had intercepted this mistake, set the record straight, and, I think, tried to prevent me from knowing what was said. I think he feared how Helen's question would fold into my understanding, generally, of Poland and anti-Semitism. I think he was worried about how I'd retell the story later, using it as an example for friends at home to support what they thought they already knew about Poland. I told Krys not to make more of it than what it was, that Helen's question was the product of ignorance, not of bigotry. But for him, her ignorance was an affront to his national pride.

Krys loved Poland. Unlike most of his friends, who had taken their college degrees and found higher-paying jobs in Western Europe or the United States, he had chosen to stay and make a life here. He didn't want the backward thinking of this narrow-minded woman to stain the whole nation. There was a piece of this, I think, in his anti-Skowroński tirade in the car on the way home. He was genuinely one of the good ones—a man with a big heart who had every right to take umbrage when Jews suggested that Poles were anti-Semites. Working in a hotel that catered to Jewish tourists, he had endured hours of anti-Polish invective without license to object. He seemed not to mind, seemed to put it in its place the same way white Americans could talk about white racists without necessarily including themselves. But I knew that it bothered him. Helen's question had offended him in a visceral way. And in the car on the way home, he made a point of distancing himself from the Helen Skowrońskas of the world.

Krys and I extended the conversation about Helen and her question, and me and my lies, through the car ride, through a walk across the old city, through a stroll to Kazimierz, and to a hidden table in our favorite dark and smoky pub—a place on the corner of two narrow streets that was filled with antique sewing machines. In the hazy red light of the bar, I played with the iron wheel on the side of our table's Singer sewing machine, rotating it back and forth with my hand. I asked Krys if maybe there were class issues here, if maybe he disdained the Skowrońskis because they were poor and uneducated. But he rejected that. "No way," he said. "Lots of people are poor and uneducated. But these people . . ." He shook his head. We had been trashing them for hours, but it didn't feel right. "I really want to like them," I said. "So like them," he answered. "But I don't."

I didn't believe that Helen hated Jews, and now that Krys had corrected her, I didn't think she suspected the use of Christian blood in Jewish rituals. But her question did expose a basic conundrum: If she had that misperception about Jews, she probably had the other ones, too. I wasn't just a Jew, I was an American Jew. I must have money to spare—gobs of it—and if I were a decent person, I would give some of my fortune to the family who had made my life possible. It wasn't Wiesław who constantly harped about the money and real estate. He chimed in, of course, and offered his opinions about what he said was promised to whom, but it was mostly his wife who brought up the property issue. This was surely because she was the one who paid the bills and felt the sting of these tribulations most acutely, but feeling like it was her whom I was trying to help was no great motivator. Helen never even knew my mom. I had no idea what her family did during the war, and somehow, I just couldn't get energized about helping the second wife of the son of the woman who had hidden my mother. I didn't know what my grandfather had or hadn't promised in 1945 when he left the house in Honorata's hands, but even if he had made the promise the Skowrońskis said he made, should his promise continue for eternity? Will my children, too, bear the weight of this debt?

Honorata's bravery had already lasted beyond her lifetime. Her act of saving my mom had led to two more lives—my brother's and mine. Our lives had triggered a chaos of events that would reverberate long into the future. It made sense that Honorata's reward should extend to the future, to her children and grandchildren, but every time they pressured me about the house, it became that much harder for me to help them. They had been undeniably hospitable. They had welcomed me into their home and submitted to personal questions about their family and their lives. I had queried them about God and work and culture—questions, Krys told me, that weren't often asked in Poland. And they had answered everything without objection. They had served meals, even with their humble resources. They always endeavored to welcome me into their home. But the blaring presence of their outside agenda continued to overwhelm their generosity. As much as I wanted to accept their kindness at face value, I had to wonder if in a small way or maybe even a significant way, they saw me as a cash machine.

I was doing what I could for them. A month earlier, I'd traveled to Warsaw to have a letter notarized at the Israeli embassy that called on the Righteous committee at Yad Vashem to award the same medal of honor to Wiesław that, twenty years earlier, it had extended to his mother. In my letter, which needed the Israeli notary seal per the museum's requirements, I argued that if Honorata had been Righteous, her son had been, too. As a teen who both helped his mother and kept her secret, he had faced the same risks that she had. I made this application hoping Wiesław would win the medal and start receiving the financial compensation his mother once had. It was something I could do in the short term while the longer-term solution sorted itself out. But while the Skowrońskis appreciated this gesture, it paled in comparison to the larger gesture that they so anxiously awaited. I knew that until they could again collect rent from their tenants, we would never have the relationship that once had been my dream.

CHAPTER FIFTEEN

YEARS LATER, WHEN HER YOUNGEST CHILD WOULD BESEECH HER for memories, my mother would insist that Poland had all but vanished from her mind, discarded like old phone numbers and long-ago assignments for school. She would have no recollection of Hono-rata Skowrońska, or of the three Skowroński sons who had seen to her needs. She would not recall the orphanage where she lived for a year, or how it was that she came to live there. Forty years later, after Swe-den and California, after high school and college in Detroit, after my mother birthed a son and then a daughter, there would remain of her life in Poland exactly one memory that she could pass to the next gen-eration: It was late in 1946, and Irena Frydrych, a few months shy of her fifth birthday, was about to be uprooted for the third time in her life. "I remember when he came for me again," Mom told me when I interviewed her for my high school newspaper. Her father had ap-peared at the orphanage and announced that he was taking her away. "This was the second time I had seen this man," Mom said. "Each time I see him, he takes me away from where I'm comfortable. I screamed."

She had no memory of the first time her father had come for her, she told me, but in this memory, of the second time, she recalled that she recognized him, that she knew his arrival portended disruption.

I pictured Mom in orphan's clothes, her red hair unkempt, her tiny fingers curled around the neck of a tattered doll, looking up at her father and bawling. Mom remembered the sting on her father's face that day. He had risked his life to save hers. He had turned over riches to a stranger for her. And now he had come for her, to reconnect with the only other member of his household who had survived, and she was inconsolable. "I screamed the whole time he was there," Mom said. "The minute I saw him, I started to scream, and I didn't stop screaming until he left." Mom remembered the trauma of the train ride to Sweden as she sat beside him, not sure who he was or where they were going. I remembered hearing this story from my mother and feeling the tug of my grandfather's heartbreak, the pull of my mother's fear.

In trying to reconstruct my mother's young life, I often considered this moment from her last days in Poland, wondering how the anguish of that time lived on in the tension that later came between my mother and her father. It was one of the few aspects of my mother's story that, since she'd given me a firsthand account and not a retelling, I considered unassailable—so solid it didn't need to be verified. I was absolutely astonished when, entirely by accident, in an archive I'd entered in search of something else, I stumbled across the news that my mother's only memory of Poland—the one moment she could recall from the first years of her life—was nothing more than the conjured figment of a child's imagination. At best, it was a concoction of other events that happened later or occurred in different ways. At worst, it was the product of fiction.

My mother's memory, I discovered, was not the only record of that final day at the orphanage. As it happened, there was a second version that, for decades, had been tucked away in the dusty files of the child-care division of Poland's Central Jewish Committee in Warsaw. And

if the child-care division in 1946 was to be believed, then my mother
never did scream at the sight of her father when he came for her in the
orphanage. She never did sit in terror beside him on a train as it bar-
reled north toward the Baltic Sea. According to the child-care division,
on the day when my mother left the orphanage for Sweden, her father
wasn't even there. The true story of my mother's reunion with her father emerged for me on a wet and windy day in mid-October, a day on
which I'd awakened before dawn to catch the three-hour express train
to Warsaw.

As on most of my previous visits to the capital, I walked immediately
from the train station, around the remarkably dominant and towering
Palace of Culture and Science, and through a network of windswept
streets to the three-story building in the shadow of a 1980s-era office
tower that housed one of Poland's greatest troves of historical treasures.
Since its founding in 1947, the Jewish Historical Institute had brought
together the surviving collections of Jewish archives and libraries after
the war. Through the Soviet years, everything that was even remotely
Jewish had ended up there, in various conditions and order. Now, with
the help of a basic database that was strikingly efficient compared to the
tattered pages and notecards at most Polish archives, the institute was
an impressive resource. The first time I visited, I came for Honorata's
Yad Vashem file, where I read her testimonies on how and why she'd
saved my mom. The second time I came for the Będzin ghetto records,
where I found documents declaring the seizure of my family's home
and factory as well as papers ordering members of my family to report
at certain hours to certain locations for certain work details. This time
I came in search of my mother's cousin Zilla, whose birth certificate
had just provided me with her name, her age, and—I hoped—enough
information to make a final attempt to find her.

I had called ahead to make an appointment with a man who, at the
time, was considered the guru of Jewish research in Poland: an American named Yale Reisner who worked at the institute but insisted, if I

ever used his name in print, that I mention the Ronald S. Lauder Foundation, which funded his position. Yale had been helpful to me in the
past, giving me tips on where to look for documents. This time I called,
described the cousin I was trying to find, and wondered if Yale could
provide any guidance. He made no promises. "It's a long shot," he said,
"but you never know. We've found people with less." I was actually
optimistic when I sat down in his cramped office and watched as he
queried his database. A part of me thought it was actually possible that
Yale would enter Zilla's information and my long-lost cousin would
emerge like candy from a vending machine. But the hopes that I had
foolishly inflated withered quickly. The historical institute's database
was driven by names. There was no way at the time to search for someone who was too young to have known her name; there was no way to
isolate children left on streetcars or even children who were adopted.
The only way to find Zilla, I was told, would be to contact nearly every
woman of her approximate age in the database. I exhaled a gloomy sigh
and sank low in my chair. There would be no reunion with Zilla. "It
may not feel like actually looking for her," Yale said at the sight of my
disappointment. "But her record's here now. If she's out there and she's
searching, she'll eventually come here. And when she does, she'll find
this." I nodded in agreement but couldn't figure how it'd be any easier
for Zilla to find me than for me to find her. I wondered why I had even
bothered to make this futile attempt. In truth, I knew that Zilla was
dead. Most likely, she'd never even made it off that streetcar.

I was so focused on Zilla, on mourning the cousin who had lived so
briefly, that I wasn't paying attention when Yale opened a new screen
and began to type. When I looked up, I could see that he'd written
Frydrych and *Będzin* into the fields. I shook my head, thinking this
wouldn't find Zilla. Then a name appeared across the top of the screen.
It said *Franka Frydrych*, a name I'd never heard. It wasn't Zilla, because
the birth date was wrong, but out of curiosity, I wrote down the name.
"This doesn't mean she was from Będzin," Yale said, "just that Będzin

is mentioned in her file. She may have passed through or lived there for a time. It's hard to know." I drew a question mark in my notebook next to her name, wondering if Franka's file would be worth reading. Then another name appeared on Yale's screen. Not sure I was reading correctly, I blinked twice to be certain. I had spent countless hours in this country tediously scanning lists of names, searching genealogical records, ghetto records, property records in hopes of spotting my grandparents, their siblings, their parents. This name wasn't one I had ever thought to look for, but there it was: Irena Frydrych.

"Someone you know?" Yale smiled as I shook my head in disbelief. I leaned in closer to read the birth date beside the name. It was February 20, 1942, and this was my mom. "Direct hit," Yale said. He clicked on the record. "It's a child welfare file," he said. I had been so upset about losing Zilla, about feeling that my quest for her was a failure, that I had nearly forgotten it wasn't Zilla who had brought me to Poland in the first place. It was the other little girl in hiding whose story I had come to discover. As Yale left to locate my mother's file, I waited anxiously in his office, thinking about how my most treasured discoveries that year were those I hadn't expected to find. I never imagined that I'd unearth my grandmother's photo in Washington or my mother's birth certificate in Będzin. I hadn't expected to locate Zilla's birth record, either. I'd been so focused since my mother died on how much I couldn't have, how much of my dream I'd had to abandon, but there were still many secrets here to reveal. I wondered if there was perhaps more truth in the pages I was reading than could be found in my mother's disinterested eyes.

Yale returned to his office with an army-green folder marked with my mother's name: FRYDRYCH, IRENA, 1946. Inside, were scattered pages— memos, telegrams, slightly yellowed on thinning pieces of paper—that, in an abstract, bureaucratic way, chronicled a year of my mother's life. The truth of my mother's journey from Poland to Sweden—with a social worker named S. Ulwainay and not, as she remembered, with her father—was the file's most stunning revelation. But other remarkable details were also brought to light, both about my mother's life at the time and about the world around her as it reeled from the shock of war. There was a confusion, a kind of postwar chaos, reflected in the memos. My mother's name was spelled in myriad ways; the details ducked and weaved. When I later showed the memos to Krys, he pointed out the interesting ways he could see the Communist structure emerging through the year as memo writers moved from addressing each other with the traditional Polish greetings of *Pan* and *Pani,* Mr. and Mrs., in late 1945 to, by the summer and into the fall of 1946, *comrade* and *citizen.* Various committees began to change their names, too, to ones that sounded more typically politburo. The Polish grammar, Krys told me, was poor, suggesting the memo writers were not native Polish speakers. They may have come from abroad to help with the refugee crisis, or they may have been Jews better schooled in Hebrew. Together, these pages told the story of a family and a world that had been shattered, of loved ones trying to reunite, and of an overwhelmed bureaucracy trying to glue together the pieces of a continent ripped apart in ways both literal and symbolic.

The first page in the file was a typewritten note on a half sheet of paper, shiny with age, that captured the sense of desperation that must have existed in the aftermath of the war:

From: The Central Polish Jewish Committee in Warsaw
To: The Jewish Committee of Będzin
November 10, 1945

We hereby refer to the committee with a request to locate Ida Fryderyk, six years old, daughter of Berek Fryderyk of Będzin. She is staying with Honorata Karwowski, living on Kołłątaja 45. It's possible that the here above mentioned stays under a different name. We are waiting for an answer as soon as possible because we would like to inform the girl's family in the United States.

       —Gen. Secretary Zelicki and Vice President Herszenhora

I was fascinated by this memo and by the circumstances that had led to its creation. It showed clearly that my relatives in Detroit knew that Beresh had a daughter and that the daughter was in the care of a woman named Honorata, but their information was sketchy. They weren't sure of my mother's name or age. They were off on Honorata's last name. Years later, when I heard the 1984 interview with my great-uncle Laybish, I learned that Honorata had reached out to my family. "That woman call," Laybish told my cousin Gloria on that old cassette recording. "She say that she got my brother's baby and we should come and get her. And then we found out that Beresh is alive so we let Beresh know and Beresh went to Będzin and took the child away." But back in Yale's office when I first saw this memo, I wondered how my family had known anything about my mom. The whole of her life had existed during a war, and essentials like her name and age must have been difficult to convey. When the war was over, the Frydrychs of Detroit did the best they could to launch a search for Ida, age six, instead of Irena, age three and a half. It's hard to know if this memo was the result of Honorata's call or if it had been written earlier. Back in Detroit, the news from Europe had landed like a bomb. Entire families had been obliterated, communities erased. As far as the Frydrychs of Detroit knew, their family back in Będzin was gone: Yisruel and Zisl were dead. Shloyme and Rudl Ester, Duvid Oyzer and Baltsha, Yankl and Heltsha, Liba and Shmil Biber. Big Gutsha, Little Gutsha, Abramek. At first they assumed that Beresh, too, had been murdered along with the young bride whom no one in Detroit had even met. But one hope remained: two babies in hiding—the daughters of Beresh and Duvid Oyzer. I imagined frantic letters to authorities in Poland, asking them to find these girls. I assumed another memo had gone out looking for Zilla, but Yale had no such record and my cousin who interviewed Laybish never asked about Zilla.

My mother's file had no documents from the early days of 1946. There was nothing announcing her arrival in the orphanage and no document marking my grandfather's return to the displaced person's camp in Germany. There was no record confirming Laybish's memory that my grandfather had contacted his family to tell them he had survived, but family folklore had it that my grandfather's family in Detroit advised him to move to Sweden, where the wait for American visas was said to be shorter. The next memo in the file, from the summer of 1946, came as my grandfather initiated that move. This was in Polish:

> To: Central Polish Jewish Committee
> From: Judiska Transmigrationskommittén, Stockholm
> Re: Irena Frydrych
> June 27, 1946
>   We hereby declare that we have submitted an application for a Swedish entry visa for Mr. Bernard Frydrych and his four-year-old daughter Irena. The father is now in Bergen-Belsen camp B1.82.M.10. According to the information from the National Refugee Service in New York, the girl is in a Jewish children's institution near Koenigshuette. We kindly ask you to contact the Swedish Embassy in Warsaw.

Koenigshuette, Yale told me, was the German name for the Polish city of Chorzów, where there had been a large Jewish orphanage. He turned to pull a file from a shelf in his office and, sure enough, located my mother's name on the registration list for the Chorzów orphanage, about halfway down the list: *Irena Frydrych, born in 1942, Będzin.* Yale scanned the list of orphans. "This is actually pretty interesting," he said. "This guy's on the faculty at Georgetown University." He pointed to one of the names. "This lady I saw the other day. She's a famous Polish writer. Oh, and I know this guy, too. He's a big Jewish philanthropist. Your mother was in good company."

The next memo, on the stationery of the Judiska Transmigrationskommittén in Stockholm, was issued two weeks later, in a grammatically challenged English:

Re: Irene Frydrich
Jewish Children's Institution, near Koenigshuette, Poland
July 10, 1946

Gentlemen,

We have pleasure in informing you that Swedish entry visa was granted
on 3rd inst. in behalf of the above. Irene being 4th years old only, we
would particularly appreciate your assisting the child in every possible
way to emigrate from Poland. As you learned from our Polish letter of
June 27th, the father of the girl is, at present, residing in Germany and
was also granted Swedish entry visa.

> *Very sincerely yours,*
> *For Judiska Transmigrationskommittén,*
> *Dr. K. Stillschweig*

With this letter, the postwar Jewish child-care bureaucracy in Poland
had simple instructions. It needed to notify Irena Frydrych's orphanage that the girl was to be prepared to travel to Sweden. But according
to the memos, there was a problem: Irena, it seemed, had been mis-
placed. Though she'd obviously been registered at the Jewish children's
home in Koenigshuette/Chorzów, orphanage officials now reported
that the child was no longer there—and they weren't quite sure where
she was. As the memos told the story, the bureaucracy went into a
scramble. Records were checked, institutions consulted. This went on
for at least two months, until September 17, 1946, when a memo
arrived in Warsaw from a *prewentorium* in a town in lower Silesia
that had just changed its name from Gieszcze Puste to Głuszyca confirming that Irena was with them. *We enclose the photographs of Irena*
Frydrych, the management of the *prewentorium* wrote to the director
of the Central Polish Jewish Committee. *The child arrived from the*
orphanage in Chorzów. She was born probably in the year 1942. We have
no other data.

I wasn't sure why my mom was in a *prewentorium*, which I assumed was a medical facility. Mom never mentioned any kind of illness. Later, when I ran this by my father, he, too, was stumped, but he offered a theory that stemmed from the time in the mid-1970s when my brother and I were rushed to the pediatrician to be tested for tuberculosis. Mom had come down with pneumonia and had checked herself in to the hospital, claiming there was no way she could recover at home with two young children there. The doctors, as a precaution, ordered that Mom be tested for other diseases and were alarmed when she tested positive for TB. I remembered the strangely shaped mark on my arm, the small square of indentations that we were told to watch. Derek and I were given little cards showing the different patterns that could appear in the square, each with a different significance. Mom, as it turned out, did not have TB, at least not at that time in the 1970s. She had pneumonia—and child-care fatigue. Derek and I were perfectly healthy. But this episode when we were kids could explain Mom's stay in the *prewentorium* back in 1946. If she'd had TB as a child, she still would have tested positive for it thirty years later.

TELEGRAM
FROM: STOCKHOLM
TO: WARSAW
OURS JULY 10 AND AUGUST 26 RE IRENE FRYDRYCH
UNANSWERED STOP FATHER ALREADY ARRIVED
SWEDEN STOP ACCELERATE DEPARTURE CHILD STOP
MATTER EXTREMELY URGENT STOP CABLE REPLY =
JUDISKA TRANSMIGRATIONSKOMMITTEN+

It was impossible to know why my mother so distinctly remembered her father at the orphanage. Perhaps the man who came for her there looked like her father, and the two became connected in her mind. Or maybe the memory of seeing him approach was something that happened later, when she first saw him in Sweden, or when he first came to visit her in the foster home. But whatever the acrobatics performed by my mother's memory, there was no question that her journey from the orphanage in Poland to the foster home in Sweden had been a difficult one. In fact, the memos chronicle a journey that was possibly even more traumatic than the one she recalled. It involved a mix of people taking her to a jumble of places over a stretch of at least eight days. My mother was delivered from one place to the next as a kind of package that needed, at every turn, to be signed for. These memos were in Polish:

To: Foreign Affairs Ministry, division of passports and visas.
October 22, 1946:

The childcare division of the Central Polish Jewish Committee hereby appoints the citizen Mgr. Ignacego Tenenwurcla to receive the passport for Irena Frydrych, a ward of the Children's Home of Chorzów. Also we would like to mention that Irena Frydrych will be under our care during her trip to Sweden.

To: The Board of the Central Polish Jewish Committee
October 24, 1946:

The childcare division of the Central Polish Jewish Committee requests 1,200 złoty in order to obtain a passport for the ward of the orphanage in Chorzów Irena Frydrych.

Handwritten note, October 31, 1946:

The passport and Swedish entry visa for Irena Frydrych has been obtained. A telegram has been sent calling Irena Frydrych to Warsaw for disposal by the childcare department.

To: Children's Home of Chorzów, Katowiscka 21, Chorzów
From: Central Polish Jewish Committee

Send Frydrych, Irena immediately to the disposal of the Childcare Division in Warsaw, Sienna 60. There is a passport and a visa.

To: The Central Polish Jewish Committee
From: Children's Home of Chorzów
November 4, 1946

We've received the passport and entry visa for Irena Frydrych. We wired Gieszcze Puste to send us the child.

To: Prewentorium for Children, Grunwaldzka 33, Gieszcze Puste, Lower Silesia

Send Frydrych, Irena. There is a passport and a visa.

To: Central Polish Jewish Committee
From: Children's Home of Chorzów
November 10, 1946

The management of the Jewish Orphanage in Chorzów, according to the telegram, sends Irena Frydrych to be at the disposal of the Central Polish Jewish Committee.

To: Children's Home of Śródborów
From: Central Polish Jewish Committee
November 11, 1946

The childcare division of the Central Polish Jewish Committee sends Frydrych Irena, five years old, to the orphanage. The girl is to stay in the orphanage until her departure abroad.

To: Temporary shelter, Warsaw, Targowa 62
From: Central Polish Jewish Committee
November 12, 1946
  We hereby send you Frydrych, Irena, four years old, who is just about to leave for Sweden.

To: Immigration Department of Central Committee, Warsaw
From: Central Polish Jewish Committee
November 13, 1946
  The childcare division of the central committee of Polish Jews requests payment of 5,000 złoty to cover the travel expenses of Irena Frydrych, a ward of the Children's Home of Chorzów, who is going to Stockholm to meet her father.

November 15, 1946
  I hereby confirm that the childcare division of the Central Polish Jewish Committee, Warsaw, Sienna 60, gave me the child Irena Frydrych, four years old, to bring her to her father in Stockholm where I am also going.
  [Handwritten] I have received the child and 1000 złoty. S. Ulwainay

Handwritten note, November 18, 1946:
  The 5,000 złoty to cover the expenses of Irena Frydrych's trip to Sweden were cleared by citizen Truskier.

In studying the cues in the memos, I calculated that my mother's journey took as long as two weeks. She started at the *prewentorium* in Gieszcze Puste/Głuszyca, Lower Silesia, in what had just become western Poland. She then returned to the orphanage in Chorzów, in southern Poland, where her father had enrolled her. She spent a night in an orphanage in Śródborów, near Warsaw, in the center of the country, where she was supposed to stay until she left for Sweden. But for some reason, she ended up in a temporary shelter in Warsaw, awaiting the day when finances and other details would be arranged so she could board a ship that would take her to her father in Stockholm. .

I wanted desperately to call my mom, to run this by her, to get her reaction, to see how she would respond. This was the kind of discovery I'd hoped to uncover in my travels with her, details to color the story I knew. Without her, these details amounted to little more than unrelated tidbits to make the outline more precise but not necessarily more complete. If anything, they only compounded the mystery of the woman who insisted she had always been loved. I could only imagine those weeks in transit—a new stop every night, a new caretaker. When she finally did come face-to-face with her father, he must have seemed like another in a series of adults who told her they would take care of her and bring her where she needed to go.

"Man, that's a bummer," said Dalton, the friend of a friend I stayed with that night in Warsaw. Over dinner, I told him about my day's finds and the melancholy circumstances around them. He shook his head. "So you're doing all this stuff about your mom, and right in the middle of it, she just checks out?" he said, still shaking his head.

"Yeah." I nodded awkwardly. I wasn't exactly comfortable with his word choice, but he had put his finger on the problem.

CHAPTER SIXTEEN

THE INTERVIEW HAD BEEN TAUNTING ME FOR MONTHS. FROM ITS perch on my desk, it glared at me—a slim miniature compact disc, no different than the others just like it, stacked in a pile. It was marked innocuously in blue ink: M-O-M, three letters scrawled by my hand. It didn't look like much, but to me, the disk that recorded my mother's February interview glowed like radioactive waste. I could neither suffer through it nor properly dispose of it. I needed to transcribe its contents, to hear what it had to say, but this recording—and the unfulfilled promise of the conversation we had agreed to finish later—was charged with too much power to be safe. When our first interview became our last, the recording became a symbol of all the questions that would forever go unanswered. The interview nagged me through June when it was in Krakow and I was in Detroit. My mother's sudden absence from my life made me crave the sound of her voice. I thought it would be a comfort, like a picture, only better. But when I walked back through the door on Ulica Staszica in midsummer and slipped the disk into the recorder's delicate metal slot, the rush of her voice through my headphones was no comfort at all.

So, ask me a question . . . Her voice flooded over me, so clear in my head, so vivid. *You're the reporter. You're the journalist. You're the in-ter-view-er.* She pronounced each syllable precisely. There she was, vibrant, crisp, her tone precise. She was both amused and irritated, humoring me. I hit stop, rewind, then play again.

So, ask me a question. You're the reporter. But I couldn't get beyond this point. The voice reproached me, laughed at me. I pulled the disk back out of the machine, then collapsed on the bed, less focused on what I'd heard than on what I'd never hear again. I wasn't sure why her familiar cadence had such an effect on me, so much more than pictures or letters or even the story of her life. Her voice was so intimate, so close, the first sound I knew, the sound I'd always known. I had similar difficulties the next few times I attempted to hear the recording. I would make it through the first exchange, then stop, afraid to continue on to what I knew would come at the end when I knew I would hear her last recorded words: *I'm getting tired of this interview, and my neck is hurting, and we're going to stop.* Then I knew I would hear myself agree. *Okay, Mom, but can we finish later?* And then I would hear her lie: *Yes. We'll finish later.*

The recording had been too painful for me, but now, headed for Sweden, I felt I had no choice. I had meant to go to Sweden much earlier in the year. It was the inspiration to bring my mother back to the place of her happiest days that had set me on this adventure in the first place, back in the heat wave that now seemed a distant past. The Scandinavian landscape of my mother's sweet dreams had initially been a major focus of my travels. But without my mom, I couldn't bear the prospect of going there alone. I pictured myself in Sweden on my own, finding her foster family, then telling them she was dead. I saw myself walking streets she had walked, knowing she would never walk them again. Through the summer, I deliberately pushed thoughts of Sweden from my head. I considered abandoning the trip altogether. But there were questions unresolved in that country, and with winter fast approaching, I was running out of time. I tried to recruit someone to go with me. I called David in Philadelphia to see if he might want to meet me in Stockholm, but while we had continued to talk on a regular basis and had discussed the prospect of his coming to visit me in Poland, he didn't have the flexibility for a last-minute trip. I offered to buy Krys a plane ticket to come along, but Stockholm in early November was not a good sell. In the end, my only option was to go alone. And if I was going to tackle Sweden alone, I would have to tackle the recording as well. I needed to walk the streets she had walked with the sound of her voice in my head.

I'm sorry, Erin, I just don't remember. What do you want from me?

But WHY don't you remember, Mom?

I just don't.

The night before my plane left for Stockholm, I forced myself to sit down with the disk and my laptop to begin as much of a transcript as I could manage. I slid the disk into the recorder, then waited, letting the voices take me back to the day when, under the pretense of making her exercise, strengthening her for chemo, I had dragged her out with me to appliance stores in search of radio-quality recording equipment. She complained when I took too long weighing my choices. *Just buy something already!* But back at home, after I had selected a slim silver minidisc recorder and a microphone with a long, thick cord, she helped me mount the plastic microphone clip onto a piece of scrap wood to make a tabletop mike stand. At the workbench in her basement, she drove three screws into the wood with her battery-powered electric screwdriver. Then I made tea for her in the kitchen, and we sat down at the table. My aunt Fran came over and sat down with us. This seemed as good a time as any. I set the mike in its new stand and pointed it toward Mom, asking if I could talk to her about Poland. She sipped from a cup of orange spiced tea. "Again with the Poland?" she asked, rolling her eyes. "Please, Mom?" I begged. She sighed. "Okay," she said. "But only an hour."

Eight months later, as I sat at my desk in Krakow, fingers poised above the keyboard of my laptop, headphones covering my ears, I took a few breaths to relax. I needed to concentrate on the words, on typing them, not on the voice that was so distractingly real as it spoke them. *So, ask me a question. You're the reporter. You're the journalist. You're the in-ter-view-er.* I inhaled, closed my eyes, focused, and typed without looking at the screen. Next I heard my own voice, softly, away from the mike, unsettled by my mother's rebuke, flailing to get the first question out.

"All right. I just want to . . . uhm, just tell me, you know, the story . . . Do you remember Poland at all?" And then I heard her answer:

"Not *really.*" her voice went high on *not* and then wavered on *really.* "I remember, like, images but they could just be dreams of, like, older boys, standing over me." I was still typing. I could handle this.

"You remember older boys standing over you?" There was skepticism in my question.

"Yeah, I think she had a couple of sons. They were probably taking care of me," Mom said. I kept typing as I listened to my mother answering some of my questions, complaining about others. "Why are you arguing with me?" she griped at one point, early in the recording, making a noise that was part sigh, part laugh. "I'm the interview-*eeee.*" I heard exasperation in my own voice as I argued that I wasn't arguing. We covered the Poland years quickly, since she didn't remember much, stopping to debate whether it was common for children to have memories of life before age four. She insisted it was uncommon, and I countered by rattling off a list of things I remembered from my early years, things that had taken place in the house we had moved from when I was four. "Well, I have no memories of being three," Mom said, indignation in her voice. "I remember my father coming for me, I told you about that, at the orphanage. And my next memory is of walking down the street with my father and screaming in Sweden. We were walking down the street in Stockholm and going to these people's apartment, and I was screaming all the way." I asked if she knew what it meant that he was her father, and she thought for a minute before answering. "No. I was *told* that he was my real father and that I was going to live with him and his wife eventually. I was told that. But I was never told the story of my life until I was on the ship coming to America."

I realized listening to Mom now that, over the years, she had become used to telling her story in a certain order. She would never volunteer the story, but when people asked, she would recall the same events, jumping through the narrative from each of those events to the next, from the orphanage to a quick stop in Sweden to the boat to the happily-ever-after in America. She reinforced those aspects of the story with each retelling. But in the interview, I was trying to slow her down, to fill the pages in between, and she was fighting me, repeatedly leaping ahead to what she considered the next important detail. "Wait, Mom," I said. "We'll get to that. First, do you remember meeting your foster parents?" Now I heard her murmur in a tone that only could have been spoken through a smile. Her voice lifted to a lilt. Hearing the recording, I pictured her during the interview, seated in her kitchen, a bright light glinting off the snow outside, shimmering in through the four-paneled window.

"They were very nice," Mom said. "She was a woman probably in her forties, but by today's standards, she looked like she was in her sixties. Her hair was wild, and she was overweight, dark hair, which was unusual in Sweden, but it was a Jewish family, and the man was, like, balding, and he was very nice, tall. They had a daughter who was fourteen, strikingly beautiful in Sweden because she had this gorgeous black, black hair." I could hear the clink of Mom's teacup as she lifted it from the saucer. The microphone picked up that sound and then, half a second later, the sound of a gulp as the liquid moved through her throat. Her voice sounded fresher when she started to talk again. "It was an apartment. It was the second floor, I think, in a building, and you walked in, it was like a hallway, and you turned right and it was the kitchen and you went further and it was, like, a living room."

I tried to push for detail. I asked about food. "I remember the cinnamon rolls," I heard Mom say as I pictured her smiling again. "I've
never tasted anything like it since." When I asked about her foster father, she told me he used to take her on his bicycle to the bar where he
hung out with his friends. She giggled when she told this part of the
story. The man worked nights and passed his days in the bar. "He was
very nice to me. Every day he brought me something, a little candy bar
or something, a little toy . . ." She adored her foster mother, too, she
said, and she remembered going to a farm in the country and playing
with other children in the street. "I remember my real father and his
new wife coming to visit me on Saturdays," Mom said, "they would
bring me candy and bananas, and I would eat all the candy, and that's
where I got my sweet tooth and my bad teeth. They would bring me
fine chocolates. And sometimes my new stepmother would take me to
buy me dresses." She chortled as she told me how her stepmother—
Grandma Fela—had once taken her to a beauty parlor to remove her
freckles and to dye her hair, which was a very bright red.

Her laugh on the recording was even clearer, more real, than the
sound of her speaking. I paused the recorder and bit my lip to keep my
composure. I exhaled a few times, took a deep breath, then pressed play
again. I heard myself ask if she had wanted her freckles removed, and I
heard her answer that she must have said something about hating her
freckles.

"You weren't cute with your freckles?" I asked.

"I was different," Mom said. "Everybody in all of Sweden was blond,
no freckles, and I had bright red hair and freckles. That made me different. I was the only one in the entire *school* that was Jewish, and my
father even accentuated that by insisting that I not go to school on Saturday. In Sweden everyone goes to school on Saturday . . . It made me
stand out. I didn't like being different. I was already different. I had red
hair." Despite this, Mom said, she liked school. She liked learning gymnastics in gym class and how to ice-skate and ski. She wasn't troubled by

not living with her father, she said, because she knew that housing was scarce in Stockholm and that there was no place for a family to live.

I typed it all, not even noticing until later that tears had slunk out of my eyes and dampened my cheek. I wiped them with my sleeve. As I feared, the interview was not very good. It was upsetting to spot holes in the narrative that I would have wanted to come back to fill in later, places where I could have followed up. Mom and I covered the broad sweep of the period but never really ventured beneath the surface. I winced when I reached the place in the interview, about twenty minutes in, when I challenged her aggressively, pushing her to anger to gauge her reaction. In retrospect, on the replay, this tactic seemed wrong. The interview had been three months before her death. At the time, not knowing how sick she was, or not wanting to believe it, I had been curious to see how she would react to my challenge.

"How come you don't care?" I asked her, almost pointing a finger at her with my tone. My question came in response to a discussion we were having about a friend of hers from school in Sweden, a Marie-Louise Lindstrom who had competed for Sweden in the 1956 Olympics in gymnastics. I suggested to Mom that if her friend had been in the Olympics, we could find her through the Olympic Committee, but Mom said she didn't care. So I asked her: "Why don't you care?"

"Right now?" She got her back up. "I don't care about much." She was sick, undergoing chemo. It was sapping her energy. If I had really known she was dying, I never would have been so insistent. At least I don't think I would have been.

"But you've never cared," I pushed. "I mean, you've never really . . ."

On the recording, I could hear Mom laughing uncomfortably. "I don't know, maybe there's something lacking in my personality," she said, half mocking me, half telling me off.

But I took her words at face value and tossed them back at her. "You think it's your personality?" I asked.

She laughed again. "Is this a psychoanalysis or is this an interview?"

she asked. I remembered lifting an eyebrow at her, trying to be coy. "I cared about you and Derek," she said defensively. "I don't care about Marie-Louise Lindstrom. Okay?"

Still, I pushed.

"But how come you don't care about your history, your past?"

And now she was officially peeved. "Because when I came to this country, my parents spent every single day of my entire childhood talking about the holocaust to everyone they greeted and they met." When she got annoyed like this, she spoke precisely, articulating every syllable of every word. She spoke quickly, shooting words like darts. "I got very sick of the story and I got very sick of the situation, and I just wanted to leave the room."

"Was this because it was disturbing?" I asked.

"No!" she said in an irritated, high-pitched voice. "Because I was *bored* with that whole story. I had heard it a million times! And it's not that I wasn't sympathetic. I was sympathetic. But after a while, you don't want to hear the same thing over and over and over again. We were a novelty. There were very few holocaust survivors in my neighborhood or my family. People wanted to hear the story, and my parents, having lived through all those atrocities, wanted to tell about it. But I. Did. No. Longer. Want. To. Hear. About. It!" She punctuated each word. "I was bored with them. I didn't want to hear it anymore, and even when there's movies like *Anne Frank's Diary* and those kinds of movies, I don't want to go to those, either. I've just heard the story too many times." I told her I'd always thought she avoided those movies because they were upsetting, too violent, but no, she said. "They! Were! Overkill! That's it. Overkill!" I felt a blush of shame now as I played this part of the interview. She was sick, trying to recover, and I was pushing.

She laughed at me a lot on the recording—and at herself—trying to keep things light despite the weight of the topic. Her voice lilted up on words she wanted to emphasize. At other times, when she was in familiar territory—like when she described the taste of blueberries in

Sweden—it rocked gently back and forth as though reciting a nursery rhyme. The notes played on in my head long after I hit stop and removed my headphones. I shook my hands from having typed so long, from having been afraid to stop transcribing, afraid I'd never have the strength and focus to finish later. Having sat through the whole thing, having played it once and then again to make the transcript verbatim— all twenty-eight minutes of it—I couldn't clear my head of her voice. It played on as I lay down in bed and tried to fall asleep. I needed to wake up early to catch my flight, but she was there, talking in my head. Eventually, I wrapped myself in the texture of the voice, tried to use it as a blanket, and it was still there when my alarm screeched in the morning, its familiar touch against my ears, calling me: *Errriiiinnn, get uh-up,* it said, kind at first, then scolding: *Erin! Get! Up!* "Sure, Mom," I heard myself muttering, "just a minute." And then an echo from another age: *Don't make me come up there!* I brought the disk with me when I boarded the plane to Sweden and listened to it again in flight, this time without the buffer of the keyboard. I let it wash over me. I let myself cry because it felt right. I ignored the flight attendants' curious looks.

Mom never wanted to see Poland. She had no particular attachment to the country of her birth. But Sweden was the smell of baking cinnamon rolls. It was sunshine and friendship and games in the street. It was Sweden she wanted to visit and Sweden where I truly wanted to take her. Now, two months after Stockholm's tourist season and far too late for me, anyway, I was going because I'd said I would. Sweden was the spiritual source of this project. It was Mom's story of crying as a child over the smudged photo of her Swedish foster mother that had started me thinking about retracing her life. And though my mission had changed, this was still the essential heart of what I was trying to do. In many ways, I was still searching for the little girl in the back of the car, still hoping that maybe I could help her.

· · ·

I wasn't sure if I'd be able to locate the Keijler girl, and if I did, I wasn't sure what I would tell her. That my mother had fond thoughts of Sweden but never got around to coming back? That I was here instead? Still, I had documented my mother's life until this point. I had her birth certificate and Zilla's. I had, from Honorata Skowrońska's Yad Vashem file, an idea of how my mom had spent the war. I had the orphanage records and the name of the social worker who delivered her here, to Stockholm, to this dazzling city at the edge of the Baltic. Now I needed the next chapter. From the window of the train that delivered me downtown from the airport, I had a sweeping view of a crowded marina and a captivating, painted streetscape. I saw hilly islands linked together by bridges and ferries, sliced open by water and air. If there was somebody living here now, all these years later, who knew my mom as the little girl with the dimpled knees whose photograph, taken at the time, hung on my wall in Philadelphia, then I wanted to find her. *And they had a daughter who was fourteen, strikingly beautiful in Sweden because she had this gorgeous black, black hair.* My mother's description from the recording lingered in my head. If the pretty girl with the gorgeous black hair was still alive, she would be around seventy and possibly still living in Stockholm. The only problem was that I didn't know her name. Mom hadn't remember the girl's first name, and if she'd gotten married, her surname would likely no longer be Keijler. The only thing Mom knew for sure was that her foster mother was Shprinsa Keijler.

I woke up early my first morning in Stockholm, put on a good pair of walking shoes, slid a notebook and a tourist map into my bag, and set out on what I feared would be a fruitless quest. I decided to start my search with the same lead that, fifty-five years earlier, had helped my grandfather find the Keijlers in the first place. There was a single synagogue listed in the guidebook, called simply Synagogan, on a street called Wahrendorffsgatan. I found this street on my map and made my way there. It was a chilly but sunny morning. The light was low in the autumn sky, giving the city a kind of golden glow. In a week or two, I assumed, all of Sweden would be frigid and dark, completely barren, but maybe because I was walking the streets in the place where my mother had spent her happiest days, the landscape felt almost sun-kissed, full of people lingering, savoring what could be one of the year's last few pleasant days. It was cold out, like a mild winter day back home, but people were crowding streetside cafés, clutching shopping bags, admiring displays in store windows. The path from my hotel led through a busy modern shopping district, full of clunky, heavy buildings in silver and black. I walked down a wide promenade of red brick that was closed to traffic and crowded with people en route to work. Eventually, I located Wahrendorffsgatan, a tiny street where I found the Synagogan. It was a striking tall yellowish structure with thin vertical windows and fine geometric detail.

I pressed the doorbell beside the synagogue's locked door and, through an intercom, asked to speak with the cantor, Maynard Gerber. Yale Reisner in Warsaw had given me the name of the cantor as someone who was involved with genealogy in Sweden. He was an American who had lived for years in Stockholm. "I'm not sure why you think I can help you," the cantor said, but he agreed to hear me out. I told him the story as well as I could, noting that the only thing I knew about the woman I was trying to find was her mother's name. "You don't even know the woman's first name?" he asked.

"Not exactly," I admitted. "I thought maybe . . . Does the synagogue keep marriage records? She might have been married here."

Gerber agreed to check the synagogue's marriage records, but he did not sound confident. "Do you even know if she had a Jewish wedding?" he asked. I admitted that I had no idea. He shook his head. "She could still be a member of this congregation, and if she's married and has another name, I wouldn't know," he said. Still, he agreed to ask around and encouraged me to come to services Friday night to meet some of the older members of the community. "Don't get your hopes up," he said. I promised to keep my expectations low.

I had some success with the Swedish Red Cross, which helped administer refugee services after the war, and called the synagogue later to tell Gerber that I now knew Shprinsa's husband's name—Benjamin Keijler—and that the family had lived at Helgageten 15. But the receptionist told me that the cantor wasn't in, that I should call back later. I considered trying the address on Helgageten, seeing if maybe the family was still there or if someone there remembered them. But Hans, the man who helped me at the Red Cross, advised me to check the Swedish national archives, which he circled on my map. I wasn't sure what I would find there, but Hans gave me instructions for which bus to take and suggested I tell the archivists that members of my family had been refugees after the war. "There should be some kind of record," he said. Sure enough, when I arrived at the archives, I was led into an open gymnasium-sized reading room and, after filling out a couple of forms, was handed six brown folders, each stamped with the name Frydrych.

There was one folder with my mother's name on it, one with her father's name, and one with Grandma Fela's. The other three Frydrych folders were marked with the names of my grandfather's three cousins: Duvid, Sukher, and Moyshe, who were the only sons of Yisruel Frydrych's brother, Yitskhok, to survive the war. Yitskhok had two daughters who moved to Detroit before the war and a son who moved to Argentina. Of the seven children who remained in Poland, only these three brothers emerged. They had stayed together during the war, trading on their skills as jewelers by making rings and necklaces for the guards at Auschwitz. After the war, they preceded my grandfather to Sweden. One of these cousins, Sukher—later known as Sol—was married to a woman named Luba Tryszynska, who was famous for saving fifty-four children at Bergen-Belsen. Decades later, she would be featured in an A&E network movie called *The Angel of Bergen-Belsen* and would write a children's book about her experiences but back in Sweden, Luba was a friend of Grandma Fela's. They had known each other in Bergen-Belsen. And it was Luba and Sukher who introduced Grandma Fela to my grandfather.

The files in the national archive looked mostly like paperwork for visa applications and other documents related to my family's immigration status. I requested photocopies for later translation, then returned to the Synagogan, eager to show the cantor what I'd collected. Before I could pull out my papers, however, he started to speak. "I found something," he said, inviting me to take a seat in his office. "This," he went on, waving an index card, "is the burial record for Shprinsa Keijler. She was buried in our cemetery in 1985." I wrote this down in my notebook. Gerber continued, "There is a woman listed as a contact for the grave," he said. I looked up expectantly. "Her name is Fannie Adolffson, and I had to assume that she's the woman you're looking for, the daughter of Shprinsa Keijler."

My hands shook as I wrote down the name. "Is there a number for her?" I asked.

The cantor shook his head. "Not on the card," he said. He was talking slowly, as though something had gone wrong, and I could feel my grin fading. I braced myself for bad news. "I hope you don't mind," Gerber said. "But I consulted the Stockholm phone book and found a Fannie Adolffson." Then he smiled and relaxed his face. "It's her. She remembers your mom." He wrote down a number on a piece of paper and handed it to me. "Call her. She's anxious to meet you."

It felt almost like a rerun. I was using the same script from the previous spring but with a different set, a revised cast. Now, the scene had some more expensive furniture, some better costumes. I was still playing the part of me, still sitting in somebody's living room, still watching as someone I'd never met examined a photo of my mother and cried. But the scene of Wiesław Skowroński's living room had been replaced by a black lacquered table, a crystal chandelier, blue wallpaper, and a spiral staircase. Wiesław had been recast as a plump older woman with a wild mane of silver and black hair and small, stylish glasses on a chain around her neck. Fannie Adolffson sat across from me, as Wiesław often had, tears in her eyes as the past came crashing down on the present and she remembered the girl who had lived with her family, then left one day without warning. "Why is this so emotional for you?" I asked Fannie through her friend who was translating. Fannie spoke some English, she said, but had asked her friend for help. "Many feelings come up," she said. "It was fifty years ago."

I had built myself up for a long and convoluted search in Sweden. I had imagined that finding Fannie would involve talking to one person who would refer me to another who would eventually lead me to someone who knew the person I was seeking. I had planned to interview strangers in nursing homes, to knock on doors in the old neighborhood, to call Keijlers at random in the phone book until somehow someone would lead me to Fannie. None of this was necessary, just as my search for Wiesław required nothing more than a knock on a door. This time the key was a burial record and a current Stockholm phone book. Forty hours after arriving in Stockholm, I had Fannie Adolffson on the phone and, a day later, I found myself in her apartment. I asked if it had been difficult for Fannie's mother when my mom left the country. Fannie blotted her face as she nodded. "*Yoh,*" she said, which I took to be Swedish for *yes.* "She was only four years old. It's a nice age with a child. She was there for four years. It was hard for her to give Irean away." She pronounced my mother's name *I-REE-an.* "And she, Fannie's mother, didn't know how . . . Was your mother's family very nice to her?" Fannie asked me through her friend.

I was confused by the question. "Was my mother's family nice to my mother?" I asked to clarify. The friend confirmed that this was Fannie's question. I thought back to the moment in the interview I'd done with my mom in which she talked of never quite connecting with her father. She described him as cold. Her word was *taciturn.* But should I tell this to Fannie? "Her stepmother was very nice to her," I said. "I don't know about her father." The friend relayed this to Fannie, who responded that her mother had told her the same thing, "that the father—your, uh, grandfather—was hard to talk to, that it was hard to see what kind of man he—" Fannie interrupted her friend's translation with a stream of Swedish. The friend stopped to listen. "He came over one day with a woman and said he was getting married and that he was going to America with *I-REE-an*. They didn't speak much about it. He just came after the wedding and they went away and they took her with them."

This surprised me. "Your parents didn't know he was taking her away?" I asked.

"They knew that he would someday take her away," Fannie said. "She was only supposed to live with them one year or two, and she was there already four years. But they were surprised about when."

"They just came one day and took her away?" I asked. Fannie nodded in a sad, methodical way. I thought about my mom, spirited away on a moment's notice without a real chance for good-bye. I thought about this woman, this mother, this baker of cinnamon rolls, who, after four years, had lost a daughter in a day. It was the same revelation I'd had months earlier about Honorata. I'd spent so much time thinking about my mom and what she had gone through. And now, for a second time, I saw how my mother's childhood had also affected the people she left behind. Here, again, was a mother's hurt, on the tearful face of her now elderly child.

"Did your mother talk about my mother later on?" I asked.

Fannie nodded and answered me in English: "Missed. Missed," she said, then added something in Swedish to her friend.

"She was wondering," the friend said, "what she was like, your mother? She says she was told that *I-REE-an* became a teacher." I told her that my mom taught school for a short time when she was young, right after graduating from college, and for a short time later, when Derek and I were in high school. She didn't like it much either time and both times quit to do other things. Fannie asked more questions, about Mom's other jobs, about me and Derek, about my dad. She asked what had happened to my grandparents and she asked how my mother had died. "Was she sick very long?" she asked. "Not so long," I said. For years Shprinsa Keijler corresponded by mail with Grandma Fela, Fannie told me. Shprinsa received a letter in 1982 informing her that my grandfather had died, but after that, there were no more letters. Shprinsa died three years later.

"Was your mother upset that my mom never wrote?" I asked.

"No," Fannie said. "She thought, She's young. She has so much to do right now. She has friends and boys and everything."

I looked down at the table. "I never understood why she didn't stay in touch with your family," I said.

Fannie waved this off. "It's hard to stay in touch," she said.

I spent the afternoon in Fannie's small, interesting apartment, cluttered with books, rugs, sculptures, and paintings. She'd filled the black lacquered table with homemade pastries, including, I noted, little cinnamon rolls. Fannie told me stories about how, when my mom was seven, she decided not to go to school. Mom left the apartment, books in hand, but detoured to a nearby park and sat on the swings until she saw other children returning home. Then she, too, returned home. "The teacher phoned Fannie's mom," the friend translated, "and asks why I-REE-an doesn't go to school. And Fannie's mom says, 'She goes every morning.' That's when they find out that she was sitting on the swing." I squealed with delight at this story. "So rebellious!" I said, thinking how this story would have made for good ammunition in the years when I didn't want to go to school. Fannie laughed as she told the rest of the story. "After the teacher called, Fannie's mother went with her every day and saw that she went into the classroom." But even as amusing as this tale was, it had a distinct sadness. Lots of kids don't like school, but to sit in a park all day by herself? At seven? I wondered at the myth of my mother's life in Sweden, the years she remembered with such fondness. I wondered if she had been happy even then, or if she spent the Sweden years missing Poland, the way she would later spend her first American years longing for the warmth of Shprinsa's kitchen.

At a different point in the conversation, Fannie told me that my mom had been a very good student but that she didn't like having to stay home on Saturdays. I told her my mom had told me the same thing. Fannie told me about going with my mom and her parents to the country and staying in a summer cottage. Then she brought out pictures taken at the cottage that I recognized immediately. The pictures were identical to some of those that hung in frames on the walls of my house in Philadelphia. There was a picture of my mom at about six or seven, sitting in a field near a haystack next to a bunch of blond children. Mom was the one with darker hair, wearing a giant white bow on her head. Fannie also had a large framed photo on her wall that hung in a smaller frame on my wall, of Mom with Shprinsa, Benjamin, and Fannie. They were all dressed for a party, he in a suit, the women in dresses, standing in a room with dozens of flowers. The flowers, Fannie told me, were for Benjamin's fiftieth-birthday party. Flowers, she said, were a birthday tradition in Sweden.

The Keijlers were not from Sweden originally. Shprinsa was born in Poland. And Benjamin, Shprinsa's second cousin, was born in Finland. Their marriage was arranged by their families, and Shprinsa was sent to Finland. The couple settled eventually in Stockholm. Shprinsa was a homemaker. Benjamin, as my mother had remembered, worked at night at the synagogue. Fannie told me his job was to sit with the bodies of the recently dead, fulfilling the Jewish obligation to never leave a body unattended before burial. A man at the synagogue approached Benjamin one day late in the autumn of 1946 and asked if he and his wife could take care of a girl, nearly five, who was on her way to Sweden from Poland. Benjamin had no time to consult with Shprinsa or hold a family meeting. He agreed and brought the girl home with him that day. "There were many families who did the same thing," Fannie said. "It was the right thing to do. They helped each other." I asked if the family had received any money for their efforts from the synagogue or from the Red Cross. Fannie shook her head. "It wasn't like that," she said. "They didn't have much, but they didn't think about this." It was a time of crisis, she said. There were not a lot of options. It was what people did.

When we finished talking, Fannie and her friend walked me back to the subway station. I looked over and noticed that Fannie was again blotting her eyes with a tissue. "What's wrong?" I asked. Fannie's friend translated her answer. "She says she's been looking forward to this day, and now it is over." I smiled and noticed that my cheeks, too, were dampening. "That's sweet, thank you," I said, and offered Fannie a hug. Then, like our mothers had fifty-one years earlier, we said good-bye and went our separate ways, unlikely to meet again.

"It was winter, December. It was very cold," Mom told me.

"Was there snow on the ground?" I asked.

"There's always snow on the ground in Sweden." She laughed.

"Oh. Of course."

"The only emotion I remember was the sadness that I felt. I was unhappy, and I cried leaving those people. I really liked those people. I lived with them for four years, and they were very good to me. I remember taking my doll. I had a very favorite doll that I sewed clothes for and hats for, and I put this doll in a little red suitcase, and I had a Swedish flag, so I remember carrying my little red suitcase with my doll and this flag."

"Did you have the sense that you wouldn't see her again?"

"That's probably why I was crying."

"But did you ever want to go back to Sweden to see where you lived?"

"I think so, maybe," Mom said. "Maybe someday I will. I would like to go to Sweden again someday."

CHAPTER SEVENTEEN

S INCE MY LAST UNCOMFORTABLE VISIT WITH THE SKOWROŃSKIS, I'd been hesitant to return to their home. I was embarrassed about the way I'd behaved there, ashamed at having lied about my mother's death, about using her manufactured illness to deflect from our ongoing conflicts. I'd been to Będzin several times since my last visit, largely in a futile effort to wrest property records from a Będzin real estate archive that was open only on Mondays from nine A.M. to one P.M. I hoped that the real estate records would, among other things, tell me where my great-grandparents were born, but the archive was run by bureaucrats who seemed to believe that foreigners interested in real estate had the singular motive of evicting Polish occupants from their homes. I had taken to returning every week between nine A.M. and one P.M., thinking that if these paper pushers knew to expect me every week, they'd eventually provide the documents I was legally entitled to see. Despite these weekly trips to Będzin, however, I stayed away from Małachowskiego Street.

I wasn't sure what had brought us to this point. Our first meeting had been such a rush, such a fun ride of expectation. That spring day when I first walked through Wiesław's door had felt like the beginning of something—one of those moments when history seemed truly capable of resolving itself. I truly believed that my dream of connecting my mom with her forgotten past would come true in a matter of months, that this old man would again come to know his sister. But here we were, more than half a year later. My mother had not appeared, nor would she. Resentments existed where I'd hoped there'd be friendship, and if the past were a book that we had hefted from a shelf, we were struggling to pry it open. Its pages were gummed and damaged, hard to read. What little we had been able to decipher had proved muddy, unpleasant, the subject of dispute. That was yet another reason to keep my distance. But there was something I needed to do, something I should I have done earlier.

It was frigid and windy the morning I set off, like I had on so many other mornings, on the highways west of Krakow. I went alone, in part because Krys was in Florence learning Italian for the month, and Magda was still in New York, but also because it was no longer fair to put someone else in the middle of a problem that I had created. The rolling landscape along the roads to Będzin that had been so succulent in summer, light and colorful in May, lush and green through July, yellowing into August and September, now looked pale and still. It was late November but already decidedly winter. It hadn't snowed yet, but the day was bitter and dark, even more gray than before. The trees had been bare for weeks. The coal dust churned out by Poland's stoves made the dark air darker, the wet air heavier. Coal stung the tissues of my eyes and nose. Gusts of wind collected on the empty fields and pushed against the sides of Ania's featherlight Daewoo as I drove. I tightened my grip on the steering wheel and gave the windows another crank to keep the chill from bleeding into the car.

In Będzin, I took the shortcut off Modrzejowska Street to the back of the house, trying to make my face look sullen as I cut the engine. I needed to bring myself back to the previous June, when this news was as tender and raw as I needed to pretend it still was. In the courtyard behind 20 Małachowskiego, there was a girl, about nine or ten, with short hair and tiny rhinestones in her ears, wearing an ill-fitting pink jacket. She was bouncing a muddy rubber ball against the side of the house. I recognized her as one of Wiesław's grandkids, one of the kids squeezed onto the sofa the day last summer when the whole family came out to greet me. Today she glanced at me as I emerged from the car, then turned her attention back to her solitary game. I was no longer a novelty here. I inhaled a breath of coal-poisoned air and positioned myself in the drear of the depressing day. I steadied my breath, slowing it down. I was trying not to be nervous. I shouldn't have waited this long to tell the truth, but once a single lie was told, the second came easily.

Instead of heading straight upstairs to Wiesław's apartment, I knocked on his daughter's kitchen window in the old brass factory to announce my arrival. Marta had a friendlier face, and I had come to see her as an ally, someone who would be easier to approach. Marta peered through the window, saw me, and waved. I could hear her muffled voice through the glass. "*Dzień dobry,* Earlyn," she said cheerfully. "*Dzień dobry,*" I responded. At some point I realized that the Skowrońskis didn't know how to pronounce my name, and now it was too late to correct them. Marta came out to open the door for me and leaned her head into the courtyard to shout at the girl with the ball. "Mal-gor-ZA-ta!" she yelled. "Go tell Grandma and Grandpa that Earlyn is here!" The girl bounced the ball a few more times, pretending not to notice Marta's instructions. "Mal-gor-ZA-ta!" Marta yelled again.

"*Słucham!* I hear you!" the girl screamed. "Just a minute!" She kept bouncing her ball until, on a return, it flew over her head and bounded into the alley. She watched the ball roll into a mud puddle near the street, then turned to run toward the stairwell that led to Wiesław's apartment. Marta laughed and invited me in.

I wanted to laugh with Marta but stopped myself. A polite, happy gesture might diminish my resolve. I wanted to ask why Malgorzata wasn't in school when the other kids usually running around the court-yard seemed to be, but I didn't ask. As I took off my shoes and followed Marta into her apartment, I wondered if I should make small talk first, if I should wait until the whole family was together to break the news. But I couldn't think of anything to say and decided to do it quickly. Marta and I walked into the hallway of her apartment, and she crouched down to dismember the vacuum cleaner she had been using when I knocked. I watched for a few seconds as she disconnected the hose and wrapped the cord around the handle. "I have sad news," I said.

"Oh?" Marta asked, rotating her neck to look up at me.

"Yes," I said, trying to form the words in my head. I wondered if the lie wasn't so bad, if I should leave things as they were, but Marta was still in her crouch over the vacuum cleaner, still twisting upward, look-ing at me, waiting for me to speak. I swallowed hard and spoke quickly, without preamble: "My mother died," I said.

Marta inhaled sharply and audibly, as though the vacuum cleaner at her knees had turned on for a moment from inside her gut and turned quickly off again. She cupped her hand over her mouth and stood to offer a gentle hug. She told me she was sorry to hear the news and clucked her distress with her tongue. She bent to pick up the vacuum cleaner, and I followed as she walked into the kitchen to store it in a cup-board under the sink. A few minutes later, we heard Helen Skowrońska enter the apartment. She came shuffling into the kitchen, carrying two plastic bags of potatoes that she set on the kitchen table. As I moved to greet her, Marta broke the gloomy news for me. "Earlyn's mother died," she said. Helen's face took on a look of surprise, and she turned to me for confirmation. I nodded and was about to fill her in on the details when again we heard the door in the hallway open and close. This time it was Wiesław entering, and I could feel the tendons tightening in my neck. I took a deep breath and listened to the sounds Wiesław made as he slipped his shoes off at the door and removed his coat.

My pulse quickened. This was the moment I'd been dreading for months, the moment I'd gone to great lengths to avoid. When Wiesław's soft blue eyes appeared in the kitchen doorway, I took a cautious step toward him, going to give him a hug before imparting the news. But before I could take a second step or raise my arms, Helen blurted out the news in a tone that was far too abrupt: "Earlyn's mother is dead." She sounded angry, and I wasn't sure why. Had she known I was lying? Was she thinking about the signature she wanted from my mom? I clenched my jaw, turning my back to her, and fixed my eyes on Wiesław. I readied myself to comfort him, to tell him—though this wasn't true—that my mother had wanted to meet him, that she had wanted to thank him and his family. But as I watched Wiesław's face, I saw that it revealed almost nothing, not sorrow, not grief.

"Let's go sit down," Wiesław said, gesturing toward his daughter's living room. I followed him to the next room and sat on a wooden chair. He settled into the overstuffed brown easy chair beside the table as Helen and Marta perched uncomfortably on the sofa. Wiesław set a pack of cigarettes on the table and searched his pockets for a match. I continued to scan his face for reaction, for pain or disappointment, maybe for a hint of the anger in his wife's voice, but the textured layers of his weather-worn face revealed nothing more than an uncanny focus on his quest for a cigarette and a match. When at last he found a dog-eared matchbook in the right pocket of his pants, he lodged a cigarette into the thin glass holder through which he liked to smoke, struck the head of a match with a flick of his wrist, and united the flame with the cigarette. He sat smoking for a stretch of minutes as Marta, Helen, and I sat in silence and watched. I wondered what was going through his head: memories of my mother as a child? Thoughts of his mother on her deathbed? His family's hope that my mother would return? I didn't want to speak, didn't want to change the subject, didn't want to take the focus away from Wiesław. After one cigarette had burned to a stub and been replaced by another, Wiesław cleared his throat, then turned to ask me a question. "So?" he said. "Have you heard anything about the property?"

Wiesław was not a man of many words. He was a not a man of social graces who knew the perfect thing to say in the face of someone's grief. I knew his question came from a place of discomfort, from a desire to thin the air of the weight of my news, and I knew it was the easiest question for him to ask, the one pertaining to the subject we discussed most often. But knowing that my mother's long-lost brother had waited exactly five minutes after hearing the news of her death to return to the topic that had become an open sore between us felt to me like the worst kind of betrayal. He didn't ask how I was doing. He didn't ask for details, whether Mom had suffered, whether I had been able to see her before she died. He didn't express sympathy. He asked only for the status of a piece of property that my dead mother cared nothing about. I turned to look at him, at the cigarette dangling from the two-inch length of glass tube that old men in Poland used as cigarette holders and that younger men seemed to use as hash pipes. He sat calmly smoking, waiting for my response, not even seeming to anticipate that I might be upset by his inquiry. I could feel my face turning red with a mix of humiliation and rage.

How stupid I had been! I had foolishly tried to spare this man the sting of bad news, and now I wondered why I ever thought he'd be anything more than mildly disappointed, why I thought he'd still venture to grieve for someone he had known only a handful of years over half a century earlier. I wondered if, all along, it had been me deluding myself into believing that he really did care, if I had wanted so badly for there to be a special connection between my mother and her "brother" that, in my mind, I made true what really was not. I felt like a dupe. Wiesław had been unmistakably emotional when I knocked on his door in May, but that might have been the shock of the moment, all those people, the pressure. Genuine tears had trickled down his face at other times, when he gazed at the photo of my mother and his, but he might have been remembering his youth, thinking back on his life, on his mother's life, on how she had been mistreated. He might have been crying for the mother he missed as acutely as I now missed mine. I wasn't sure what reaction I'd expected. People respond to events in different ways. We don't all exhibit our emotions. But even if he didn't care much about my mom, he could have shown some sympathy for me.

I was tempted to say something rude, to stand up and walk out. I was tempted to burst into tears to make them feel sorry for me. Instead, I swallowed the mouthful of bile that had gathered in my throat and decided to answer his question. "Well," I said, attempting to speak. Helen and Marta had sat silent on the sofa, watching me as I watched Wiesław. But now it was as though the room, which had been frozen, had surged back to life. Helen became animated at the sound of her favorite topic and leaned forward with interest to hear what I would say. A buzzer went off in the kitchen, and Marta jumped to tend to it. With nothing else to do or say, I launched into an explanation of what I had done in the interest of the property. I told Wiesław and Helen that I'd talked to a number of lawyers and had settled on a firm in Katowice, the big city adjacent to Będzin. I told them that the lawyer they'd met, Tomasz Borcz, had decided not to take the case because it would be too much trouble for him, but he was still offering advice. I gave Wiesław the name and number of the attorney I'd retained and told him that I'd instructed the lawyer to be accessible to him and his family.

I struggled a bit when my Polish failed me but, as well as I could, spoke of the work I was doing to collect the necessary papers. I told the Skowrońskis that I had solicited the aid of three of my cousins, one from each surviving branch of the family, and that these three cousins and I would collectively inherit the property. Once the property was transferred to our names, we would endeavor to correct the confusion with the tenants for the Skowrońskis. This was, for me, a compromise. I wouldn't name all of my great-grandparents' heirs, but each branch of the family would be represented. As I laid out the details, I noticed that

I wasn't annoyed or angry as in the past. What I was feeling was regret. I'd had good intentions—at least I'd like to believe that I did—but the Frydrychs and Skowrońskis, it seemed, were never meant to be friends. Our family connection had been an extraordinary event, a woman's remarkable act of bravery during an inconceivable time. Sixty years later, the virtues of right and wrong were not as clear as they had been, and gestures in one generation were not necessarily destined to have an effect on the next.

After about an hour, I stood to leave. This was a short visit for me, and Marta came out of the kitchen to stop me. "Stay for lunch, Earlyn," she said. "I made soup." I shook my head contritely. "I'm sorry," I said. "I have to go." I told her I had some records to check at the Będzin town hall, which would be closing soon. "So come back after," she said. "You've never stayed the night here. Why don't you stay tonight?" I considered this. Marta's hopeful look when she made the offer was a touching contrast to the conversation I'd had with her parents. Marta was the only one in her family who had expressed genuine remorse at the news of my mother's passing. And she, if not her parents, seemed to be reaching out to me. I'd realized recently that Marta and I were roughly the same age. I had thought she was older because she was married and had a five-year-old, but in fact, she was born just a year before me. I wanted to talk to her, to hear, without her parents around, what she had to say about her family and mine. I wondered if maybe reconciliation was meant to skip a generation, to be left to those of us for whom the past was not so personal.

I thought about leaving for an hour, then coming back to spend the evening with Marta and her husband and son. I should have been honored to spend the night under the roof that once sheltered my family, but the truth was I didn't wanted to stay. I didn't like having to speak Polish, which sapped my strength. I didn't like seeing the cracks in the crumbling walls and lamenting the way my great-grandparents' ambitions of home and success had been neglected over the years. I was disappointed in Wiesław and Helen. And at that moment the only things I wanted to do were leave, go home, call David, and crawl into bed. "Maybe next time," I told Marta. "Next time I'll stay the night." As I slid back into the driver's seat of Ania's car, it occurred to me that I had come to see this house of my mother's infancy in much the same way I had once seen the house where Mom and I lived together. In my teenage eyes, my mother's house was a house of judgment. It was a place where I was too fat, too lazy, not good enough for her. Her house welcomed me as the only home I'd ever known, but it demanded a great deal more from me than I thought I could give. I wondered if the Będzin house would have a second act for me, too, as my mother's house eventually had. I wondered if this house would live on in my mind to become a happy place of precious memory—a refuge cleared of emotional liens.

I drove the three blocks from Małachowskiego to the Będzin town hall so I wouldn't have to come back for my car and risk having to confront the Skowrońskis again. I parked in the small lot in front of the building and wandered in to find the Urząd Stanu Cywilnego, the bureau of civil records, rather quiet, a welcome respite from the noise in my head. The clerk who usually helped me wasn't in, so another clerk offered to let me read the birth, death, and marriage books on my own. "As you know," she told me, "these books are under control of the personal-property law. We're not supposed to show them to you, but we trust you to be careful." This was a pleasant surprise, and I thanked this woman profusely and promised to put everything back where it belonged. I'd have to bring flowers for her, I thought as she gave me further instructions. I'd never had total access to the records; I'd always had to submit my requests to the clerk, then wait for her to return with a response. But now the records were mine to peruse at my leisure. I still hadn't figured out where my great-grandparents were born and had not yet determined whether my grandmother had older siblings who might have survived the war. Since I didn't know if I'd ever have this level of access again, I decided to read as many of the aging Jewish record books as I could.

I started with 1945, hoisting that heavy volume off the shelf, dropping it softly onto the table, and cracking it open to the familiar smell of old paper and mold. I read back in time, through 1944, through 1943, through 1942. In 1941, in the volume's second index, I found something: a record for the marriage of Beresh Frydrych and Sura Leah Rozenblum. The clerk had always insisted that she had no record of my grandparents' marriage, and since Sura Leah was listed as single on her daughter's birth record, I assumed that the marriage either never took place or wasn't recorded. But, in fact, according to the record in question, which was written in German, my grandparents had married— and on a date that was instantly familiar: December 7, 1941.

I tried to calculate the time difference between Poland and Hawaii, wondering if, at the hour of my grandparents' vows, the Japanese bombers were still cruising across the Pacific or whether the attack on Pearl Harbor had already begun. I wondered if Pearl Harbor was even news in Poland, where the war was already in its twenty-eighth month. The Jews of Poland had long been stripped of basic rights. Would they have seen the American entry into the war as a harbinger of Allied victory? Or would events in Hawaii have been just another piece of distant news? Here was a young couple getting married in the middle of a war, taking a step that, under normal circumstances, would have been charged with hope. But could they have been hopeful? I had heard survivors talk of rumors at the time that married women would fare better in the war than single women, that the Nazis wouldn't touch young marrieds for fear that they were pregnant. This proved untrue, but was the rumor behind my grandparents' decision to marry? Or was the story true that they had fallen in love amid the whirl of war? *It was wartime*, Mom told me. *But my parents wanted to be together.*

And soon there was a child. I did another quick calculation and was amused to discover that, counting back from my mother's birthday in February 1942, Sura Leah would have been six and half months pregnant on the day the Japanese sneak-attacked the U.S. naval fleet at Pearl Harbor. I smiled to myself, thinking how furious my mother had been a generation later when, after her divorce from her first husband—the man she married before my father—my grandfather sent her an abrasive letter. Jewish women didn't get divorced, he told her, and her decision to do so had dishonored his family. Now I took a moment to side with my mother in her lifelong quarrel with her father, wishing I could call her with this touch of vindication.

With full access to the archives, I also found two missing birth records for my grandfathers' eldest siblings, Faygl and Moyshe, who, though they were born two years apart, were both recorded on the same day in 1896, just after Moyshe was born. And, I located a 1904 marriage record for Yisruel's brother, Yitskhok, the jeweler whose three jeweler sons would later connect with my grandfather in Sweden. I couldn't read any of these records—they were in Russian—but I carried the 1896, 1904, and 1941 books to the lady down the hall, who made photocopies. She smiled agreeably and swept each book from the counter to the copy machine, pressing the appropriate buttons. But as I reached into my pocket for money to pay her, the clerk who had earlier granted me "trusted" status in the archive came running from her office, shaking her fist at me and shouting. "What's wrong?" I asked. "Can you slow down, please?" But she kept screaming at me, shaking her fist. She grabbed my photocopies and ran back to her office.

"I'm very sorry. Excuse me. I don't understand," I said, following her. "Did I do something wrong?" It took me a while to figure out that the clerk had apparently asked me to check with her before making any copies so that she could verify that I wasn't in violation of the personal-property law. When presented with these instructions, I had answered yes and said that I understood. Clearly, I had not understood. This was the folly of proficiency but not fluency in a language, especially when combined with my stubborn refusal to acknowledge deficiency. I was too proud to admit how much I didn't understand and, for months, had gotten away with largely faking it in Polish, pretending to comprehend with a smile and a nod. But this woman was rightly convinced that I'd been trying to scam her, and she had *trusted* me. I apologized and tried to explain myself, but she was enraged. She told me she could get fired for this. Or anyway, I think that's what she said. I could no longer rely on myself to say. It took all of my shaky Polish negotiating skills to pry the documents out of her hands. She eventually released them to me and overcharged me by only a couple of złoty, but as soon as it had been afforded to me, my special status at the Będzin Urząd Stanu Cywilnego—one of the few things in Będzin that had seemed to be going my way—was revoked. I was officially banned.

Come home, Krys, I need you! I e-mailed him that night in Florence and told him that when he came back to Poland, I had a job for him. I offered to pay him whatever he was making at the bar to work as my guide and interpreter. My savings had gone a lot further in Poland than I'd expected. Life was inexpensive here, and Krys was worth the price. He had a degree in history and could speak both Polish and Russian. Recalling my other communication gaffes and emotional breakdowns at Polish archives, I thought how much easier it all would have been if Krys had been by my side, helping me navigate cultural subtleties and idiotic rules.

When I called David early the next morning, I confided that I was losing my drive. "I don't know what I'm doing here anymore," I told him. I wanted to come home to him, to see if maybe we could try to build a life together, far from this country and its ghosts. But I didn't feel ready to go home, not yet. There was still so much I wanted to do or felt like I should do. I admitted that I was unhappy in Poland most of the time but told him I was considering another year away. He told me that if this was my choice, he would come join me, that somehow we would try to be together.

CHAPTER EIGHTEEN

THE FROTHY LAYERS OF SNOW THAT BLANKETED THE TOWN SQUARE consumed both of my feet and most of my shins as I trudged through the weather toward Krys. Feathery snowflakes collected on our coats. The sky disappeared beneath a whitewash of cold. That was when I thought I could see him. Out across the snowy field, on the other side of the creek, I could almost make out of the form of a proud father walking up the hill with a nine-day-old boy in his arms. I could almost see the joy on his face, and also the concern. I could almost see December 1839, and the man, Pinkhes Frydrych, who had just become the father of a son. Furious storms had hammered the village for days, and mounds of snow, thick and heavy, had piled on the roof of the little house beside the flour mill that Pinkhes rented from the town council.

Aging beams strained under the weight of accumulated winter. Pinkhes had wanted to climb to the roof all week, to shovel it clear, but it had been too dangerous. Each groan of suffering wood was a new reminder. Pinkhes looked up to the roof and beyond. "May you last another day," he said. Zlata was washing Fraydela's soft, dark curls in a metal tub on the same kitchen table where, the day before, the mohel had carved a slice off the baby. The men had elbowed each other, pushing and craning to get a better look, to watch, or if not exactly watch, to peer through wincing eyes while trying to block lingering memories of their own original injuries. They watched, or not exactly, as Shmil Frydrych, born eight days earlier, received his token drop of wine, felt the metal pierce his tender flesh, and released a shriek so powerful and painful it bounced off the snowy roof, back down the mohel's newly bloodied knife, and into the pants of each of those who flinched in sympathetic observation. "*Mazel tov!*" they yelled, patting the father on the back and holding the baby, still screaming, high above the sea of black hats. A *simcha.*

But now Fraydela's hair needed washing. Sura stood on the stool beside the stove, heeding her mother's instructions to *never stop* stirring the soup. Fraydela was trying to be a good girl and not complain about the *cold* water and the stinging lye. Pinkhes was pulling his hat down over his head and preparing for the walk up the hill to the town square. The czar had decreed that all nations living in Russian lands register their newborns with the civil authorities for means of taxes and conscription. Zlata hinted that it might not be a terrible idea if Shmil were, you know, not a matter of public record, but Pinkhes reminded her what had happened to Moyshe Alterman when a midlevel Russian officer in Kielce reported to his superiors that Moyshe's second-born son, Lem, had never been recorded. Shmil would be recorded, Pinkhes announced. And so, on the day after his son's circumcision, he wrapped the boy in a gray woolen blanket, tucked him into his coat, hoping this might keep them both warm, and steadied himself for the burst of cold that awaited them outside. "I will return," he said as he opened the door to the first smack of icy air and stepped out into the snow.

The hills and their shadows had vanished beneath the pallor of winter, erased until spring, when Pinkhes Frydrych set off from the mill, across the frozen creek, and up the hill toward the center of town. It took much longer to cross the town in winter. The ten-minute walk in summer meant twenty minutes in winter, slogging through bulky, wet snow and walking into the wind. Pinkhes, who was himself born thirty years earlier in this same town, had followed in his father's footsteps to become a miller. His son, too, would work the mill, he thought, as would his son's sons. Pinkhes watched his feet disappear into the snow, rescuing them one after the other, then plunging them back through the wet. The baby was starting to squirm. "Shhh," he whispered. "We're almost there." The market square looked frozen and empty as father and son approached. Beyond the square, smoke rising from the chimneys of the Christian homes danced around the white steeple of the church. The Christians had always lived at the top of the hill, in front of the church. The Jews had always lived at the bottom, behind the synagogue. The two sides had always met in the middle, crowding the square on market days, Tuesdays and Fridays, to bicker over the price of bread. But there were no meats or spices this day, no men announcing that their finely carved bowls were more finely carved than any in three surrounding towns. On this day there was only cold and white, a single merchant hunched over a bucket of thick-skinned potatoes, and a few other shivering souls rushing to finish whatever it was that had forced them from their stove-toasted homes and into December's bitter air. Pinkhes rushed across the square, holding tight to the baby for warmth.

It was just before three P.M. when Pinkhes arrived at the office of the town clerk, off the main square. He pulled the baby from his coat and set him down on the table. "This is my son," he said proudly. He wasn't happy to expose the boy to future conscription but was happy to show off his firstborn son. "I'd like for him to be registered." The scribe lifted the heavy Jewish book, bound in red, from the shelf behind him and turned through eleven months of born babies, through some who were already crawling, some already forming their small pink tongues around the beginnings of their first words, and through quite a few who had already been recorded a second time, in the back of the book. The clerk turned until he reached the first blank space in the birth section. He instructed Pinkhes to ask the adjacent shopkeepers to step in and serve as witnesses. Then he dipped his quill into ink and began to write: *It happened on December 12, 1839 at 3* p.m. The clerk guided his quill across the page. He was writing in his native Polish. The town of Działoszyce had been controlled by czars for half a century, but Polish was the most-spoken language among the Christians in the village. It had been the language of the Polish kings, including the one who granted the town its charter four hundred years earlier. And so Polish was the official language for record-keeping. The clerk asked Pinkhes the relevant questions and then wrote down what he was told:

> Pinkhes Frydrych, a 30-year-old renting a mill in Działoszyce, appeared in the presence of Abraham Łazęga, 64 years old, and Dawid Zelmanowicz, 40 years old, both merchants, both residents of Działoszyce. He presented a child of the male sex, born 3 December this year at 7 a.m. from his wife, Zlata, 26 years old. The child, during circumcision, was given the name Shmil Frydrych. This act was read to those present and signed by them.

Each man then dipped a quill into ink and signed his name. Pinkhes signed first in Hebrew letters, then in Polish ones. Then he wrapped his son back in the blanket and set across the snowy market square, having fulfilled his religious and civic obligations as the father of a boy. And so it was that, for legal, religious, secular, and symbolic purposes, Shmil Frydrych became a member of the human race, of the great nation of Ashkenaz, and of the small town at the confluence of two tributaries of the Nidzica River that the Jews called Dyaloshits, the Poles called Działoszyce (Jow-oh-SHEETZ-ah), and the czars called Russian land.

At least it could have happened that way. Or something close to that way. The details of the story have vanished along with Pinkhes's footsteps in the snow. But the spirit of that day would live on in the redbound volume that the clerk lifted from the shelf that day at the behest of my great-great-great-grandfather Pinkhes to record the birth of my great-great-grandfather Shmil.

The day would reveal itself 162 years later, on another snowy December day in a town not far from Działoszyce when the news of Pinkhes's newborn son would be read by the once inconceivable notion of an English-speaking daughter of the daughter of the son of the son of the newborn baby who came officially into existence on that presumably frigid day in December 1839. My great-great-great-grandfather Pinkhes may have believed his only mission that day was to comply with a czarist edict. But in doing so, he was also reaching out across the years, across the fall of an empire and the rise of another, across two world wars, an industrial revolution, a Russian retreat, a German advance, and another Russian retreat to send a message in a bottle to a distant heir, inviting her back to his time.

I spent months searching for the town where my great-grandfather Yisruel Frydrych was born. I made countless interminable drives to distant villages and spent hours in their archives, searching in vain for a hint or a clue. Then, on a morning in mid-December, Krys called to say he'd solved the mystery. He had returned from Italy and agreed to work with me, then immediately began translating a stack of Polish and Russian documents I'd collected into English. Among them was the marriage record of my great-grandfather's brother Yitskhok Frydrych, which was one of the documents I had begged free from the grip of the angry Będzin clerk the day I inadvertently disobeyed her. Weeks after that incident, Krys reported that when Yitskhok registered his marriage, he listed his birthplace as a town called Działoszyce. "It's up near Kielce, on the road to Warsaw," Krys said. "If Yitskhok was born there, Yisruel probably was, too." We made plans to drive there the following day.

The narrow roads north of Krakow were slippery with ice and snow, and it took us nearly three hours to wind our way along a route that, in warmer weather, would have taken no longer than an hour to drive. Unlike the modern highway that zipped west to Będzin, the older roads to the north had crosswalks for pedestrians and drew rural traffic of old ladies with jugs of water and donkey carts piled with wood. We found our way to Działoszyce, then continued a little farther to the slightly larger town of Pińczów, where someone directed us to the fourteenth-century stone barn that housed the records of dozens of little towns in this part of Poland. Within an hour, a search that had dragged on for months without success became instantly, magically easy. Like a cluster of fireworks, each explosion triggering the next, Krys and I not only found the long-sought birth record for my great-grandfather Yisruel Frydrych, we also found the record for his father, Shmil. We found records for his father's older sisters, Fraydela and Sura, and for his father's younger brother, Yankl. We found birth, marriage, and death records for aunts and uncles, cousins and kin going back as far as the first Działoszyce Jewish book in 1809, and we emerged two hours later with thirty-seven different Frydrych documents spanning the length and breadth of the nineteenth century. Within a few hours, we had gathered an entire century of family history.

It was that easy. There had been no conflict, no begging. Krys had done the talking, telling the archivists that he was my cousin and we were researching our family. No one became alarmed about a foreigner in the building. I just had to sit and wait, my only suffering the sight of irreplaceable record books sitting in puddles on the floor, covered with loose plastic sheets. After months with my face in these moldy volumes with incremental victories, I was instantly transported conclusively and substantially back beyond the story I knew, beyond a narrative that to me had always begun with a young couple falling in love in a ghetto. Będzin had been the only Polish city I'd ever heard in connection with my family. But now the story could find its way back at least another century. My mom was born as her family was slamming so hard against history that all stories that preceded her—all family heirlooms—were blown away like nearly every Jewish town in Europe into indecipherable bits, impossible to reconstruct, let alone rediscover. But now it was all there for me to imagine. I could arrive at the home of a small-town miller named Pinkhes Frydrych on the day he wrapped his firstborn son in a woolen blanket and carried him up the hill to record his birth in a volume bound in red.

I'd never given much thought to a past this distant. With a cataclysmic event like the holocaust in my family history, there was never much point in wondering what came before. But as I unearthed these early roots of the family tree, I found that their discovery was almost transcendental. They lured me in, showed me the life that had thrived in the years between the fall of the Second Temple and the ovens at Auschwitz—the years they skipped when they taught Jewish history in Hebrew school. In the age of Zionism, Jewish history was taught to me as the story of before and after. There was before, in the land of milk and honey, and there was after, in the land we needed to fight for. If anything happened in between, if Yiddish culture flourished for hundreds of years among the flatlands and rolling hills of Eastern Europe, if music or politics or scientific theory emerged from the shtetls and towns where Jewish people lived, they were explained to me as times of terrible suffering, of weeping and longing, that culminated in the most catastrophic of global events. But now the between years had names and places. An entire ancestral garden had sprouted and bloomed in those years, and I sensed how much more there was to discover. It was the same sensation I'd had on Rosh Hashanah, of history coming alive and speaking to me, presenting itself for me to imagine.

I wondered how far back I could go: back to Moses and the flight from slavery in Egypt? To the Second Temple? To the fall of Rome, when the Jews living throughout the empire scattered north into Western Europe to form the Jewish communities that came to be called

Ashkenaz? I could go back as far as the fourteenth century, when a Polish king invited Jews to Poland and offered to protect them from the pogroms and inquisitions that they'd confronted in England and France, then Spain and Germany. Or maybe just as far as Działoszyce, to the small-town miller and his newborn son in the nineteenth century. I could romanticize his life, conjure details like the smell of Zlata's soup or the sweet black curls of his daughter's hair. I could stand in a foot of snow in the market square with Krys and see Pinkhes coming up the hill with his nine-day-old son in his arms. The day when Krys and I explored the little town while snow drifted from the winter sky, I could see how much could pile on a person's roof there. So maybe I could picture that and give a tiny breath of life to a time that had been largely forgotten.

When Krys and I arrived in snowy Działoszyce, we saw the white steeple of the church at the top of the hill, then coasted slowly down the winding road into the market square. Działoszyce's square had buildings on only three of its sides. On the fourth side was a yawning field bisected by a frozen creek. There was an hour left before the early winter sunset, so we studied the facades of the buildings around us, looking for the synagogue, for clues embedded in stone that would show us where the shul had been. Across the square, I spotted an older woman sitting at a bus stop and suggested to Krys that we ask her where the synagogue once stood. Krys agreed but then paused. "We might start a pogrom," he said with a wink. I could tell he was joking but was surprised to hear him say this. "You think?" I asked. "No," he said, shaking his head. "But in these small towns"—he shrugged—"you never know." With that, he took a step through the snow toward the old lady, then stopped. "Hey, Erin," he said. "Come look at this." I moved toward Krys and followed his long pointing finger to an abandoned building that stood by itself across the frozen field. It was missing its roof and had no glass in its narrow slit windows, but we both could tell what it had been.

We made our way across the field and walked in through a small opening at the back of the building. All that remained of the structure were four walls of heavily built brick and clay. There were cutouts where windows and doors had been and a chill white sky in the open space where a roof once offered shelter. We saw bits of wood against the front wall where an ark had been and two halves of a sloping divider that once separated women from men. There was even a shallow indentation on one side of the clay divider where, in better times, the community had placed a *tzedakah* box to collect money for charity. The building wasn't much more than a ruin—an empty shell around a winter sky—but it was proud and regal, even now. It sat on a bend in the creek, completely by itself, a quiet reminder of what was missing. Its slim windows stood at attention around the rectangular perimeter. Once there might have been art on the walls and tile on the floor. But now, in place of people and ceremony, there was a rich, dramatic light glinting on the floor of snow. Inside, we saw what might have been the detritus of teenage parties—discarded beer cans, cigarette butts, some patches of yellow in the snow along the walls. I could see why local kids would gather here. It was quiet and mystical, away from the watchful eye of the community. I hoped that at least some of these kids stopped on occasion to imagine this place back when 65 percent of Działoszyce's citizens were Jews, back when the shul was full and the community thrived.

Krys and I assumed that the synagogue had been torched, like others in this country, in the early days of the war. But the man at the community center who sold us a book on the history of Działoszyce told us that the synagogue had survived the war untouched. When the roof collapsed in the 1980s, he said, it was a casualty of neglect, not of war. According to the history book, when the Działoszyce synagogue was built in 1852, the town had seventeen hundred inhabitants, mostly Jews. The Działoszyce memory book, compiled by Jewish town survivors after World War II, recalled that most of the Jewish townsfolk were craftsmen or merchants. They collected goods from the fertile farm-lands in the surrounding hills and sold them on Tuesdays and Fridays in the central square. There were two flour mills in town during the nineteenth century and six in the vicinity that were managed or leased by Jews. Pinkhes Frydrych must have had one of those leases.

I considered Pinkhes and Zlata at the opening ceremony for the new shul. They may have stood with their four children—Sura, born in 1834; Fraydela, born in 1838; and the two boys: Shmil, born in 1839, and Yankl in 1842. Maybe the aging couple recalled the celebra-tions they'd made in the old shul and wondered what events would take place in the new one. Maybe it would be to the new shul, where, in the 1860s, Shmil Frydrych would go after marrying Liba Mari Hen-kos. And maybe Shmil would pass that shul in 1868 when, like his father before him, he started up the hill toward the market square with a squirming nine-day-old baby in his arms.

It would be summer—June 4, 1868—on the day that Shmil Fryd-rych would instruct the clerk to record the birth of his son Yisruel. Like his father before him, Shmil would sign the document first in He-brew, then in the official language, which would no longer be Polish. An uprising would have caused the czar to crack down on the speaking of Polish so that by the time of my great-grandfather's birth, Russian would be the official language for record-keeping. Shmil Frydrych may have assumed that Yisruel would one day make the same walk with his children at the hour of their births, but the world was about to change. The small-town life that Pinkhes and Shmil knew would no longer be enough for modern men like Yisruel and his brother Yitskhok. The brothers would come of age at the dawn of industry as a new cen-tury approached. When they became men, Yisruel and Yitskhok would travel west so that their children could be born in a modern city at the westernmost tip of the czar's sprawling reach. In Będzin, Yitskhok would apprentice to become a jeweler. In 1904 he would marry a girl named Pesela Najman, and they would have ten children. Yisruel and

Zisl would buy a house at 7 Modrzejowska Street, where they would raise eight children. They would start a family brass business and one day upgrade to a bigger house at 20 Małachowskiego Street that, due to circumstances no one could have predicted, they would continue to own even sixty years after their deaths.

CHAPTER NINETEEN

After nearly a year in the land of my mother's birth, Poland had given me a home. It was not a sentimental home, warmed by the fires of time, but a real home where leaks needed fixing, occupants required attention, and people wanted feeding and care. I had a strained relationship with the family I'd come to Poland to find and no idea how to repair the damage. But here in the country where I once thought I'd be hated, I had found a connection with the land and its past. The well of my search drew now from the sweeter waters below, where the taste of blood was diluted by the flavors of music and books, language and arts, created here by my family and others. Somehow, after everything, I had come to feel welcome.

I had a small group of close friends, including Krys and a mix of Poles and expats whom I had met throughout the year. As winter settled in, we were bunkering into a cozy life of thick Polish soups and honey vodkas with tea. David came to visit in December, and Krys took us home to spend Christmas with his family in a snow-covered village near the mountains of southern Poland. For New Year's Eve, thirty of us piled into a ski lodge near the Slovakian border. It was mostly Krys's college friends who'd come home from England or France to spend Christmas with their families. As one year faded into the next, I increasingly found that I wasn't ready to leave. I was due back at my job in Philadelphia. I had been granted a year off from work but had lost several months to my mother's illness and death. Now, I wondered what would happen if I didn't go home, at least not yet. I missed Philadelphia. I missed David. I missed my friends and my job. But then I thought about Krakow in the spring, about watching the Planty bloom again, and about seeing the somnolent wintry market square surge back to life. I thought about how much I still had to learn, about how I still hadn't found my grandmother's Rozenblum siblings or the name of the town where Zisl Frydrych was born. I hadn't even begun to look for the woman who left Zilla on the train.

An important part of me wanted to stay another year. David insisted that he was serious about coming to live with me in Poland if I decided to stay. He was a computer programmer who could work remotely and had already talked to his boss about telecommuting. Thinking about it, I could taste the fantasy I'd conjured back in Amsterdam about Hemingway and his cosmopolitan café life, about being young and in love and trying to do good work. David and I talked dreamily about our plans of staying in Poland. I would use my mother's birth certificate to become a Polish citizen, not just because it would make the taxes cheaper on the family home but also because I loved the idea of actually belonging in a country that never fully considered my mother a citizen. To come back these years later and become what she should have been had a triumphant feel of "so there," the sensation of planting a flag on a hillside after a victorious battle. With enough time, I thought, I could improve my Polish enough to befriend even non-English-speaking Poles, and with Dave as my partner, I could wholeheartedly invest myself in the place where my mother was born. I thought maybe I'd convince Krys and Magda to set up a tour agency with me. We could take

Jewish families on customized tours of their own shtetls and towns. We could help them do the research for their families that Krys and Magda had helped me do for mine. Dave, too, would make friends here. We would travel the continent, see the world, and fall deliciously in love with each other.

It was an exhilarating idea but it was also impractical. I would run out of money. I would have no job to return to. And I knew that David didn't really want to move, that he would rather I return to Philadelphia. Either way, I needed to make up my mind. If I did intend to leave, I needed plane tickets, and I needed to notify the friend who was renting my house. But as much as I wanted to resolve the question, and as much as David deserved a conclusive answer, I couldn't make any decisions without determining what the future would hold with the Skowrońskis. The thought of never having to visit that family again was, frankly, a prominent pro on the side of going home. But leaving things as they were would have felt like climbing a mountain halfway to the summit, then turning back at the first drop of drizzling rain. If I truly planned to stay on in Poland for another year, then I had to make peace with the Skowrońskis. I had to make them my partners in whatever I endeavored to do here. Without them and their connection to my mother's childhood, I might as well have been living in Moscow or Prague. I might as well have moved to any other place in any other part of the world.

I set January 7 as my decision date and promised both Dave and myself that I would have a final answer by the end of that day. Then, on January 6 I set off to at last accept Marta's gracious invitation to spend the night inside my family home. As I drove west to Będzin on that icy January day, I wondered if this would be my final drive along the familiar route, or if I could turn it into a different kind of visit, one conducted on different terms. I wasn't sure what I would discuss with Marta, whether I'd be able to speak Polish through an entire night without an interpreter. I worried about other things, too, selfish things, like where I would sleep and whether there'd be room for me in Marta's two-room apartment. I spent the entirety of my drive to Będzin concocting excuses for why I wouldn't be able to spend the night after all. But I was curious, too. I wondered what would happen when Marta and I dropped the formalities and began to consider ourselves less as heirs to a business deal and more as possible friends. I wondered how it would feel to sleep in the very house where so much of my family story had unfolded. I wondered if I'd be able to sense the presence of my aunts and uncles and cousins who had lived in the house—who possibly had died there.

When I pulled into the courtyard, Marta greeted me warmly, extending a hug that conveyed a sincere anticipation of my visit. I made an effort to mimic her enthusiasm and be both a good sport and a gracious guest. I lavished praise on our dinner of chicken soup and potatoes, which really was wonderful. And when Wiesław and Helen stopped in to say hello, I complimented them, too, told them they were looking well. Maybe because they didn't mention the property, or maybe because they were only there a short while, the encounter was among the least stressful I'd had with them in months. Soon my trepidations about the night began to seem needless. I felt encouraged. This was where I needed to be now, with Marta and her family, eating dinner and exchanging cordialities. After dinner, I followed Marta, her husband, and their son, Marek, to a third-floor apartment in one of the back properties, beyond the brass factory, where Marta's brother and sister-in-law lived. Marek was put to bed with the other kids in that apartment, and I joined the adults on a sofa in front of a large TV. Someone produced a jug of sweet German wine. Another of Wiesław's daughters arrived with a bottle of vodka. Another man and a woman arrived. I wasn't entirely sure how they were all related, but the apartment quickly became a full-fledged party. Helen even dropped by for a couple of drinks. She told jokes and laughed with the others. My Polish was still spotty, and I missed a lot of the conversation, but it was clearly dusted with the sort of laughter that accompanies gossip and merrymaking. I thought how lucky it was for an entire family to live within steps of one another like this, to be able to come together and socialize every evening after the kids had gone to bed. They were making me feel like a part of their family, and for the first time in months, I genuinely felt that there could be something between the Frydrychs and Skowrońskis, something that could be salvaged.

As the wine and vodka flushed over me, I smiled with the joy of a sad story acquiring a happy ending. We were writing a new finale to a tale that began in this very house sixty years earlier. I could at last envision a time when we could ride off into the sunset at the end of our war story. That was the moment, more or less, when I made up my mind: I was going to stay. I would return to Krakow the following day, call my editors, and beg them to extend my leave. I would call David to tell him that I would take him up on his offer to join me in Poland. I would devote myself to learning Polish as intensively as I did when I first arrived, when I needed the language to survive, and I vowed that when I next returned to Będzin, it would be with the ability to laugh at jokes and appreciate linguistic nuance. Marta and I would become friends, and we would one day discuss our families and figure out how things had become so complicated. She and I—the next generation— would find a way to make peace between our families, both now and in the future.

Someday, I thought, bubbling with anticipation, I would bring my entire family here to Będzin for a reunion. I would bring the cousins and aunts and uncles who, like me, had been severed from their heritage by an ocean and the culture of a foreign land. I would hope that they might find the same allure in the landscape of our legacy and find meaning in this old story and this run-down house. Maybe, I thought, a family reunion in Poland could be even more important, and even more significant, than the more modest reunion between a brother and his long-lost sister that had been my grandest dream. The new dream, the larger reunion—without my mother, sadly, but with many more people—could be impressive enough and vital enough to fill the black hole left by the implosion of the old dream. It could give me something to strive for.

That moment, in a roomful of laughing, smiling Skowrońskis, would have been the happiest of all possible endings for me, the one I had craved since the first time I walked up the path from Małachowskiego Street. But, like many such giddy nights, this one woke to the jarring splash of morning light when I went upstairs to Wiesław's apartment to say a quick good-bye and found my mother's long-lost brother lying in bed, apparently drunk. Wiesław didn't usually drink, I'd been told, because of the medication he took for his heart, but he must have made an exception that day. He must have gotten up early and started to drink, or else he'd been drinking so late the night before that the stink of it still clung to his skin in the morning. And when he saw me, he sneered at me. I wasn't sure why he was upset, whether he was mad that I spent the evening with his daughter and not with him, or whether there was something else bothering him. Whatever it was, he greeted me not with his usual warmth, not with a hug or a smile, but with pointed questions about why I wasn't doing more to solve his family's property problems.

I was stunned by his tone and tried to answer as best I could, but his questions simmered into accusations that surged into a tirade. He pointed his crooked finger at me and upbraided me, telling me, with a slur in his voice and venom in his face, that my grandfather had given this house to his mother and that he had promised to come back and fix things and that he never did and that my grandfather had created these problems and that his family now had to deal with them. Wiesław told me that I had come here and said I would help but that I hadn't helped, I hadn't done anything at all, or if I had done something, it wasn't enough. And, well, I didn't catch it verbatim, but my Polish wasn't so bad that I could miss the timbre of this particular rant. It was the same one I'd heard a dozen different times from him and from his wife, in a dozen different forms and on a dozen different occasions, but I'd never heard it quite like this before, never so menacingly and, frankly, never so mean.

I knew that Wiesław was a gentle soul. I knew he never would have hit me. But standing there in the doorway between his kitchen and his bedroom, in an apartment that may well have been the very apartment where my mother was born, I looked up at the wrath in Wiesław's eyes and thought that he actually might. I thought he might raise his hand and slap it hard across my face. At that moment the pendulum that had merrily settled on *stay* the night before swung swiftly back in the other direction, completely and irreversibly veering my decision away from *stay* and hurling it resoundingly back toward *leave*. I shook Wiesław's hand. It was the same hand I'd once taken with enormous if timid anticipation, with a tremble in my throat, and with an overwhelming sense of history in resolution. Eight months later, a few days into a year that I hoped would be better than the last, I shook Wiesław's hand with curt finality. "Good-bye, sir," I said. "Thank you." Then I left. I walked down the stairs from his apartment, out into the courtyard, past my family's former *meshingiser*, and into Ania's car. I started the engine, put the car in reverse, pulled into a three-point turn, and drove forward onto Modrzejowska Street behind the house. I drove back to Krakow, carefully on the plowed but slippery highway, and announced to Krys when I walked in the door that I had made up my mind: "I'm done," I told him. "I can go home now." And even though Marta called me later that night to say she'd heard what had happened with her father, and even though she said that he wanted me to know he was sorry, and even though she sounded sweet when she told me she hoped I wasn't angry, and even though I told her no, I wasn't angry, and even though I meant what I said, that I really wasn't angry, it was, I knew, too late. I had made up my mind. It was time to go home.

Exactly three weeks later, I gave Krys a box of things I couldn't bring with me and tearfully hugged him good-bye. I mailed Ania's car keys to her parents and told them where they could find her Daewoo, then I flew to Chicago where, by prearrangement, I met Ania at customs. She handed me the keys to my car and asked me to drop her at a friend's in the city. I drove down around Lake Michigan and across my home state to Detroit, where I stayed for a week with my father before moving my storage boxes from a pile in his basement to the trunk of my car. Then, in the first week of February 2002, I set out across Ohio and Pennsylvania on the very same drive I'd made with my mother two and a half years earlier, in the middle of a heat wave, when she told me a story that would set me on a journey that would ultimately end in defeat. At least it would feel to me like it had ended in defeat. It would feel that way for a while.

I had gone in search of something—my mother? the truth? myself? the past?—and had emerged on the other side with no clear answers about any of the above. I had set out seeking resolution and returned without any at all. I hadn't learned much more about my mother, beyond the fact that her memory was imperfect in places and acutely accurate in others. She remained mostly a mystery to me, a woman I would always admire while eternally craving her approval. But just as my mother's story didn't end with her dramatic voyage across the ocean for a new life in a new country, my story didn't end when I landed at Chicago O'Hare. I didn't know what would happen to the Skowrońskis or the Frydrychs. I couldn't predict the fate of the house where our families had lived. But even back then, even back when I nursed the shame of what I thought was my failure, I knew that the story would live. I knew that my mother had invented her first happily-ever-after, that her triumphant voyage to America had been more about myth than reality, but I knew also that an actual happy ending eventually arrived in my mother's life. I knew that she eventually found herself a home, a family, and a time in her life when she truly was always loved. And so I knew that my story hadn't ended, at least not yet, that my happily-ever-after was still just finding its way.

EPILOGUE

MORE THAN FIVE YEARS HAVE PASSED SINCE MY RETURN FROM Poland, and the knotted saga of 20 Małachowskiego has only stumbled and tripped. Though I did everything that my lawyers instructed, though I gathered all of the birth, marriage, and death records on their extensive list, and though I had all the records appropriately processed, the legal case has crawled along at a slower pace than even Tomasz Borcz predicted. My great-grandparents wouldn't be declared dead by a Polish court until 2003. They wouldn't receive their death certificates until a full year after that. The Skowrońskis, meanwhile, would become even more impatient with the lagging process and would eventually take matters into their own hands. In 2004 they would file a claim under a Polish squatter's law that could enable them, as longtime occupants of the property, to become its owners. If they're successful, their names will appear on the deed to 20 Małachowskiego, and my family will lose every right we ever had to the home my great-grandparents sacrificed to buy. I would be shaken by this maneuver, not because I wanted the property or because I didn't want the Skowrońskis to have it. I would be shaken because the family I once tried to help, the family I once felt honor-bound to assist, had essentially become my legal adversary. In the eyes of the Będzin court, their squatter's claim would stand in active opposition to my bid to inherit the land.

The squatter's law was something we discussed back in 2001. Though I wasn't clear on this at the time, the document they had wanted my mother to sign at the Polish embassy in Washington was a declaration confirming that they had lived as good-faith owners of 20 Małachowskiego for the twenty years required by law. The squatter's claim was something the Skowrońskis had discussed before I even arrived on their doorstep, they told me; they had never taken that step, partly because they needed testimony from my family, but mostly because they needed money to pay taxes and fees that could surge as high as ten or twenty thousand dollars. One of their requests in 2001 was for me to support their claim and pay the taxes, but I told them this wasn't possible, that while the inheritance claim came with similar expenses, I would have a chance to recoup those costs by selling off units in the building or structures at the back of the lot. I assured them that I would guarantee them a place to live in the building, but that I couldn't be a part of their claim.

What changed between 2001 and 2004 was the Będzin tax collector told the Skowrońskis that, because they were poor, they could become exempt from the costly fees associated with taking ownership of the property. They went promptly to the court and filed their claim. I couldn't blame them. I surely would have done the same. But when I heard about their claim from my lawyer, I felt like I had been slapped. I had already spent several thousand dollars and countless hours on an inheritance claim that I was bringing, ostensibly for them, and now they were moving to stop me. My lawyer suggested that the best course for me would be to drop my case and throw my support behind theirs. With my testimony, he said, the Skowrońskis' claim would go faster than mine. I wanted to take my lawyer's advice and, despite my dismay over their seemingly sudden gambit, I wanted to support the Skowrońskis. But as with everything else connected to that house, it wasn't that simple.

One problem was the Baytners. When the Skowrońskis filed their squatter's claim, they didn't just file for my family's half of the property. They filed for the entire property. I e-mailed Hannah Baytner in Israel to inform her that if she wanted to keep her family real estate, she needed to act quickly. She called me, enraged, loudly insisting that we needed to stand together against Helen Skowrońska. "To the street!" she shouted into the phone when I told her I wasn't sure how I wanted to proceed. "To the street you must throw her! She is a Pole. You are a Jew. For you she does nothing! There is nothing that you owe her!"

Another problem was the Frydrychs and the more than four dozen shiny paper plates that stretched across the wall of the hotel ballroom at my long-ago family reunion. It was one thing to get my cousins' cooperation for a plan to inherit a home from our dead ancestors. Asking them to give our ancestors' home to a Polish family, even one connected to the woman who had saved my mother, was a different matter entirely. "I don't know what to do," my cousin Lillian sighed into the phone. "I don't want property in Poland, but I remember how important that house was to my parents. It just doesn't seem right that these people should have it."

After months of hair-pulling rumination over how to proceed, I told my lawyer that I wouldn't oppose the Skowrońskis' claim but that my family could not collectively support it, either. When I traveled to Poland in September 2006 to testify in both legal matters, I told the judge in the squatter's case that I personally did not oppose the motion, but that I couldn't speak for any of my many cousins. I also told the judge, in case it was relevant, that I had seen a document my grandfather gave to Honorata Skowrońska in 1945 that gave her the right to manage the property and to act as its owner. I wasn't sure if that statement would help the Skowrońskis or stand in their way. As of today, neither case has been concluded. They remain as unresolved and ambiguous as the relationship between the two families involved.

I'm not sure what will happen when the court cases conclude, how I'll feel about the house or about the Skowrońskis. I'd like to think there might still be a chance for a friendship to bloom someday, but my skepticism hasn't diminished. In fact, I became even more skeptical after a disturbing encounter I had with the Skowrońskis' downstairs neighbor on a visit I made to the house in 2004. The neighbor quietly approached me as I made my way up the stairs one day when I was visiting with my lawyer. She silently motioned me into her apartment, sat me down and implored me not to give the house to Helen Skowrońska. "They're terrible people," she told me. She said Helen had told her that as soon as the "rich American" gave her the house, her first act would be to evict this neighbor. "I don't want to be evicted," this woman pleaded. "Please don't give her the house." Her pleading speech contained many of the same complaints that a neighbor had made about Honorata in a letter to my grandfather forty years earlier.

Dismayed by the dragging property saga and determined to produce something worthwhile from my time in Poland, I contacted the public radio program *This American Life* in 2002 and pitched a story about the popularity of Jewish culture in Poland. I thought that by broadcasting the story of young Poles embracing Jewish culture, I could soften the harsh edges that defined the American Jewish view of Poland. I even interviewed Magda, who did fulfill her goal of converting to Judaism, but never seemed to experience the life-changing reinvention I suspect she was after. These years later, she's still trying to define herself as a Pole or a Jew or the something new that her nation has become since joining the European Union. Even now I think she's still struggling to figure out who she is and what she wants to be.

I had grand hopes for the radio piece. I believed it might lend some perspective to the resentment that lingered between Poles and Jews.

But when the show aired in September 2002, the Poles who heard it took offense. They heard me say at the beginning that "I'd always heard Poles were anti-Semitic," and that even though my mother was saved by a Pole, I'd heard the family "only did it for the money." And though this was the setup, the myth I would debunk in the piece, the Polish listeners took it as proof of my bigotry and considered me another Jew accusing Poles of crimes they hadn't committed. They sent me angry e-mails and lit up the program's online comment board with accusatory invective. They called the piece "replete with ignorance, ethnic hatred, and lies" and salted their comments with words like *inaccurate, arrogant,* and *insulting.* Then Jewish listeners entered the debate, sniping back that the Polish listeners needed to acknowledge their crimes and accept responsibility for what they had done. One of the Jewish writers accused the Poles of "shrill defensiveness" and "blatant anti-Semitism." My relatives, meanwhile, were dismayed by my portrayal of Poland. "I'm glad you met some nice people there," one of my older cousins told me. "But they still hate us. They always have." And with that, my dream of building cultural harmony and understanding evaporated along with my other aspirations. As much as I tried to put the fad into context, the people who heard the program—Jews and Poles alike— heard only what they wanted to hear.

At some point, I had to acknowledge that I had set my hopes too high, that I had tried to do more than any one person could, that the conflicts around me—the personal ones between my family and the Skowrońskis, and the global ones between Poles and Jews—were just too charged. There were too many agendas and too many sacred suppositions. I met many people in Poland who were anxious to deal with the legacy of what had happened there. I met young Poles embracing the multiethnic past of their now homogenous land, hoping to redefine their country as an international nation, free from the stereotypes pinned on their parents. I met Jews who, like me, were desperately researching family histories against a ticking clock of a survivor generation that is already nearly gone. And I met those, like the Skowrońskis, who stayed behind when so many others departed. Their country was put on ice for forty-four years, and when that ice melted in 1989, they discovered that old demons were still there, still alive, still on the deed, still needing to be dealt with like the ghosts that walked the streets of Kazimierz or slept beneath the open sky of the Działoszyce shul. These demons lingered on, haunting the living.

The government of Poland owned thousands of properties—no one knew exactly how many—that its predecessor governments had illegally seized but that the current government would never have the money to restitute. It therefore created a bureaucratic structure to stand between people like me and our ties to the past, drafting personal-property laws to make archivists wary of foreigners. My legal case was one of possibly hundreds or thousands that affected properties with unclear deeds and with occupants of ambiguous standing. But the courts were corrupted by antiquated laws and by a government unwilling to confront the past. These were intractable problems, and in the end, I had no choice but to admit that I had been foolish to believe I could solve them.

The perfect literary way to end this book, I've always thought, would have been with the birth of a red-haired daughter to whom I would give the name Irena. In this ideal ending, I would promise to raise the child as attentively—and with the same high expectations—as my mother raised me. And I would hope for my daughter to someday try again in the next generation to do what her mother and grandmother could not. This book would end as it began, as the story of a mother and a daughter and of legacies passed on through generations. But though David and I are still together, and though he has the red hair that could theoretically give me the child of literary perfection, he refuses to let me have a baby for the purpose of an epilogue. So, in the absence of that, I shall end this book with the news that I did see the fulfillment of one of my dreams. It was the vision I had the night I sat drinking with Marta and the other Skowrońskis in January 2002 when I vowed to host a family reunion in Poland.

A year after my return to Philadelphia, I sent invitations to more than fifty relatives, the living descendants of Yisruel and Zisl as well as the descendants of Yisruel's brother Yitskhok. Roughly twenty people expressed some interest, but there were concerns about cost and school schedules and quite a few objections from those who told me they would never step foot on Polish soil. In the end, twelve of us made the trip, including my brother, my father, David, and five of my mother's cousins, ranging in age from twenty-one to eighty-nine. We met in Poland in September 2003 at the dawn of 5764 on the Hebrew calendar and spent Rosh Hashanah in the tiny Krakow synagogue where I had taken my father two years earlier.

On the first night of the holiday, which was also the Sabbath, I stood around a table before the service, watching my cousin Jane light a pair of tiny tea candles with the strike of a single match. She said a prayer, lit first one wick and then the other, then circled her hands over the flames and covered her eyes. When she was done, I repeated the gestures, followed by two of Jane's daughters, Karen and Patti, and by Karen's daughter, Emily, who at twenty-one was the youngest member of our group. After Emily, the next candles were lit by Jane's sister Annie, who, at eighty-nine, was the oldest traveler. Annie was legally blind but determined to see what she could of the country where her mother was born. Then the lot of us, the female half of our family history tour, stopped and watched the little fires burn.

We stood there silently, watching a tray of burning lights until someone—I can't remember who—asked the question that made it worthwhile: "Isn't it wonderful to do this here?" she asked. And it was. The trip had been a hassle to put together. I had fired the travel agent in a disagreement over airfares and had ended up planning all of the details myself. I booked the flights, reserved the hotel rooms, hired the drivers, planned the tours, scheduled the meals, and took the heat of everyone's individual needs and agendas. It had been an extraordinarily taxing ordeal, but that night, with the candles burning, none of that mattered anymore.

We went to shul to hear the ancient music lofting in rafters, led by the Brooklyn rabbi who still made certain that Krakow's high holiday services were divine. Then two days later, after the holiday ended, I led our twelve-person entourage, plus a driver and interpreter, up the path to 20 Małachowskiego. As we approached, nearly everyone in the group—my father, my cousins, my brother, my boyfriend—was looking up at the house, at its three stories of pinkish brick. But I was looking at Jane. It had been almost seven decades since Jane, at age six, had last stepped foot on this property. It was 1934 when Jane came with her parents and her sister Gloria to spend the summer with her grandparents. She remembered showing off her American roller skates to her old-country cousins and squealing when she had to use the outhouse. Sixty-nine years later, as I led her down the same walkway she'd walked as a child, I could see her body shake when she realized she knew where she was. She stopped halfway from the sidewalk to the door and stared as though hypnotized at the archway that led through the house. "Would I go in there?" she asked me, pointing. Her tone was methodic, like a child reciting a poem. "Yes, Jane," I said. "It's through there."

I had barely known Jane before my mother died. When she talked to me at my mother's funeral, I wondered which of my mom's many cousins she was. Now, having worked with her on gathering documents for the Polish legal battle, and on collecting family photos and stories for my research, I was struck by how much she reminded me of my mother. Jane's skin was the same all but translucent white as my mother's. Her face had the same blanket of freckles that nestled in the creases around her mouth. Jane's hair was the same shade of red that once disguised my mother's identity and saved her young life. Jane was fourteen years older than my mom but had always been the likeness of her baby cousin. She'd watched out for her, she told me, since the day

Mom arrived as a scared little kid on a boat from Europe. "I had to look out for her because she was another redhead," Jane said. Traveling with Jane and her family, I noticed that she and my mom had similar expressions, both vocally and facially, the same pair of laughing eyes, though Jane's were hazel, like mine, not blue, like my mom's.

My mother never would have been as emotional standing in front of the house as Jane was that day. My mom would not have remembered having been there, but standing there, watching what looked like my mother's face showing the kind of passion that, in my wildest fantasies, my mom's would have had, I could feel my hands and my heart and my head and my spine and my fingers and toes all swelling with an overwhelming mix of sorrow and joy. The sensations of the last few years came flowing back at once, arriving together. Jane's big hazel eyes stretched open with amazement as she stood in the archway that ran through the house. "I was only six years old, my God!" she said, shaking her head as though trying to free herself from a trance.

Later, when I watched the video of that day, I saw that Helen Skowrońska had been standing in the front walkway, watching us as we arrived. We had passed her on our approach to the house, but because my eyes were so focused on Jane, I hadn't seen Helen until we were all crowded in the courtyard behind the house, taking pictures, like tourists in a cathedral, of the spot where Jane was certain the outhouse had been. I blushed when I saw Helen and approached to greet her. In the time since I'd last seen her, Helen had dyed her gray hair blond. She was wearing a bright green sweater. I introduced Helen to some members of my family while some of the others fanned out around the courtyard, peering into windows. I hoped Helen wasn't made nervous by this massive invasion. I had called ahead to warn her that I was coming with twelve other people, but I knew I couldn't control what my family would say or do, and I didn't want a repeat on a larger scale of the smaller conflicts that once were common between us. To my relief, Helen didn't seem to mind our invasion. She invited us upstairs, where she had cakes and, though it was ten A.M., wine and vodka to drink. We followed Helen up the stairs that Jane claimed one of Zisl's chickens used to climb every morning to lay an egg in a basket under the kitchen sink.

At the top of the stairs, I knew the door wouldn't open to Wiesław's gentle face. He had died in July 2002, only six months after I left Poland. Marta had sent me a two-line e-mail the following September that said, more or less: *Please contact us immediately. Since the death of Wiesław Skowroński, we are concerned that we will be evicted.* There was no cushioning of this information for me as I had once done for them, no suggestion that I might care in any way other than how this would affect them financially. In fact, I didn't care, though I once might have hoped to. I forwarded the e-mail to my lawyer in Katowice, who said it wasn't much of a threat, that it would take years for an eviction to go anywhere in Poland. He offered to call the Skowrońskis to assure them of this.

We all crowded into the living room, which had been completely redone with a new beige paint job and furniture that I recognized from Marta's apartment downstairs in the former brass factory. After Wiesław's death, Marta and her family had moved upstairs because Helen did not want to live alone as a widow. One of her sons had wanted to move in with her, but, Helen said, he tended to be angry and combative when he drank. "My husband was the same way," she said, prompting Marta to giggle and remind her mother that "Earlyn remembers." We mingled around the apartment for a few minutes, marveling at how well Jane remembered the place as it had been in 1934. She knew, before Helen could tell her, that the kitchen had been moved from one side of the apartment to the other and that the living room had been subdivided into two rooms from one. Then we all settled into what became a kind of raucous family meeting. Our interpreter was Krys's friend Agnieszka, who volunteered for the trip when Krys said he couldn't stand the thought of going to Będzin or seeing the Skowrońskis again. Magda had returned to Krakow after eighteen months in New York, but during my family visit, she was cramming to complete her long-delayed master's thesis and couldn't spare the time for a day trip. With Agnieszka translating above the din of a few simultaneous conversations, Helen told my family how much she had suffered with her real estate problems. She repeated many of the statements she had made to me in 2001, only now they were remixed for a larger audience, and the pressure was no longer on me alone.

When people began to stir after about an hour, I announced that it was time for us to go. "But wait!" Helen stopped me. "We haven't resolved this." I turned to her, surprised that she expected some kind of resolution. I told her we had run out of time, that I wanted my family to visit the castle before returning to Krakow. "But the castle will always be here," Helen objected. "We have problems now." Two years earlier, Helen's dismay over our leaving would have upset me. This time I said I was sorry, but it was time for us to leave. We filed back down the stairs and into the front yard, where we stopped to pose for a group portrait before moving on to the castle and the old Jewish cemetery and the memorial to the Great Synagogue of Będzin.

When Helen filed her squatter's law claim about six months later, I wondered if her manuever was rooted at all in her annoyance with me for ending that meeting. I wondered if I could have done or said something that would have convinced her to hold off. But even if we had stayed a little longer, even if we had been kinder or more understanding, there was nothing more we could have offered Helen that would have soothed her concerns. I suppose we could have given her money, but I couldn't guess how much would have been enough.

At the top of Modrzejowska Street, beside the vacant lot that once contained the house where my family lived before moving to Małachowskiego, it was my cousin Annie's turn to alight with childhood memory. Annie was nine in 1923 when she visited her grandparents at this first house. The brass business was so small then, Annie said, that her grandmother Zisl sold brass pressing irons and doorknobs from the kitchen table. Annie was born in Detroit in 1914, a year after her mother, Faygl, emigrated from Będzin. As a young married woman in the 1940s, Annie moved from Detroit to Los Angeles with her husband and children, followed soon by her mother. It was Annie who hosted my mom and her parents for a few months in California in early 1951. My mom spent her heartbreaking ninth birthday in Annie's house on Genesee Avenue. These years later, Annie was a petite woman of eighty-nine, shorter than five feet tall, with a shock of bright white hair that curled around her head. She was legally blind but could see shadows and large objects. As Jane clutched Annie's elbow to guide her, and as I showed Annie the clearing where the house at 7 Modrzejowska Street had been, she swore that it all looked familiar.

"Oh my God, I don't believe it!" she said as she turned her body in a circle to see what she could of the panorama. "This must have been the hill that I went down." She pointed her fine white knotted hand in the direction of the hill. "What I remember is we went down that slope," she said, moving her finger back and forth in a horizontal line. "And there was a little street. I remember turning left." That, she said, was how she traveled to the home of her uncle Yitskhok the gold maker. And Annie was exactly right. I knew where Yitskhok's house had been, and she had remembered its location precisely. She turned back to the lot that stood in front of us. Today it was a vegetable garden, but Annie didn't see that. She didn't see the graffiti on the cemetery wall up the hill or the loud highway at the bottom of the hill with its clanging streetcar. What Annie saw was 1923.

"There were stairs going up to the house," she said. "It was a low, flat building, and inside the house were just two rooms, divided in the center." As the rest of us crowded around her, Annie described the long table around which the brothers and sisters of the enormous family sat and dined together. "At this end," she said, gesturing with her slight arms, "was the kitchen where they cooked." Annie covered her cheek with her right hand. "Oh my God, I can't believe it!" she said. She noted how much smaller this cozy property had been compared to the massive complex of buildings the family owned later on Małachowskiego, but as she saw it then, it was plenty. "There was a big yard here," she said. "And ducks were there, and geese were there, and little animals." Her face took on a happy grin. "For a kid, it was a barnyard! It was beautiful!"

My family trip to Poland was not a total success. The driving tour we took of the Jewish quarter in Warsaw was boring. The bland fried Polish food was a source of complaint. And because my family insisted on touring the camp at Auschwitz, the trip was a lot more focused on death than I wanted it to be. As a result, some of my cousins left Poland not with warm feelings of connection but with the other reactions that Poland tends to stir among Jews: fury and blame. I was disappointed. I had wanted my family to see the full sweep of history instead of only the holocaust, but it had taken me months to overcome that rage and see the country as anything other than a single war. I shouldn't have expected my cousins to arrive at that place in only a week.

Wiesław Skowroński is not the only person essential to this story who has died since its telling began. My grandma Fela died, too, in January 2003, a month shy of her eighty-first birthday. She had a stroke or a series of small strokes from which she never recovered. She was the last remaining holocaust survivor in my family. With her death, the story of what happened in those horrible years and in the happier years that preceded them left the realm of memory and became a secondhand tale that could never be completely understood. I had tried to prove aspects of my family's narrative, but much of it would exist now only as legend. There's a line in the Jewish burial ritual, spoken graveside, that struck me sadly at Grandma Fela's funeral. It was a dreary day in Atlanta. There were not many people at the grave, just me and my brother and father, my uncle Harold, his wife, their two daughters, and a handful of Grandma Fela's other relatives and friends. The rabbi was a middle-aged Israeli woman who explained during the ceremony that in Jewish law, we die two deaths. The first is our actual death, and the second is the death of being forgotten. This is a reminder to the living to never forget the dead, but to me, that day, it was also a reminder—an excruciating one—of how much we lose every time we bury a survivor. Grandma Fela was from Łódź, one of three survivors in her family, and she was the last to die. I shuddered to think of how many people died their second deaths on the day when Grandma Fela died her first.

The holocaust mantra has always been "Never forget," but too often what's remembered are the crimes committed, not the lives that came before them. And so, despite the hours I spent berating myself for having failed, I can take comfort in knowing that in a year spent turning dusty pages, I had done justice to memory. I reached out across time to Pinkhes and Zlata, to Shmil and Liba Mari, to Yisruel and Zisl, to Beresh and Sura Leah. My mother told me once that a great regret of her life was never knowing what her mother had looked like. It was, to her, as if Sura Leah had never existed. But a few months before my mother died, I changed that for her. I brought her a picture of her mother, albeit a small one. And whether or not that picture meant anything to her, it hangs now in a frame above my desk. Sura Leah looks out at me, at the granddaughter who's preventing her from dying her second death. For her, for my mother, for her cousins, for her grandparents, the best I can do is remember. I can not only remember them myself but also deliver them, their stories, and even the ground on which they walked to those in my family today and those who will come in our wake.

ACKNOWLEDGMENTS

L ONG BEFORE I LEFT MY HOME FOR A LIFE IN THE COUNTRY WHERE my mother was born, an invaluable collection of friends and strangers offered advice without which my journey might never have been possible—or would at least have been very different. Sharon Musher and Daniel Eisenstadt were the first to provide me with an essential list of contacts. Jeff Cymbler—the guru of Będzin research— handed me a virtual road map for everything I would do next. David Lee Preston, whose family story so surprisingly intersected with mine, offered the lessons he learned in his own search. Karen Auerbach clued me in to what I could expect in Poland today, while Dasha Rittenberg introduced me to the Poland she once knew.

I owe a debt of gratitude to my colleagues in Philadelphia, to Zack Stalberg, who generously allowed me the time to go, then let me come back, then let me repeat the cycle, and to Mark McDonald, Gar Joseph, Ron Goldwyn, Bob Warner, Jim Nolan, and all my other friends at the *Philadelphia Daily News* who kept me posted on what was happening back home. I am especially obliged to Dave Davies, who taught me everything useful I know about reporting and encouraged me at every stage of this book.

I made many welcoming and supportive friends in Poland including Darek and Marta Rozmus, who names unfortunately vanished from this book, but whose contributions were crucial to everything that happened from the first chapter on. Allen Haberberg, Zdzisław Les, and others in Kazimierz provided the venues of connection, the places where I could take refuge. Jagoda Krzywda, my Polish teacher, gave me a voice in a place where I was speechless. Annamaria Orla-Bukowska provided the context for what I was seeing around me. Henryk Rand offered advice that I wish I had heeded. Ewa Chrusciel, despite what happened later, was a good friend and a skilled translator. Jarosław Krajniewski was a hospitable ambassador in Będzin, and Yale Reisner deserves great admiration for making documents appear with a wave of his magic wand. I also owe a debt of thanks to Jakub Piechota who went far beyond the legal call of duty and put up with much more from me than most people would. In Sweden, the people who helped me included Liam Wasley, Hans Lindstrom, Lars Halberg, Maynard Gerber, and, of course, Fanny Adolffson. In Israel, Rina Kahan introduced me to many thoughtful Bendiners, Hana Bayter offered an important link to my family's past, and Dana Miller, who so generously opened her home to me, also tracked down a treasured photo and documents vital to this story.

As anyone who has read this book well knows, my dearest friends in Poland, Magda Bartosz and Krzysztof Adamiec, were the wonderful surprise that greeted me in Krakow. Their wisdom, their humor, their insight—not to mention their knowledge of the best Krakow bars—made up for every irritation I would find outside our Staszica Street home. I also want to thank the Skowrońskis, Wiesław, Helen, and Magda. Through everything, through their impatience and my disappointment, through the years when the courts could do nothing, they always opened their doors to me. They welcomed me. They shared their lives. I regret that I couldn't do more for them and hope they'll forgive me if, by telling my side of the story, I trampled unfairly over theirs.

Later, after I came home and returned to my little house in Philadelphia, and after that, after I gave up on this book and moved to New York, there would be countless drafts of this story that would be read and reread by clever and talented friends. I hesitate to try to name them all, certain I will forget more than a few, but the book improved so much over the years it would be thoughtless not to at least recognize a few of my generous readers. Among them were Matt, Elaine, Meredith, Carol, Nancy, Nicole, Jay, Dave, Bill, Christel, Steve, Anne, Stacie, Allison, Leah, Rachel, Tanaya, Jennifer, Corky, and Carrie. Becca Kolasky Spain and Rachel Scheier distracted me when I most needed distraction. Other friends, such as Michael Alpert and Mira Binford, offered suggestions and perspective. The semester I spent in Michael Steinlauf's Jewish history class at Gratz College lent a dimension to the book that would otherwise have been lacking. Paul Glasser at Yivo helped me decide how best to spell Yiddish family names. Michael Traison helped me cope with the ongoing legal saga that has extended far beyond the last page of the epilogue. The Bendiners I interviewed, including David Klajman, Lila Zaks, Esther Shlitzel, Izzy Hollander, Charlie Spitzberg, Marysia Borden, Arnold Gleitman, David Spitzberg, and Arnold Shay helped me understand the lost culture I was trying to discover. Miriam Eckert, Heidi Warren, and Anne Barnard all provided translations.

I will be forever grateful to Wendy Dorr, Julie Snyder, and Ira Glass at *This American Life* who gave this story a stage when other curtains had closed, and to my editor, Meghan Stevenson, who happened to hear a rebroadcast of one of those pieces and took the time to track me down. In a matter of weeks, she changed the fate of a project I had given up for dead, then skillfully guided it through to completion.

This book could not have been written without any of these people and it would not have been worth the effort if not for my family—the family I've always known, Aunt Fran, Uncle Bob, Stephanie and Ian,

Joel and Carole—who offered unconditional support at every stage, and the family I came to know from doing this research—Lillian, Jane, Ida, Dorothy, Annie, Rhonna, Marcy, and all of the other Fredericks, Friedricks, and Frydrychs, who share with me this important tale. David Miller provided crucial groundwork and was the first person to preach to me on the glories of Ashkenaz. My grandfather, Beresh Frydrych, carefully preserved key documents from his past for me to discover, and my Grandma Fela passed those records on to me, shared her painful story and indulged me in this adventure. She never forgot where she came from or what she had survived and she made sure that I would understand. I'm also grateful to my uncle Harold who, like his sister, never had much interest in this story but who, I'd like to think, is glad it's being told.

My brother, Derek, has always been and always will be the person who knows me best, and my father has always been my most unyielding supporter. They were there for me no matter what happened, whether I succeeded or failed, whether I wrote a book or merely told the story to them over dinner and a bottle of wine. I am also indebted, overwhelmingly, to David, my partner, my best friend. Though it took me longer than I wish it had to appreciate what we could become, he was by my side from the beginning and through the ricochets of fate since then, on the nights when I would break down in tears, and in the mornings when the sun would rise on a new chance for celebration. And, above all, the person I need to thank most is my mom—not because this is her story or because she trusted me with its telling, but because she always believed in my infinite possibility. While I have struggled at times under the weight of her high expectations, they were born of her grandest dreams for me. She inspired me.